MOTORBOATING &SAILING's

AUTHORITATIVE GUIDE TO MAINTENANCE, REPAIR AND IMPROVEMENT

D1508910

THE NEW BOATKEEPER

Edited by Bernard Gladstone

AVON BOOKS  NEW YORK

AVON BOOKS, INC.
1350 Avenue of the Americas
New York, New York 10019

Copyright © 1999 by Hearst Communications, Inc.
Cover and interior illustrations by Wendy Pagano and Tess Kuehnl
Published by arrangement with Motor Boating & Sailing
ISBN: 0-380-79934-0
www.avonbooks.com

Library of Congress Cataloging in Publication Data:

The new boatkeeper / edited by Bernard Gladstone.
p.   cm.
Includes index.
1. Boats and boating—Maintenance and repair Handbooks,
manuals, etc.   I. Gladstone, Bernard.
VM322.N48   1999   99-20867
623.8'2'00288—dc21   CIP

First Avon Books Trade Paperback Printing: June 1999

AVON TRADEMARK REG. U.S. PAT. OFF. AND IN OTHER COUNTRIES, MARCA REGISTRADA,
HECHO EN U.S.A.

Printed in the U.S.A.

QPM   10   9   8   7   6   5   4   3   2   1

THE NEW
BOATKEEPER

CONTENTS

SECTION 4: PROJECTS AND IMPROVEMENTS

SECTION 5: CRUISING POINTERS

SECTION 6: SPRING COMMISSIONING AND FALL LAYUP

INTRODUCTION

One thing I have learned in more than thirty-five years of boating experience—including more than twenty years of writing and editing the Boatkeeper section of *Motor Boating & Sailing* magazine—is that the vast majority of pleasure boat owners take tremendous pride in their boats, regardless of whether it is a ten-foot sailing dinghy or a sixty-foot luxury motor yacht. They are constantly on the lookout for new and better ways to maintain the appearance and operating condition of their boats and are always eager to learn and read about new techniques and materials.

The Boatkeeper section of *MB&S* (which has long been one of the most popular and widely read sections of the magazine) has always served as a forum for the exchange of just such information—in fact, many of our readers have been clipping and saving these sections for years. It was as a result of this that the first *Boatkeeper* book—a compendium of the "best" of the Boatkeeper articles that had appeared in the magazine up to that time—was published.

Several years later the first volume was followed by a second called *More Boatkeeper*—a new edition that added more of the "best" of Boatkeeper to the original volume.

This latest, *The New Boatkeeper*, is a completely new and updated edition that includes many additional Boatkeeper articles that have been published in *Motor Boating & Sailing* magazine since the last *Boatkeeper* book was released. It contains many additional boating improvements, boat maintenance pointers, and other time- and money-saving hints that may not have been published in the first two volumes—in addition to updating some articles that did appear in those earlier editions. Step-by-step instructions and more than one hundred detailed drawings clearly explain how any boat owner can properly maintain and improve his or her boat—even if that owner is hiring someone else to do the work. The information supplied in these pages was derived from interviews with many professionals, as well as from my own years of experience of owning and operating powerboats and sailboats of all sizes— and actually living full-time aboard my own boats for more than thirteen years.

By studying the information contained in these pages, every boat owner—whether a beginner or seasoned veteran— will know at least what work *should* be done and at best *how* it should be done *properly!*

The Contents at the front of the book enables the reader quickly to locate articles about a particular subject, while the detailed index at the back of the book will speed up and simplify the problem of finding the exact answer to all kinds of boat maintenance problems and boat improvement projects.

BERNARD GLADSTONE

SECTION 1
MAINTENANCE AND REPAIRS

When fiberglass pleasure boats were first introduced, extravagant claims were made about the wondrous qualities of this new boat-building material. Among other things, fiberglass was claimed to be completely waterproof and virtually maintenance-free—but experience has taught us that many of these claims were somewhat exaggerated. It is true that few of us would want to go back to the days of wood boats when rot, attack by marine growth, and the need for complete repainting every year made boat maintenance an almost constant project. But we now know that fiberglass boats are *not* completely maintenance-free, and that they are not absolutely waterproof (experts acknowledge that all marine laminates allow some water to permeate or pass through them, and most agree that the composite laminates used in boats will deteriorate to some extent if not properly maintained).

Fiberglass laminates (referred to in the industry as fiberglass reinforced plastic, or FRP) consist of multiple layers of glass fibers and cloth that have been reinforced and bonded together with a plastic resin—usually a polyester or epoxy resin. When the resin cures, it hardens into a solid mass, with the embedded glass fibers and fabrics serving to reinforce and strengthen that mass, much in the way that steel reinforcing rods serve to strengthen poured concrete.

The glass fibers come in three different forms: woven cloth made from glass fibers, chopped strands of glass fiber that have been laid into mats of various thicknesses, and strands of glass fiber that are bunched together and formed into a coarse woven cloth called roving. In most laminated boat hulls, alternating layers of all three are used, but the number and combination of layers, as well as the sequence of these layers, varies tremendously. In fact, the composition and layup of FRP laminates is a constantly changing technology that has made the maintenance, repair, and care of fiberglass boats much more complicated than was first believed. And, just as there were early misconceptions about fiberglass on the part of the boating public, today, too, there are numerous misconceptions about the care and repair of fiberglass and gel coat. Here are some of the most frequently misunderstood facts and fantasies about fiberglass laminates:

• Although most manufacturers of fiberglass boats use polyester resin, not all polyester resins are the same. Strength and water resistance may vary according to the quality of the resin, the type and amount of catalyst used, mixing techniques, temperature control, and the workmanship involved in laying up the laminate. This is especially true of large repairs and modifications made after the boat is built. If resins are not allowed to cure properly, the laminate will be more subject to damage from long-term soaking in water (softening, flexing, or fatigue cracking). Vinyl ester resins and epoxy resins are much more waterproof than polyesters, but they cost considerably more (that's why they are generally not used by manufacturers) and in some cases may be more difficult to work with.

• When mixing resins for a fiberglass repair, never guesstimate when measuring out the small amount of catalyst required, regardless of how experienced you are. Always *measure* the amounts needed—usually between 1.25 percent and 3 percent of the mixture (by weight). There is very little room for error; too much or too little catalyst will almost always result in improper curing and bonding, as well as weakness of the laminate.

• Inadequate stirring of resins and gel coats is another common error when mixing. If you want consistent results, it is absolutely essential to mix all ingredients thoroughly for at least two minutes. If colors, inhibitors, fillers, or other ingredients are to be added to the resin, these should be stirred in first, adding the catalyst before final mixing.

• In order to thicken resin so it won't sag or run when making repairs on a vertical or overhead surface, you can add fillers such as microballons or Cab-O-Sil. *Don't* try to add more catalyst to make the resin set up faster, and *don't* lay it on thicker. For small repairs and patches that do not have to be reinforced with fiberglass cloth, use an epoxy resin with a filler or thickener added.

• When making repairs that require several layers of cloth, make sure each layer of glass cloth, mat, or roving is thoroughly saturated with resin, leaving no dry spots or air bubbles in the fabric. Do not try to build up thickness quickly by using a single heavy layer of chopped mat, rather than several layers of cloth. Regardless of the type of resin used, remember that several thin layers of fiberglass cloth or roving will always be better than one thick layer. That's because there will be less shrinkage and less distortion after it cures, particularly if there are curves or bends involved.

• When making a patch, the edges should be scarfed or sharply beveled so that each layer of new material overlaps the old material. A 10:1 bevel is recommended for most scarfing with polyester resin; for epoxy resins an 8:1 bevel is usually adequate. Each layer of cloth should overlap the one under it around all sides, with the last layer overlapping all of them so the patch "feathers out" to leave no abrupt edge around the perimeter (blunt edges can lead to distortion of the laminate).

• Although the cracking of the gel coat is often regarded as merely a cosmetic problem, this can sometimes be an early-warning indicator of cracking in the laminate underneath. If gel coat cracking occurs in a fairly new boat, it could mean there is a defect in the original layup, or in how the gel coat was mixed or applied. In an older boat it could mean there is some stress cracking of the laminate under the gel coat.

• When mixing and applying gel coat, don't thin it with acetone; this will interfere with proper curing. Styrene solvents are not advisable either; they will cause the gel coat to yellow and become brittle as it ages. There are solvents that can be added to gel coat, but they are normally available only from the manufacturer or from distributors of fiberglass products.

• You can use a top-quality paintbrush to apply gel coat on small patching jobs, but it's best to use a special thickness gauge (available from manufacturers and dealers) to make sure you apply the gel coat in the proper thickness (16 to 20 mils when wet). If you apply too thin a layer it may not cure properly; if you apply it too thick it is likely to shrink, crack, or discolor, and it will be more porous than it should be. Spraying is best, but this requires specialized equipment and some experience in spraying in order to do the job properly.

FIXING NICKS, SCRATCHES, AND GOUGES IN GEL COAT

Most fiberglass boats have a lustrous, shiny layer of gel coat on the outside that is purely cosmetic in function—it adds little or nothing to the structural integrity or strength of the laminate. Maintaining that glossy finish requires frequent washing, plus the application of a good coat of wax at least once or twice a year. Although gel coat is a lot tougher than paint, it is still a comparatively thin coating and is susceptible to crazing (a weblike pattern of hairline cracks) and minor scratching, as well as small nicks and gouges.

Most boat owners feel that repairing gel coat is a job that must be turned over to a professional, because they have neither the experience nor the expertise to do it themselves. Yet in many cases all they need is a little patience and a willingness to experiment—and at today's labor costs the effort is well worth it. You can't really do any harm to your boat; if it doesn't come out right you can always scrape out what you've done and start over.

Gel coat forms a thicker, tougher coating than paint, and it forms a stronger bond with the surface under it. Gel coat requires the addition of a separate catalyst that is mixed in just before you apply it, and depending on the amount of catalyst added, it cures quickly (anywhere from one to four hours in most cases). Cured gel coat is brittle and won't flex much, especially if applied in too thick a layer, or when allowed to "puddle." It is also subject to cracking or crazing when under excess or uneven stress—for example, when bolts or screws that go through it are overtightened.

How Laminates Are Made

⚓ Most fiberglass boats are built of alternating layers of fiberglass and resin. The cloth provides strength and rigidity, while the resin bonds everything together. The laminate is "laid up" inside a mold that forms the outside shape of the hull, so layers of cloth are applied by working from the outside in.

Several different types of fiberglass are used in building up the laminate, often in alternating layers. Chopped fiberglass fibers (called fiberglass mat) are often used for bulk and rigidity, and in most cases this is combined with woven roving, a coarse heavy cloth that serves as a primary source of structural strength and adds impact resistance. Fiberglass cloth is the most expensive material, but at least one layer (and sometimes more) is used behind the gel coat to give a smoother finish and to add strength to the laminate. Cloth is also easier to form where curves are required.

Since the laminate is formed from the outside in, it is obvious that any imperfection inside the mold will show up as an imperfection in the gel coat and in the finished laminate. To avoid such defects, the mold must be carefully cleaned and polished before the first coat of gel coat is sprayed into it. The gel coat must be sprayed on in even layers, after which alternate layers of mat, cloth, and roving are applied and saturated with resin until the required thickness is built up.

Instead of being a solid laminate, some boats are built with "sandwich"-type construction that contains a center core of balsa, plywood, or other material. Over this there are actually two layers of laminate—one on the outside, and one on the inside. This creates a strong, rigid hull that is much lighter than a solid laminate of equal strength.

If a crack or gouge is relatively small and shallow and the damage does not go through to the laminate underneath, then filling that crack with gel coat is the method most often used to repair it. However, if the crazing is due to a structural defect, or if it is being caused by uneven stressing, make sure you reinforce or repair these defects beforehand (for example, bolts that are so tight they crush the gel coat, or fasteners unevenly tightened that create hidden stresses in the laminate).

Start by chipping away loose particles and flaking edges; then cut the crack out to widen it and to bevel the edges in order to provide better bonding for the new gel coat. One effective tool for this job is an ordinary can opener similar to the one shown in Figure 1.1. You can also use a small abrasive bit chucked in a high-speed electric drill. Widen the crack until it is at least ⅛

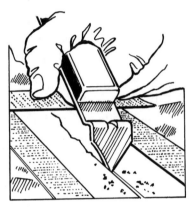

Figure 1.1

inch wide and about ⅛ inch deep, then sand the inside with a small, folded piece of medium-coarse sandpaper (#80). Dust thoroughly and wipe with a rag moistened with solvent just before you apply the gel coat.

Before starting to fill the crack or gouge, it is a good idea to apply masking tape around all sides of the damage. Don't use a cheap masking tape because this can often leave a thick edge on the gel coat and the tape may be hard to remove. Apply the tape as close to the damage as possible and press down firmly along the edges.

To apply the gel coat you can use either a small artist's brush or a flexible plastic spreader (Figure 1.2) cut to size (larger patches are usually coated by spraying). Normally gel coat is about the consistency of cream, so if you will be using

Blistering: Some Causes and Cures

⚓ All FRP laminates are permeable to some extent and will allow moisture to pass through them, but this is not actually what causes blistering. Blisters occur when water gets trapped inside the laminate, causing osmotic pressures to build up *inside* that laminate, or between it and the gel coat. Trapped moisture causes some of the solidified resins to break down while also dissolving some of the water-soluble glycols, metals, and acids that are present inside the laminate.

This forms a solution that can no longer pass safely through the other side of the laminate the way plain water can, so the tiny drops of watery solution collect in the microscopic voids found inside the solidified resin—creating what is referred to as osmotic pressure inside the laminate. This pressure builds up until it eventually causes blistering of the gel coat and in some cases even delamination of the composite.

Much research has been done on this blistering problem, but some of the causes are still not completely understood. Blistering can be severe when the manufacturer was careless about layup procedures, about mixing and catalyzing the resin, or about proper application of the gel coat—but this does not mean that blistering is always the fault of the manufacturer. It can and does occur even in a perfectly formulated and carefully laid-up laminate.

The best protection against blistering seems to be applying an epoxy barrier coat that is formulated for just this purpose— preferably if applied before painting the bottom for the first time. On boats that are already blistering, the best repair strategy is to strip off all of the old bottom paint and gel coat, using a special "power peeler" or "planer." (If there are only a few blisters, these can be cut out individually without taking all of the gel coat off.)

If there are still signs of blistering or delamination after the gel coat has been removed, or if there are hidden pockets of moisture in the laminate itself (a moisture meter is invaluable for detecting such pockets), then you may have to use the power peeler to remove several layers of the laminate until you get down to solid material.

The next step is to dry out the hull thoroughly, then do whatever patching and repairing is necessary to achieve a smooth, faired bottom. Apply new gel coat if required; then coat with a top-quality waterproof epoxy barrier coating, making certain you follow the manufacturer's directions exactly.

a brush it often helps to let the colored gel coat sit for fifteen or twenty minutes before you add the catalyst. This will allow it to thicken slightly as solvents evaporate, making it less likely to run or sag. For additional thickening—often desirable when using a spreader to fill in a gouge or nick—you can add a small quantity of microballons (also called microspheres) before adding the catalyst. This is a fine white powder that is sold in marine stores for just this purpose.

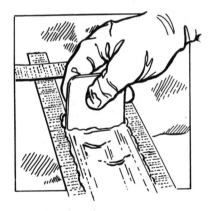

Only after everything is ready should you add the catalyst to the gel coat *because you won't have much working time after this*. The amount of catalyst to add is usually anywhere from two to four drops per tablespoon of mixed gel

Figure 1.2

coat—but this is not critical because if you add too little it will just take longer to cure. However, if you add too much it may

Mixing and Matching Gel Coats

⚓ One of the trickiest parts of any gel coat repair job is matching the existing color, especially dark colors like blue or red. If the boat is not too old, and if the manufacturer is still in business, your best bet is to order some of the original gel coat from the builder. However, even if you can do this, or if you have some of the original gel coat, don't expect it to match perfectly—colors tend to oxidize and fade or darken after only a few months of exposure, especially in the darker shades. This means that some tinting is almost always required. You can also buy gel coat in a neutral color (no pigment added) or in white from some marine supply outlets and mail order distributors, and then add your own colors.

To ensure the closest possible match, use rubbing compound on a small area next to the damaged area in order to strip off wax and soil and expose the true color. Then try to tint your gel coat to match this shade, rather than the oxidized version. It will be slightly lighter in color at first, but in a few months it will oxidize to match closely the rest of the boat.

Like paint, gel coat can be colored with tinting pigments that come in tubes or vials. An assortment of such colors is included in many gel coat repair kits, or they can be purchased individually from marine supply outlets. Actual matching is basically a trial-and-error process. Add the colors needed before you add the catalyst and before thinning the gel coat. Add colors very slowly, a drop or two at a time, and stir thoroughly. Test the color by smearing some tinted gel coat onto a small piece of nonporous plastic or hardboard. Tape this sample up against the boat next to the cleaned spot, then stand off and view the sample from at least an arm's length away. When the color of the sample matches that of the boat, you know you've got a good match. If you must err slightly, settle for a little too light rather than too dark. Once you've got the color right, you can mix in the necessary thinners and then the catalyst, stirring thoroughly to ensure a uniform mix.

"go off" (start to harden) too fast, or it may darken the color. So if in doubt, it is usually best to err on the light side. After filling, level the patch off flush with the top of the masking tape so that when the tape is removed the patch will be slightly higher than the surrounding surface.

The gel coat will never cure completely if left exposed to air, so the patch should be covered or coated to seal out air while it is curing. Pros accomplish this by spraying the patch with polyvinyl alcohol (PVA), but this is not easy to find in local stores, especially in small quantities. Just as effective is a piece of thin plastic kitchen wrap that can be smoothed on over the surface of the gel coat. Hold one end of the plastic down by pressing it firmly against the surface to one side of the patch, then "squeegee" the rest of it down on top of the gel coat with a plastic spreader. Smooth the plastic into firm contact with the gel coat to squeeze out all air bubbles and to form the gel into a smooth finish. Allow to cure until hard (usually from one to four hours), then peel off the masking tape and the plastic. The patch should have a smooth, glossy finish that is slightly higher than the surrounding surface.

Sand this flush with wet-or-dry abrasive paper wrapped around a wood or hard-rubber sanding block, and avoid scratching up the surrounding surface if possible. The first sanding should be with #400 paper, used wet. Dip the paper into water frequently to flush away grit and lubricate the abrasive action. Sand until the patch is flush and you can no longer feel a ridge around the edges, then switch to #600 paper to remove the scratches left by the first sanding, again dipping into water frequently as you work. The final step is buffing with fiberglass rubbing compound, using a high-speed electric buffer or a buffing pad chucked into a high-speed electric drill (at least 2,000 rpm). Then finish with a good marine wax.

Pointers on Spraying Gel Coat

⚓ Although small cracks and nicks can be filled with gel coat using a small brush or plastic spreader, covering an area that is more than a few square inches in size will require the use of a sprayer because gel coat dries too fast for brushing. However, for very small jobs, you don't have to go out and buy a compressor and spray gun. You can use a small, inexpensive, aerosol-powered spray unit that is widely sold in hardware, marine, and auto supply stores, as well as in hobby shops. One of the most widely sold brands (Figure 1.3) consists of an empty jar that threads onto the bottom of a pressurized aerosol-type can. You fill the jar with the paint or gel coat, then simply press the nozzle on top to spray the material out of the jar.

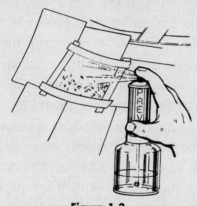

Figure 1.3

Even better are miniature spray units called "air brushes" that are sold in hobby shops and art supply stores. The least expensive models are also "powered" by a disposable can of aerosol-type propellant or compressed air, but they are more versatile than the type mentioned above because they come with an adjustable nozzle that enables you to regulate the spray pattern.

When gel coat is to be sprayed, it must be thinned with acetone or with the solvent recommended by the manufacturer to about the consistency of skim milk. Add the thinner a little at a time, then stir to check the consistency. You can always add more if it is too thick, but you would have to start over if you add too much thinner. If the gel coat is too thin, it will run and drip and may not cover as well as it should. If it's too thick, it may not come out of the sprayer or it may come out very unevenly.

Do your thinning before you add the catalyzer so you will have time to experiment with the spray pattern and viscosity before it starts to set up. Experiment on scrap pieces of cardboard or plywood. If the gel coat spits or spatters—or won't come out at all—it's probably too thick, or, in the case of a unit with an adjustable nozzle, the nozzle may need to be adjusted. When you finally get an even spray pattern, add the catalyst and go to work, keeping in mind that it's best to spray in short bursts. You must always keep the nozzle moving while it is spraying and remember that several thin coats are always better than one thick coat.

HOW TO FIX FIBERGLASS

Although major structural repairs to a fiberglass boat are usually left to the services of a professional, most smaller fiberglass repairs can be safely tackled by any do-it-yourself boat owner who is willing to learn a few basic techniques. With a little patience and practice, he can easily repair hairline cracks in the gel coat, scratches, gouges, dents, and even holes that go clear through the laminate.

A weblike pattern of fine hairline cracks in a small area— usually referred to as crazing—may seem to be only a cosmetic problem, but it should not be ignored. Crazing can be caused by uneven stress in the hull and could be a sign that the laminate needs to be reinforced in that area. Or the stress may be due to the fact that some fasteners may have been greatly overtightened near that crazed area.

If these hairline cracks are only in the gel coat, you won't have to cut out and fill in each crack separately—you can cover the crazing with several coats of matching gel coat (unless the surface was previously painted, in which case all the paint will have to be removed first). Start by sanding the crazed section with #120 grit paper, using a backing block on flat surfaces to avoid creating ripples. Sand until the cracks are almost invisible, then wipe down with a solvent to remove all wax and polish.

Unfortunately, matching the existing gel coat color is seldom easy. If the boat is not too old, your best bet is to obtain some of the original gel coat from the builder, but even then some minor tinting may be needed (see page 10 for more information on this).

Larger cracks must be individually cut out, using a small pointed abrasive bit in an electric drill or the point of a puncture-type can opener (sharpen the point with a file first). After cutting out the crack, brush away dust, particles, and sand with #150 or #180 paper. Wipe down with solvent and apply strips of masking tape on each side of the sanded section. The tape will not only protect the surrounding area, it also serves to build up a slight extra thickness that will simplify "feathering out" the patch later on. If the crack is less than ⅛ inch wide and does not go all the way through into the laminate, it can also be filled with gel coat, but the gel coat will have to be thickened to a puttylike consistency by adding microballons or chopped fiberglass as a filler before mixing in the catalyst.

After tinting the gel coat, use a plastic spreader to pack it into the crack and cover the sanded areas between the masking tape. Press firmly to eliminate air pockets and scrape off excess gel coat so its surface is flush with that of the masking tape. Cover the patch with a piece of thin plastic kitchen wrap to seal out air while the gel cures, using a plastic spreader to smooth the plastic down on top of the wet patch so no air is trapped underneath. Tape down the edges around all sides.

After the gel coat has cured, peel off the plastic and sand

with #150 paper to remove excess material and to "feather out" the edges of the patch. Wet-sand with #400 wet-or-dry paper to remove scratches left by the first sanding, then wet-sand again with #600 paper. Burnish with fiberglass polishing compound, then wax the surface to restore the luster.

Cracks that are more than ⅛ inch wide or that are deep enough to go into the laminate are best filled in with an epoxy putty (or an epoxy resin that has been thickened with filler to a puttylike consistency). Cut the crack out as previously described, then clean with solvent before filling.

If the crack is more than ¼ inch wide, use a small grinder or a sheet of coarse sandpaper to bevel the edges of the crack and create approximately a 12:1 slope on both sides (widest at the surface). Apply the epoxy with a plastic spreader, packing it down firmly to eliminate air pockets. Deep cracks should be filled in two or three layers, allowing each layer to harden before adding the next one. Trowel the final layer smooth and remove all excess before the epoxy starts to harden. After the epoxy has cured, wet-sand the patch with #220 paper, then with #400 paper. Finish by coating with matching gel coat or paint.

Holes that go clear through the laminate, and are more than an inch or so in diameter, will have to be patched with fiberglass cloth and resin. This is best done while working from the inside, if possible. First cut away all damaged material using an electric saber saw or grinder. Then use a grinder or disk sander to bevel the edges of the cutout so as to create at least a 12:1 slope around all sides. Wipe down with acetone to clean the surface and to remove sanding dust, soil, and wax.

A backing will be required to temporarily support the resin-impregnated fiberglass cloth patch, and for this you can use a piece of hardboard or plastic laminate that is a couple of inches larger on all sides than the hole. Cover this backing with a sheet of plastic film and press it firmly against the *outside* of the hole, securing it in this position with tape, clamps, or a temporary brace of some kind. A patch, or filler, for this hole is built up by applying successive layers of resin-impregnated cloth to a temporary backing that consists of a scrap piece of plywood that has been covered with a sheet of plastic.

Cut the first piece of cloth to match the widest part of the bevel, then cut a series of additional pieces, each slightly smaller than the previous one. Lay the first piece of cloth on the plastic-covered plywood, then mix up as much epoxy resin and catalyst as you will be able to use up in about fifteen or twenty minutes (it starts to set up after that). Brush the resin liberally over the first piece of cloth to saturate it, then lay the next, slightly smaller, piece on top and coat it with resin. Continue until you have built up enough layers to equal the thickness of the laminate, then brush an extra coat of resin around the tapered edges of the hole. Lift the stack of saturated cloth off the scrap plywood and press the whole thing in place over the hole, squeegeeing it firmly against the backing previously applied to the outside. Make sure you eliminate all air bubbles and press hard around the edges to ensure firm contact with the beveled edges of the hole. When ready, this patch will be applied *from the inside.*

Wait until the patch has cured before removing the backing on the outside. You should be left with a smooth, flush patch showing on the outside. Wet-sand this with #220, then with #400 paper, then finish with gel coat or paint to match.

In those cases where you cannot get at the inside to make the repair, you will have to work from the outside. After cutting away all damaged material, use a grinder or sander to taper the edges of the hole on the outside as described above. Even though you cannot get at the inside, you will still have to create some kind of backing *on the inside* to provide a form against which you can press the layers of cloth and resin needed to fill the hole. Here's how this can be done:

First cut a piece of stiff cardboard or thin plastic for a backing. It should be a little larger than the hole. Lay this backing flat and cover it with several layers of resin-impregnated fiberglass cloth. While all layers are still wet, push a length of flexible wire through the cloth and cardboard, then loop it back through a second hole as shown in Figure 1.4.

Hold on to the two wire ends firmly with one hand while you push this backing through the hole from the outside (you will have to fold or bend the corners of the cardboard in order to push it through the hole). After this is through the hole, pull on the wires from the outside to draw the backing in tight against the back side of the fiberglass hole. Secure them in that position by tying the wires to something solid on the outside or by wrapping them tightly around a stick that is long enough to reach across the hole. Leave this in place until the resin bonds the backing against the inside of the hole, then cut off the projecting end of each wire.

Now you can patch and fill in the hole by laying up multiple layers of cloth and resin as described above. Be sure you wet each piece of cloth thoroughly with the catalyzed resin before applying the next piece, and make sure you squeeze out all the air bubbles each time. Fill the hole slightly above the surface, then sand flush for the final smoothing. Finish with gel coat or paint.

Figure 1.4

Bonding Plywood Bulkhead to Fiberglass

⚓ To install a plywood bulkhead, shelf, or divider inside a fiberglass hull, the usual method is to bond the plywood in place with strips of fiberglass tape that have been saturated with resin. One mistake that is often made is allowing the edges of the plywood to butt directly against the fiberglass hull, creating a "hard spot" that can cause distortion of the fiberglass and potential high stress in that area. To prevent this and to provide room for expansion and contraction of the plywood, there should be a spacer installed to keep the edge of the plywood from pressing directly against the fiberglass. The spacer can consist of a small piece of rigid plastic foam or a pad made of two or three folds of fiberglass cloth.

The strips of fiberglass cloth or tape should overlap each other along the edges so that they leave no abrupt change in thickness where the cloth strips meet the surface of the fiberglass or the plywood. One way to accomplish this is to use strips of tape that get progressively wider so that each layer overlaps the one under

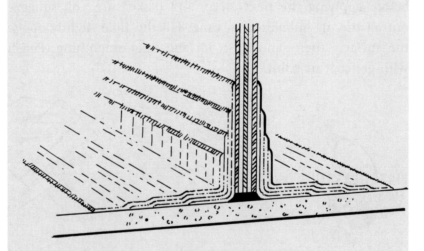

Figure 1.5

it. The edges of the tape will then taper off or "feather out" so as to blend in gradually with the surfaces on each side.

Another way to get the same effect, one that is favored by many pros because it permits using strips of cloth that are all of the same width, is to simply offset each layer of cloth to one side—alternating between the vertical and horizontal surfaces as shown in Figure 1.5. Here's how this works:

Say you're going to apply four strips of glass tape, all 5 inches wide. The first strip would have only 1 inch of this width folded up against the fiberglass hull with the other 4 inches folded up onto the plywood. The second strip would have 2 inches folded against the fiberglass with 3 inches folded up against the plywood. The third strip would have 3 inches against the fiberglass and 2 inches against the plywood, and the fourth strip would have 4 inches against the fiberglass and only 1 inch up against the plywood.

You can apply successive cloth strips to the joint one layer at a time, saturating each one with resin as you go; or you can apply all strips at one time by first laying them out on a sheet of cardboard with the proper offset for each layer. However, you must then soak each strip with resin before placing the next one on top. Lay a sheet of waxed paper over the whole stack, then turn it over and remove the cardboard. You can then pick up the waxed paper and use this to press the resin-coated multiple layers of glass cloth into the joint.

FIBERGLASSING OVER WOOD

Covering a plywood cabin top, deck, or cockpit floor with fiberglass not only serves to seal permanently against leaks and water intrusion, it can also add to the integrity and strength of that structure or surface (depending on how many layers

Fastening to Fiberglass

⚓ Sheet metal (self-threading) screws should not be used to fasten hardware to fiberglass—even for light loads—because they often cause gel coat to chip and they usually have little holding power. If there is wood under the fiberglass, then the appropriate fastener to use is a wood screw of proper length so it grips firmly in the wood, but a clearance hole should be drilled through the fiberglass first so that the screw passes through without chipping the gel coat.

If you have to fasten into a rigid fiberglass laminate, the proper fastener is a stainless steel machine screw threaded into a tapped hole in the fiberglass. Driving a machine screw in is a lot easier than driving in a sheet metal screw—and it will not cause the gel coat to chip. Of course, drilling and tapping does require a set of threading taps, and does require drilling each hole the exact size required for that particular thread. Fortunately, most boats will need only a few different size bolts to handle the majority of all fastening jobs, so only a small assortment of taps and matching drill bits will be required.

are applied). If properly applied over sound wood, a fiberglass covering will last the life of the vessel.

Although often thought of as a rather mysterious process that only a highly experienced technician can safely tackle, fiberglassing over wood is actually a fairly simple process that requires no special skills or unusual tools—all it takes is the ability to follow instructions with a reasonable amount of patience and care. There are certain safety precautions you must observe: Wear protective clothing and keep your skin covered as much as possible (coveralls with long sleeves and long pants are best) because some of the materials can irritate the skin. Make sure the area is well ventilated, and wear protective goggles and a mask when sanding. Don't handle fiberglass cloth with your bare hands, and keep the fabric in a plastic bag when you are not using it to prevent fibers from floating around in the air. And finally, remember that the solvents used are highly flammable, so make sure there are no sparks or flames in that room.

Fiberglassing over wood involves laminating layers of fiberglass cloth onto the surface of the wood, using a hard-drying resin that not only impregnates and fills in the pores of the cloth, but also serves to bond the fiberglass permanently to the wood and seal it against attack by moisture and insects. In these applications, it is the cloth rather than the resin that adds most of the strength to the laminate; the resin serves as a binder and a sealer.

There are actually two different kinds of resin used for fiberglassing—polyester and epoxy resins. Polyesters require the addition of small amounts of a catalyst just before use. This catalyst causes the liquid to harden through a polymerization process that changes the resin from a liquid to a solid. It comes in small bottles or tubes because only a few drops are needed to start the curing process.

The speed at which the resin cures will vary with the temperature—lower temperatures slow down the curing process and higher temperatures speed it up. The amount of catalyst used can be varied to some extent to speed up or slow down the curing time. Increasing the amount of catalyst will speed up hardening time, while decreasing the amount will slow down hardening time. But these proportions can be varied only slightly—too much or too little catalyst can ruin the resin.

Epoxy resins differ from polyesters in that they are thermosetting—they cure by heat that is generated when the resin is mixed with its hardener. Epoxies tend to be thicker than polyesters, and the hardener is mixed with the resin in much larger proportions, usually in ratios of one part hardener to anywhere from one to four parts resin (instructions on the package will specify the proper proportions). Unlike polyesters, the proportion of hardener to resin should never be varied in an effort to speed up or slow down curing time; always mix in the exact proportions recommended. You can speed up curing time if necessary by applying mild heat from a portable electric heater or a heat lamp.

Polyester resins cost considerably less than the epoxies do— anywhere from 30 to 50 percent less in most cases—and most people find that polyester resins are easier than epoxies to work with because polyesters are more liquid and thus make it easier to completely "wet" the fiberglass cloth thoroughly (thorough "wetting" of the cloth is essential to the success of a good fiberglassing job). In addition, polyester resins are relatively immune to attack by ultraviolet rays (epoxies are subject to attack by long exposure to sunlight, so they should be painted after laminating is complete). With a polyester resin you can add color to each coat in order to eliminate the need for painting later on.

Polyester resin is adequate for most fiberglassing jobs over wood, and it is the most popular type for this purpose; some, however, have switched to using an epoxy resin because it forms a stronger and more water-resistant bond than the polyesters do. Epoxies are more resistant to cracking and will bond better to hard or oily woods such as teak, redwood, and oak, as well as to metal and other nonporous materials. There is one other difference in working technique between the epoxy and polyester resins: Since each layer of epoxy will dry to a very hard finish, sanding between coats is a must if more than one coat of cloth or resin is to be applied. Polyester resins come in two classifications: bonding or laminating resin (also called air-inhibited resin) that cures to a tacky surface so that no sanding is required between coats, and marine or finishing resins (non-air-inhibited) that dry to a hard, nontacky surface for the final coat.

Laminating resins that dry to a tacky finish make it easier to apply more than one layer of cloth and resin because no sanding is required between coats, but they also make it more difficult to feather edges where pieces meet or overlap (tacky edges are hard to sand). Since finishing resins dry hard they must be sanded before paint or gel coat can be applied over them, or before application of another coat of that same resin can be applied.

Preparation of the old surface is extremely important before fiberglass cloth can be laminated over it. All paint or varnish must be completely removed down to the bare wood, either by sanding and scraping or by using a marine-grade chemical paint remover. Don't use a torch or heat gun to remove the paint—this will drive the oils deeper into the pores where they may interfere with proper bonding of the resin. After stripping, fill all cracks and holes and sand to a smooth surface, but don't use a filler that contains any type of oil. Use either a water-mixed wood putty or, better yet, an epoxy-based putty (if you will be using an epoxy resin for laminating the cloth). If you plan to use a polyester resin, use the patching compound recommended by that manufacturer.

Bear in mind that one layer of fiberglass cloth will add only a little extra strength to that surface—multiple layers will add more (alternating layers of mat and cloth can be built up to create a strong, thick laminate that will be even stronger than the wood underneath, but this adds considerable weight to the boat). The main purpose of fiberglassing over the wood is to permanently seal and protect that surface, but it is important that the fiberglass only be laminated over sound wood.

After patching and smoothing, remove all hardware, deck fittings, and moldings, then sand the wood thoroughly with coarse paper. When sanding, round off sharp outside corners that will be covered with fiberglass, and make certain inside corners are rounded off by adding a fillet or inside "cove" such as a hard-drying epoxy or polyester putty. Don't use bedding or caulking compound or any kind of patching and filling compound that contains oils. After sanding, vacuum up all sanding dust and wipe down with a rag moistened with solvent.

There are two methods for fiberglassing over wood: the wet method and the dry method. In the wet method, a coat of resin is applied to the wood first, then pieces of the fiberglass cloth are applied over the wet resin and smoothed into the resin with a roller or squeegee. In the dry method, the cloth is applied directly to the dry wood, then resin is spread over the cloth to saturate it thoroughly. Most amateurs will find it easier to use the dry method (this is also the method recommended by most manufacturers of epoxy resins). This allows you to "wet out" larger sections of cloth at one time—which means you can mix larger batches of resin at once without worrying about it starting to set up before you have a chance to use it all. Also, since you can work with larger pieces of fabric, there will be fewer joints to bother about.

If you are using an epoxy resin, it is a good idea to precoat the bare, clean wood with a thin film of the mixed epoxy before you start. This seals the wood and ensures uniform porosity so the wood won't draw too much resin out of the cloth when it is applied. After this dries, sand lightly, then wipe with a rag moistened with acetone to remove the dust and the waxy residue left by most cured epoxies.

For most fiberglassing jobs, a medium-weight fiberglass cloth is used (7½ to 10½ ounces). Cut pieces of cloth to fit over the area to be covered, making them as large as possible to minimize the number of seams or joints required. If an area cannot be covered with a single piece of cloth, overlap joints or seams a couple of inches wherever the pieces meet. Excess cloth will be trimmed off after the resin has been applied and before it cures completely. Cut all the cloth needed to cover the entire area, then lay each piece in place dry. Fasten it down with tape or a staple gun (use only Monel staples), and on curved surfaces, make small cuts where necessary to make the fabric lie flat and to minimize the amount of sanding and filling that will be required afterward.

Start by mixing only small amounts of resin—especially if you are using a polyester, which sets up much faster than an epoxy—because once the resin starts to set up it must be thrown away. With polyesters, mix no more than about one pint at a time. (If colorant is to be added, mix the color in with the resin before you add the catalyst to allow maximum working time after the catalyst is added.) With an epoxy you should be able to mix as much as 12 to 16 ounces at one time.

Spread the resin onto the cloth by pouring it on over the cloth in a zigzag pattern, then use a foam roller or squeegee to spread it around, working it well into the cloth to eliminate air bubbles and to "wet out" the cloth completely. Most people find it easier to use their hands (covered with disposable plastic gloves) rather than a roller or squeegee (see Figure 1.6). Work excess resin from the wet areas into dry areas and make sure you squeeze out all air bubbles. When properly saturated, the cloth should have a semitransparent look with the weave only barely visible.

On vertical surfaces (where you can't pour the resin), use a bristle brush to saturate the cloth, dabbing and rubbing with the side of the brush and working it well into the weave with repeated strokes. Then use a squeegee or a roller to complete the "wetting out" process.

Before the resin has a chance to cure, trim off excess fabric wherever the pieces of cloth overlap, using a sharp utility knife to cut through multiple layers of cloth down to the base wood. Peel off this excess cloth on one side of the cut just made, then lift the edge of the cloth on the other side of the cut and peel

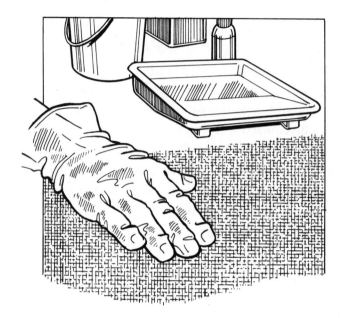

Figure 1.6

away the excess again. Press down on the seam firmly to ensure a perfect butt joint.

Allow the first coat of resin to cure completely, then sand the entire surface smooth with a medium-fine grit paper (#120 or #150). Be careful not to cut through the cloth with the sandpaper at any point. Wipe down with solvent to remove all sanding dust, then apply a coat of the resin alone (unless you will be applying additional layers of cloth to strengthen the surface). Apply this final coat of resin with a foam roller or short-nap roller recommended by the dealer so as to completely fill in the weave of the fabric. When this cures, give it a final sanding with #220 paper and finish with marine paint in the usual manner.

....
PROTECTING AGAINST DAMAGE
FROM CHAFE AND ABRASION

Wherever a dock line, water hose, or electric cord rubs against wood, metal, or fiberglass, or wherever any part of the hull or superstructure comes in contact with a dock, piling, or bulkhead, there is a potential for chafe damage. Fortunately, preventing this damage is not very difficult—all it takes is a few common-sense precautions.

Line chafing is probably the most common type of chafe damage—not only causing damage to the line, but also to the boat. On every properly equipped boat, dock lines and mooring lines should be guided overboard through smooth, well-rounded chocks that are strategically positioned so that the lines will not rub against, or come in contact with, any other part of the boat—wood or fiberglass. They should also be positioned to serve as a fairlead—in other words, to minimize sharp bends in the line whenever possible.

In addition to installing chocks that will provide antichafe protection for the lines, you also need to protect nearby brightwork and gel coat where dock lines might come in contact with these surfaces as they enter or leave the chocks—for example, where a line passes over a toe rail on its way to the chock, or where

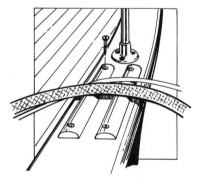

Figure 1.7

a line rubs against the gel coat near the chock on its way in or out of that chock. Chafe can also occur where a stern line is pulled tight around the corner of a transom, or over the covering board or deck edges around the perimeter of a cockpit.

Merely wrapping the line with chafing gear is usually not

Using Fender Boards to Protect the Hull

⚓ When tying up against a fixed dock, bulkhead, pier, or piling, fenders alone may not be enough to protect against scrapes, scratches, and dents. If the fenders are hung in the usual vertical position, they will often roll off to one side of the piling as the boat moves, allowing the boat to come into direct contact with the piling. If you hang fenders horizontally, there is still a good chance that the fenders won't be long enough to stay in constant contact with the pilings while the boat moves back and forth as the tide or current changes.

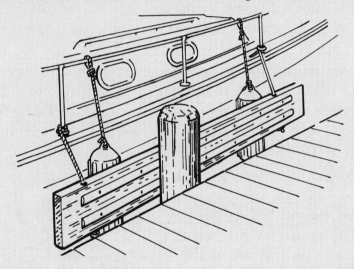

Figure 1.8

Therefore, most experienced skippers of medium- to large-size cruising boats carry fender boards similar to the one shown in Figure 1.8. Consisting of a length of two-by-six that is from three to five feet in length, with all corners and edges sanded smooth and rounded off, this board has two ½-inch-diameter holes bored through the width of the board, from one edge to the other. Two lengths of ⅜-inch nylon line are fed through these holes and knotted at one end to keep them from pulling through. These lines are then used to hang the fender board over the side by tying to a handrail or suitably located handrails or stanchion bases.

Two fenders are then strategically located behind this fender board when it is hung over the side to keep the board from coming in contact with the boat. The fender board then serves as a buffer between the boat and the piling or pier because the board prevents contact between the hull and the piling or dock. To keep the fender board from getting stained with creosote, and to minimize wear and tear when the board is up against rough bulkheads, two long strips of stainless rub molding are screwed to the outside face as shown in Figure 1.8.

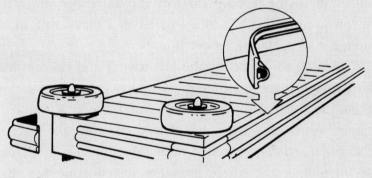

Figure 1.9

It's usually best to hang the fenders over the side first, then position the fender board over the outside of them. Try to position the center of the board against the piling and try to space the fenders so they are equidistant from each end of the board. Where possible, do not tie the fender lines to the same cleats or railing as the fender board lines.

enough—damage can still occur on any surface that this line rubs against. The best way to protect against this is to install strips of teak or mahogany or, better yet, half-round strips of stainless steel similar to the type shown in Figure 1.7 on page 27. In the case of electric shore cables or water hoses that are not under tension, a simpler solution is to suspend them below the handrails with loops of canvas or rope, or with some vinyl fender straps.

Chafe damage can also occur from small fender lines that are carelessly tied to wood handrails—a practice that is common on many cruising boats. Wrapping a fender line around the handrail in the place where the fender is needed may be fine if your handrails are made of stainless steel; but if they are of varnished wood, then there is the likelihood of considerable chafe damage to the finish after the line is untied. Prevent this by first wrapping the handrail with heavy canvas at that point, or by using flexible vinyl or canvas fender straps that snap on around the handrail and have a metal ring at the bottom for securing the fender line.

In addition to protecting the brightwork and gel coat from chafe damage, it is even more important to protect the docking lines by adding chafing gear wherever there is a chance of abrasion so that any wear that does occur will take place on the sacrificial chafing material, rather than on the line. This is especially important where lines are forced around a sharp bend, even if the line is fed through a smoothly rounded chock, because wear is much more severe when a line that is under tension is also pulled around a sharp curve.

Although many different types of material can be used to protect lines against chafing, the most popular type is the slit, tubular-shaped chafe guards that are made of rubber or resilient plastic. A length of heavy garden hose slipped over the line also works well and is very popular with many boat owners—not only because these homemade chafe guards are much less expensive than store-bought units, but also because the hose can be cut to any length needed.

None of these chafe guards will help much if they slide out

of position—away from the point where abrasion is likely—so it is essential that the protective material be securely tied, taped, or sewn to the line at that point. Plastic "wire wraps" of the kind used to bundle or secure electric wires and cables can also be used to keep chafe guards in place. Wrap the plastic tie tightly around the outside of the chafe guard and draw it up tight, then thread the free end through one of the rope strands. Store-bought chafe guards usually come with leather thongs or small-diameter nylon rope ties that are used to secure them, but simply wrapping these around a dock line and then tying a couple of square knots around the line will not be enough—the knots can slip or work loose, allowing the guard to slide out of position. Prevent this by weaving the nylon tie or leather thong through the strands of the dock line.

In an emergency, chafing gear can also be held in place with multiple layers of duct tape. Just remember that under severe stress or in a strong blow, nylon lines will stretch and move around a lot, so regardless of what kind of antichafe gear you install, make sure the covering is long enough so that part of it will always remain inside the chock or alongside the point of possible abrasion.

Protect Your Boat and Trailer

Here is a simple method that anyone can use to protect his small boat and trailer from the weather when it is out of the water—without the expense of having a custom-fitted cover made. Back the trailer up to a conveniently located tree or tall post, then block the wheels and block up the trailer's tongue to keep it well above the ground. Unwind the trailer's winch cable until it is long enough to reach the tree or post behind the boat, then tie it to the tree, but high up enough to create a sloping "ridge pole" for the "tent" you will create over the

Figure 1.10

boat as shown in Figure 1.10. Use one of those blue plastic tarps that are sold in all marine supply stores to form this tent, and make certain the tarp is big enough to completely cover the boat when draped over the taut cable. Tie the corners of the tarp to the trailer, or tie the corners to concrete blocks to weight them down and thus keep the tarp in place.

Trailer Chocks

Simple wood trailer chocks can speed up and simplify the process of loading your boat onto your trailer at a launching ramp. You can easily make a pair of your own chocks out of two 10-inch-long pieces of four-by-eight pressure-treated lumber. Screw an eye hook into one side of each block and then tie a length of elastic shock cord to each eye hook. After backing onto the ramp, all you have to do is set one of these chocks behind each rear wheel of the trailer, then tie the free end of the shock cord to the trailer carriage. After the boat is loaded, you can then simply pull it up the ramp and out of the way—the chocks will follow. The shock cord can then be

Dock Protection for Your Boat

⚓ When docking at a marina there is always the danger of accidentally rubbing against or slamming into the dock—especially when you are alone and can't get the fenders down in time. To avoid the scrapes, dings, or scratches that such mishaps often cause, many boat owners install dock padding or bumpers of some kind (conscientious marina owners should, it is hoped, install this type of dock protection on their own). If your home dock or slip does not have this protection, you can easily install your own, since all marine supply outlets sell a wide variety of plastic dock bumper materials that can be installed along the sides and edges of any dock.

Probably the most dangerous part of any dock or finger pier is the sharp corner that juts out at the end. If an errant wind or poorly judged turn brings the boat's hull in contact with this corner, it is almost certain to cause scratches, dents, or other damage. To prevent this, install one of the various commercial dock bumper materials that are sold for this purpose—preferably one of the preformed shock-absorbing corner cushions that wrap right around such corners.

For sizable boats, the best protection for dock corners is a "docking wheel" similar to kind shown in Figure 1.9 on page 29. Available from most marine supply outlets, these cushioned wheels spin on a vertical metal axle that bolts to the dock so the wheel's "tire" sticks out beyond the corner of the dock, causing the boat to always come up against this before it can touch the actual dock. With one of these in place, the boat will simply roll around the corner on this wheel while pressing up against it. The wheel will also permit you to come in close, allowing the hull to ride in as it turns, without you having to worry about scratching or tearing the other dock bumpers loose.

used to tie the chocks to the trailer until the next time you
need them.

....
MARINE CORROSION

Galvanic corrosion, the kind most often encountered in boats,
is caused by the presence of moisture or immersion in an electrolyte (seawater or contaminated freshwater), plus the presence of two pieces of metal that are electrically dissimilar.
Corrosion may seem to be only a cosmetic problem when it
occurs on deck hardware and fittings, but it can lead to far
more serious problems—for example, when a through-hull fitting is so weakened by corrosion that it literally falls apart, or
when corrosion does serious damage to your rudder, propeller,
or other piece of underwater hardware. That is why it is so
important that metal protection and corrosion prevention be
part of your routine maintenance program.

Galvanic corrosion (which differs from electrolysis) occurs
when two different metals are immersed in an electrolyte such
as seawater while the metals are electrically connected by a
conductor—even wet wood. This creates a simple one-cell battery that generates its own current, which flows through the
electrolyte from one piece of metal to the other. Different metals vary as to their electrical potential, and all metals can be
rated according to this potential—as shown in the galvanic series chart shown on page 38. Those with the lowest electrical
potential are higher up on the list (stainless steel, silicon
bronze, nickel, etc.) and are the least likely to corrode (these
are usually referred to as the more "noble" metals). Metals
lower down on the galvanic scale (zinc, cast iron, mild steel,
copper, etc.) will corrode more rapidly and thus are less
"noble" and often referred to as the base metals.

The flow of current in a galvanic cell is always from the
less noble metal (the anode) to the more noble metal (the

cathode). The anode is the metal that corrodes and deteriorates first because it loses ions into the electrolyte solution before the cathode does, thus keeping the current flowing. This is what happens in a flashlight battery; current flows from the zinc outer shell of the battery (the anode) through the electrolyte inside this shell to the cathode in the center of the battery (a carbon rod or special alloy made of noble metals). Flashlight batteries are not really dry; they are filled with a damp paste. When the paste dries up, or when the zinc is almost eaten away, the battery is useless.

Galvanic corrosion works the same way—two metals are involved and the less noble of the two gets eaten away while the other metal remains virtually untouched. For example, if a bolt made of stainless steel is used to fasten an aluminum cleat in place, galvanic corrosion of the aluminum would be very likely to occur in a short while (after the addition of moisture). An electrical cell would be created with current flowing from the aluminum (which becomes the anode because it is less noble) to the stainless steel bolt (which becomes the cathode because it is more noble). The result would be corrosion and deterioration of the aluminum with little or no damage to the stainless steel. The rate of corrosion (sometimes mistakenly called electrolysis) will vary according to how far apart on the galvanic scale the two metals are, as well as with the temperature, the relative sizes of the two pieces of metal, and the conductivity of the electrolyte solution (the saltier and more contaminated the water, the better a conductor it becomes).

Bear in mind that the metals do not have to be completely submerged for galvanic corrosion to occur. It can attack fittings that are well above the waterline or even inside the hull—all it takes is the addition of moisture. A drop of salt water or a drop of contaminated freshwater could seep into a microscopic crevice, and this water then becomes the electrolyte between two dissimilar metals.

Fortunately, there are a number of steps that can be taken to prevent this type of corrosion:

1. Whenever possible, use fasteners made of the same metal and alloy as the piece of hardware being fastened in place.

2. When joining two metal objects, avoid using dissimilar metals if you can. If this is impossible, select metals that are fairly close together on the galvanic scale.

3. When you *must* use dissimilar metals or fasteners made of a different metal, make sure you electrically insulate the metals from each other. Use gaskets, shims, or insulating washers of plastic, rubber, or other nonconducting material between the metals where they touch each other. Also, use an insulating sleeve or epoxy coating to insulate around bolts, screws, and other fasteners that go through the metal.

4. Use corrosion-resistant metals that are high on the galvanic scale, such as type 316 stainless steel, silicon bronze, copper-nickel alloys, Monel, etc.

5. Keep moisture away from the metal by covering it with a suitable coating such as a rust-resistant paint or waterproof varnish—anything that will keep air and moisture from coming in contact with the metal.

6. Spray a moisture-displacing penetrating lubricant or corrosion inhibitor into all crevices and around all fasteners to keep moisture out.

7. Use sacrificial zinc anodes (zinc is the least noble of all marine metals) to provide protection for metal hardware and fittings below the waterline. When properly installed, the zinc serves as the anode for any galvanic action that takes place in its area; therefore, the zinc will be "eaten away" by any galvanic reaction instead of the hardware that you want to protect (rudders, propellers, shafts, etc.).

Figure 1.11

Bear in mind that the zinc must be submerged in the water at all times and it must make good electrical contact with the metal it is supposed to protect. Rudders are protected by zinc "buttons" that are bolted to each side (Figure 1.11), as are trim tabs and underwater metal struts. Propellers and propeller shafts are protected by split zinc "collars" that are clamped around the outside of the shaft.

It is obviously impossible to bolt zinc anodes directly against the metal items that need protection *inside* the boat because the zinc would not be underwater. Metal fuel tanks, seacocks, and similar metal items that need protection against galvanic corrosion are usually connected to a master bonding system that electrically connects all metal components with a continuous heavy copper cable. This cable is then connected to a large "master" zinc that is bolted to the outside of the hull below the waterline. This large zinc serves as a sacrificial anode to protect all of the metal components that are electrically connected to it. It will get eaten away by any galvanic action that occurs before any of the other metal items on the inside are attacked.

It's important that these sacrificial zinc anodes be replaced

Galvanic Series Table (Starting with Most Noble Metal)

1. Stainless steel, type 316 (passive)
2. Monel
3. Nickel
4. Silicon bronze
5. Manganese bronze
6. Aluminum brass
7. Copper
8. Tin
9. Brass
10. Iron and mild steel
11. Aluminum alloys
12. Zinc

regularly—once or twice a season, or as soon as they are about one-third eaten away. If you wait until they are all gone, you will have waited too long and there may already be damage to the other metal items. Also, remember that the zinc should never be painted; this would negate its effectiveness. When replacing the zinc, make certain that it makes good electrical contact with the metal against which it is bolted by cleaning off all paint, corrosion, marine growth, and other foreign matter before mounting the new one.

Protecting Stanchions

Water that gets trapped inside metal bow rails and stanchions during the winter can freeze, causing the stainless steel tubing to split and warp as the freezing water expands into ice. A simple solution to this problem is to drill a small drain hole near the base of each stanchion long before winter arrives. That way water will drain out harmlessly without accumulating. Stainless steel is very hard to drill with ordinary drill bits, so for best results use cobalt bits rather than ordinary high-speed bits. Make sure you use a center punch first, and use a variable-speed drill to keep the bit point from skittering around while you try to get the hole started.

Electrolytic Corrosion

⚓ The other type of corrosion that boat owners have to watch out for is electrolytic corrosion (commonly referred to as electrolysis). Like galvanic corrosion, this is also an electrochemical reaction that involves a flow of current through an electrolyte, but while in galvanic corrosion there is no outside current involved (the cell generates its own current), in electrolytic corrosion the current comes from an *outside* source (usually leakage from the ship's batteries or from AC shore power).

Another major difference is that in electrolysis the metals do not have to be dissimilar, although the anode will be eaten away much faster if one metal is much less noble than the other. The damage resulting from either type of corrosion is the same—one metal (the anode) gets eaten away by the flow of current. In fact, this is what happens in the electroplating process. For example, in chromium plating, a bar of chromium metal is used for the anode, and the metal to be plated serves as the cathode. When outside current is applied, it serves to eat away the chromium bar while carrying its particles through the electrolyte and depositing them on the surface of the object being plated.

Electrolysis will only occur if you have two pieces of metal that are surrounded by an electrolyte solution so that charged particles can flow from one metal to the other. The current can come from either the AC or DC systems—usually due to poor grounding or leakage from the boat's batteries. Leakage from a heavy shore power can allow current to leak into the water surrounding your boat and cause electrolytic corrosion of your underwater hardware. Even current leakage from a poorly grounded boat near you in a marina can cause problems on your boat. The rate and severity of the damage will vary with the amount of current leakage, as well as with the temperature and salt content of the water.

The surest way to protect against stray currents from any shore power supply or dock is to install an isolation transformer on your boat, and to make sure all of your boat's wiring is properly grounded. When in a marina where stray currents are suspected, extra insurance can be provided if you suspend a few zinc "guppies" overboard (oversize zinc anodes, usually shaped like a fish). Heavy electric cable is used to connect these to shafts, metal rudder posts, and other hardware that needs protection on your boat.

Preventing damage from stray battery current on board usually involves considerable sleuthing. The current can be caused by connections that are constantly damp or poorly insulated from bilge water. Tracking down the source usually requires a sensitive meter that can read very low current levels, and in many cases it will take the services of an experienced marine electrician to pinpoint the source.

Protecting Outdrives from Fouling

When inboard/outboard (I/O) boats with stern drives are left idle in the water for weeks at a time, there is often a problem with fouling and marine growth on the underwater part of the outdrive. A simple way to prevent this is by "bagging" the prop and the outdrive with a sturdy bag made of plastic or other waterproof material. Pull the "bag" up over the outdrive from below, then tie it securely in place over the top to keep out water. This bag will then enclose the props and underwater part of the drive unit, keeping away barnacles and other growths that would otherwise form on the drive unit.

You can have such bags made up by any canvas shop or awning maker. Make certain they attach three straps around the top, with snaps at the end of each strap so that you can quickly fasten the top of each bag to the stern of the boat with matching snaps. Be sure that when the bags are in use, a large warning sign is placed across the ignition switches to remind you that the bags must be removed before the engine can be started.

WINNING THE BATTLE AGAINST MILDEW

Mildew is an insidious fungus growth produced by a microscopic plant known as mold. The invisible spores are actually in the air around us all the time, but it is not until they find conditions in which they can thrive—and a surface on which they can settle and grow—that they cause problems.

In addition to the objectionable musty odor that is characteristic of it, mildew can also weaken and eventually destroy fabrics, leather, paper, cardboard, carpet, wood, and most other organic materials (including many ingredients found in paints and adhesives). Mildew can grow on almost any surface, including inorganic fiberglass, because it can feed on a film of dirt, grease, or oil on that surface. As a rule, it thrives better on soft, porous, and rough surfaces than it does on smooth, shiny surfaces (that's why you will seldom find mildew growing on glass or on a mirror—unless that surface is very dirty).

Mildew spores thrive in damp, dark, poorly ventilated spaces that are also relatively warm. Yet it often shows up inside a boat after a cool spell because when warm, moisture-laden air comes in contact with a cool surface (like a fiberglass liner) condensation forms, and this provides the dampness essential to the growth of the fungus—especially if the location is dark and poorly ventilated.

Because mildew needs moisture to thrive, eliminating dampness on the inside is one of the first measures the boat owner should take—especially when the dampness is caused by inadequate ventilation and condensation. Ventilation is needed in all the closed-off spaces inside the boat, including hanging lockers, cabinets, lazarettes, heads, and galleys.

Never stow wet boots, foul weather gear, or wet towels and rags inside any locker or cabinet—dry them first. If this is impractical, stow the wet articles *outside* until they are dry. And remember that mildew feeds on dirt or anything organic, so avoid stowing any items below that are soiled or stained with food or perspiration. Galleys are particularly susceptible because food particles, grease, and dirt provide excellent food for the fungus, so make sure you keep counters, tables, and sinks clean, and never leave wet towels or rags lying around while the boat is closed up.

Dampness is also likely to be a problem in the head (especially if you have a shower) so get in the habit of drying out this area completely before closing up the boat. Never leave wet or soiled towels or wet bathing suits hanging in the head or, worse yet, bunched up in a corner. If you have a shower, be sure you spread out the shower curtain after each use so it will dry quickly.

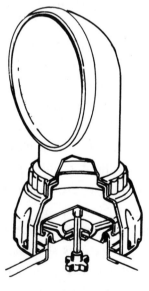

Figure 1.12

Do everything you can to provide as much ventilation as possible for the interior of the boat, and don't forget closed-off compartments and lockers since mildew grows best in dark and poorly ventilated areas. Dorade-type vents (Figure 1.12) are a big help in this respect because they allow fresh air to circulate even when the boat is closed up. However, make sure you face those at one end of the boat *into* the prevailing wind and those at the opposite end of the boat *away* from the wind to ensure a more effective flow of air through the inside.

Boats that do not have Dorade vents can get similar results with low-profile "mushroom"-type exhaust vents (Figure 1.13) that can be installed in cabin tops and hatches. Many of these provide light as well as air. They keep water out when the boat is closed up, yet allow fresh air to circulate through

Figure 1.13

the inside of the boat. Some are solar-powered for maximum efficiency—that is, they have a small solar-powered fan that can either draw air in or exhaust it out to provide continuous ventilation.

To ensure adequate ventilation of lockers, cabinets, and other closed-off compartments, you should install louvered vents in all doors and access panels. Marine supply outlets sell round or rectangular-shaped stainless steel vents in various sizes for just this purpose, and for maximum efficiency it is generally best to install two vents on vertical surfaces or doors—one near the bottom and one near the top.

Since the two worst enemies of mildew are sunlight and fresh air, it's a good idea to leave curtains open as much as practical to allow sunlight into the boat, even when you are not onboard. When leaving the boat for weeks at a time, leave locker doors, cabinet doors, and drawers open wherever possible to allow air to circulate. Prop up upholstered cushions and mattresses, and tip vertical cushions forward to allow air to flow under and around these upholstered pieces. Unfortunately, keeping the inside of the boat clean and dry and providing as much ventilation as possible is not always enough. Chemical mildew inhibitors—usually granular compounds that attract and absorb moisture—can also be used, but remember that these must be renewed periodically as they become saturated.

Another effective method for keeping things dry and thus inhibiting mildew is to add mild heat on a continuous basis. One way to provide this heat is to keep a small 40- or 60-watt lightbulb burning continuously inside the hanging lockers. This generates enough mild heat to dry out dampness, but bear in mind you have to be very careful with lightbulbs in an enclosed area when there are flammable materials nearby (like clothing). Even the smallest bulb will get hot enough to scorch or start a fire if brought into contact with paper or cloth—and things can easily move around when the boat rocks.

A safer and more efficient way to eliminate humidity problems is to use small electric dehumidifiers that are made for marine use. Actually low-level heaters, they are sold under the brand name GoldenRod; these rodlike heaters draw very little current and never get hot enough to start a fire or scorch anything, even if they come in contact with the material. They are installed by simply attaching two small clips and then snapping the tubular rod into the clips. The electric cord is then plugged into any accessible outlet. There are several sizes available to suit the space being protected.

Moth balls will also do a good job of inhibiting mildew (if you don't mind the odor), but only if used in a relatively small, closed-off area that is sealed off from much air movement. Scatter them liberally inside hanging lockers, cabinets, and drawers, or wherever clothing or canvas materials are stored, but remember that moth balls will evaporate and disappear as time goes on, so they must be replaced periodically even if the boat remains closed.

MOUNTING DECK HARDWARE

Items of deck hardware such as cleats, chocks, mooring bits, stanchions, pulpit bases, and handrails must be securely mounted so they will not tear loose under severe stress or the

Removing Mildew

⚓ In most cases the first step is to take all removable items outside and air them thoroughly in the sun. This includes clothing, cushions, curtains, carpets, cordage, cartons, books, etc. Where possible, send affected items to the cleaner or take them home to be laundered, but don't vacuum or shake them around inside the boat—this only spreads the spores on the inside.

Mildew stains on vinyl, fiberglass, and painted surfaces can be removed by spraying with a commercial mildew remover—usually without the need for much scrubbing. Just spray on, wait a few minutes until the spots and stains disappear, then rinse off with plain water. If necessary, repeat the spray-and-rinse process once more. Make sure there is plenty of ventilation when working in confined areas, because inhaling the spray can cause irritation. Be careful about using these products on clothing or colored fabrics; these chemicals may affect the color or damage the fabric.

For these materials, your best bet is to wash with soap and water as soon as possible. If the item is not washable, sponge with alcohol or with a foam-type upholstery cleaner. Allow to dry, and if any mildew stains remain, you can try bleaching them out with lemon juice and salt. However, experiment on a small inconspicuous area first to make sure this won't harm the fabric or its color.

constant vibration incurred by all boats when under way. Each piece must also be mounted in such a way as not to cause damage to the deck or hull, or to result in leaks through improperly sealed fasteners. Sometimes additional backing plates are needed under the deck, but at other times it will be necessary to completely replace poor-quality fittings and their fasteners.

There are three types of fasteners used to secure hardware and fittings: wood screws, self-tapping screws, and bolts that go completely through the laminate and are secured by nuts on the other side.

Wood screws are used to fasten directly to wood, or when fastening hardware against a thin fiberglass laminate that is backed with wood. However, they are used only for comparatively light loads where the pull is more or less parallel to the surface—not where the load or stress will tend to pull the screw straight out. *Never use screws to secure mooring cleats, mooring bits, stanchions, or handrails and grab rails that are needed for safety.*

Even though wood screws do not go through the wood in most cases, it's important to use bedding compound under each piece of hardware. Also, squeeze a small amount of compound into each pilot hole before driving the screws home to keep water from entering the wood.

Self-tapping screws are used to fasten hardware to reasonably thick fiberglass laminates the same way that wood screws are used—but these also should be used only for relatively light loads where the pull will be nearly parallel to the surface—for example, for fastening a small halyard cleat to the side of a cabin or cockpit on a sailboat, or for fastening small fender cleats to the side of the boat. But don't use self-tapping screws for fastening to laminates that are less than $3/16$ inch in thickness—unless you will be using an expansion-type anchor that "mushrooms" out behind the laminate when the screw is tightened. When using screws, stick to stainless steel because aluminum screws are just not strong enough.

Fiberglass is much harder than wood, so it is absolutely necessary that you drill a pilot hole of the right size for each screw. If the pilot hole is too small, the screw may crack the laminate and/or the gel coat when you drive it home, or the screw may be so hard to drive home that you will end up breaking it. On the other hand, if the pilot hole is too large the screw will not grip properly and will tend to strip the hole when it is tightened. It's not hard to determine what size drill bit to use. The bit should be equal in diameter to that of the solid body of the screw without its threads. Hold the screw up to the light and then hold the bit in front of it at about eye level. If the drill bit is the right size it should just block out the body of the screw, allowing you to see only the threads of the screw sticking out on each side.

The use of bedding compound is just as important when self-tapping screws are used in fiberglass as when wood screws are used in wood. Water can work its way into fiberglass laminates and can cause blistering or separation later on.

Bolts that go completely through the fiberglass and are secured by nuts on the inside are by far the preferred method for mounting all types of deck hardware—especially fittings that must withstand considerable shock and heavy stress. The most common practice is to install large, heavy washers under each nut; but for secure mounting and best protection of the laminate, it is far better to use backing plates of thick wood or heavy-gauge metal. Backing plates should be a little larger in overall size than the base of the fixture being mounted, and holes that go through this backing plate should be drilled slightly oversize to allow for any slight misalignment of the bolt holes. If wood is used, the plate should be at least ¾ inch thick; if aluminum is used, select a piece at least ¼ inch in thickness.

Make sure you use a good bedding compound under the base of each fixture and under the backing plate, as well as under the heads of the bolts. Force a small amount of the same bedding compound into the bolt hole before pushing the bolts through, and tighten the bolt by turning the nut, if possible, rather than by turning the bolt's head. Turning the bolt instead of the nut will tend to squeeze out the compound under the

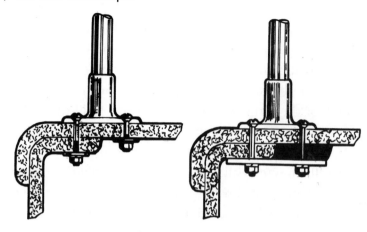

Figures 1.14a and 1.14b

head, while tightening the nut will leave the compound undisturbed. All bolts, nuts, and washers should be made of corrosion-resistant bronze or stainless steel and should be drawn up tight enough to prevent loosening, but not so tight as to crack or distort the laminate and the gel coat. To ensure against eventual loosening without overtightening, insert a lock washer under each nut or use two nuts on each bolt (tightening the second one firmly up against the first one).

When a deck fitting is bolted to an area where two parts of the hull mold overlap so that there is a definite variation in thickness, installing a backing plate is difficult because the plate will get badly distorted when the nuts are tightened. This will create uneven stresses in the laminate, as well as in the hardware. Some boat builders solve this problem by placing a large washer under each nut, rather than a single solid backing plate (Figure 1.14a). But such washers are never big enough to spread the load properly. The best way to provide a solid backing that is uniform in thickness is to fill the gap left by the two different thicknesses of laminate as shown in Figure 1.14b, using either a two-part epoxy putty or an epoxy resin that has been thickened with microballons or fiberglass fibers. Coat the backing plate with wax on one side so the epoxy won't stick to it, and wax the threaded ends of the bolts where they will come into contact with the epoxy. After everything is in position, pack the putty in behind the backing plate and tighten the nuts only enough to make solid contact and squeeze out excess compound. Trim this excess off before it hardens, then wait till the epoxy cures completely before tightening the nuts all the way.

Epoxy filler can also be used to provide a flat surface for a backing plate when bolting to a laminate that is very rough or uneven on the back. Spread a thick film of the epoxy over the area, then press the waxed backing plate up against it. Push the waxed bolts through and tighten the nuts just enough to squeeze out excess and form a flat surface under the plate. Wait till the compound hardens, then finish tightening the nuts.

NO MORE "HEAD" ACHES

Although most marine toilet problems are a result of someone throwing something into the toilet that shouldn't be there, or failing to properly observe operating instructions, there are times when the trouble results from poor maintenance and/or neglect on the part of the skipper. Modern marine toilets are much more dependable than they used to be, but they still are not as dependable as your typical home toilet—which is why preventive maintenance is particularly important with marine units.

All manufacturers sell parts and overhaul kits that include everything needed for periodic maintenance, but don't wait until something wears out or breaks down before using one of these kits. In the spring, replace the rubber joker valve, the flapper valve, and other parts subject to wear, and lubricate all moving parts as recommended in the owner's manual. If you have an electric head, spray the exposed terminal connections

Securing to Laminates with a Wood or Plastic Core

⚓ Many boats are built with "sandwich" type construction—an inner and outer "skin" of fiberglass with a lightweight core of balsa, plywood, or foam in the center. Bolting deck hardware to this presents a problem because if the bolts are tightened too much they may crush the lightweight, softer core and deform the thin layers of laminate on each side.

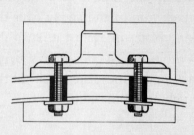

Figure 1.15

To solve this problem, insert metal or wood plugs as shown in Figure 1.15, then bore through these to insert the bolt. Tightening the nut will then exert compression pressure on the plug or insert without squeezing the core material. The insert or plug should be bonded in place with epoxy resin. Also, you should coat the exposed edges of the core material with epoxy after you have drilled the hole for the plug and before inserting it into the hole.

Instead of inserting solid plugs of metal or wood, you can also form plastic "plugs" of hardened epoxy putty as indicated in Figure 1.16. To do this, simply bore out an oversize hole

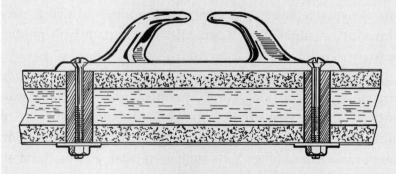

Figure 1.16

(¾ inch to 1 inch in diameter) through the laminate "sandwich," then fill this with epoxy putty. You then can either insert a bolt of the right size to create the needed hole, or wait till the epoxy hardens, then drill it out to create the proper-size hole for the bolt.

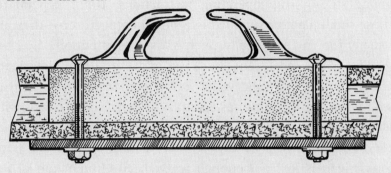

Figure 1.17

An even better way to mount heavy-duty deck hardware on core construction is shown in Figure 1.17. You merely cut through and remove only the top layer or "skin" of fiberglass to expose the core material over an area that is slightly larger than the base of the fitting to be installed. Then dig out the balsa, plywood, or other core material, leaving the bottom layer of fiberglass intact. Now you can fill the cavity that remains with a two-part epoxy putty. After this hardens in place, you can drill through the epoxy to provide holes for the mounting bolts. On the back side, use a backing plate that is slightly larger than the epoxy "plug" you just created so that it overlaps on all sides of the plug. You will then be able to tighten the nuts as much as necessary without fear of crushing either the core or the laminate.

with a moisture-displacing spray at least once a month to prevent corrosion.

Probably the most important preventive maintenance procedure is to make certain that every member of the family knows how to operate the head—and knows what *not* to throw into it. When guests come on board, make sure they are also instructed, preferably by an actual demonstration. Post a clearly printed, prominently located card or placard next to the head giving step-by-step operating instructions. Don't depend on those small plaques supplied by some manufacturers—they are usually too small to really catch a visitor's attention.

One of the most frequent causes of eventual trouble is inadequate flushing of solid waste and paper. Many users tend to stop pumping (flushing) as soon as the bowl looks clean (with electric heads they tend to release the push button as soon as the bowl looks empty). Unfortunately, flushing until the bowl looks clean is just not enough to flush all effluent out of the discharge hose that connects the toilet to the holding tank or marine treatment device. There will still be some solid waste and paper remaining inside the hose, especially if the hose is a long one or if it has several bends and/or elbows in the line.

If this effluent remains in the hose for days at time, it will greatly hasten the buildup of sediment and scale, thus reducing the effective inside diameter of that hose. In as little as six months of regular weekend use a typical 1½-inch-diameter discharge hose may be reduced to less than 1 inch in diameter, severely restricting flushing efficiency and eventually clogging the line.

To prevent such buildup, the toilet should be given an extra-long flush when there is paper or solid waste in the bowl. On manual toilets this means giving the pump at least ten to fifteen extra strokes after the bowl is empty. On electric toilets the push button must be held down for at least fifteen to twenty seconds longer than it takes to clean out the bowl.

An even more common cause of sudden "head aches" is people dropping foreign objects into the toilet. Most marine toilets are not designed to handle sanitary napkins, paper towels, and bulky wads of double-ply toilet paper (that's why many recommend using only single-ply paper, or the type that is specifically sold for marine toilets). Even small items like a filter-tip cigarette or a wooden match stick can get stuck in a rubber joker valve or flapper valve, causing waste to back up into the bowl when flushing. Or the toilet may not flush at all the next time it is used. As a rule it is best to insist that nothing but human waste and toilet paper can be dropped into the bowl.

Another thing boat owners must be careful about is the indiscriminate use of home-style toilet bowl deodorants and cleaners. Many can be harmful to plastic or rubber seals and valves, as well as other internal components. If in doubt, check with the manufacturer of your particular unit to see what they recommend, or read your owner's manual.

Here are some other things to check and maintenance procedures to follow to prevent unexpected breakdowns during the boating season:

1. Make certain that both the inlet and discharge seacocks are open all the way. If your boat has gate valves instead of regular seacocks, they may have corroded on the inside. Gate valves should be replaced as soon as possible anyway, because they are not safe for use as a seacock when used below the waterline.

2. The discharge hose may have too many bends and elbows in it (each elbow adds the equivalent of about eighteen feet to the length of the hose). It's also possible that the discharge hose leading from the toilet to the holding tank or treatment device may be too long (the manual will tell you the maximum length recommended).

3. If the discharge hose is more than two or three years old, disconnect one end and examine the inside with a

bright light to see if there is a heavy buildup of salt and other sediment that is partially clogging the hose, thus cutting down on its inside diameter. If so, the hose should either be cleaned out or replaced.

4. Make sure the Y-valve that directs effluent to the holding tank or the marine sanitation device (MSD) is not clogged or frozen in one position. Move the handle back and forth to free it up, and then run plain water through in each direction to make sure both ports are clear. If in doubt, take the valve apart and clean it out, then lubricate the inside before reassembling it.

5. If the toilet is below the waterline, there should be a vented loop in the discharge line to prevent water being siphoned back into the bowl—even when it is not in use. If water does accumulate in the bowl, it's possible that the vent opening (the small hole in the little vent at the top of the loop) is clogged. Unscrew the cap on this little vent and clean out the vent opening with a pin or needle so that air can enter freely. Then check the vent disk (or miniature joker valve inside the vent) to see if it needs to be cleaned or replaced. (This vent disk allows air to enter, but keeps wastewater from escaping as it is being discharged.)

6. Most marine toilets use raw seawater for flushing, so there will always be a certain amount of eel grass, marine growth, and other floating debris drawn in with the water. An intake strainer in this line is necessary to prevent clogging of the inlet hose and pump, and this strainer must be checked frequently to see if it needs to be cleaned.

7. If you have an electric head, check the terminals and connections to make certain that the fasteners have not corroded or loosened. A poor connection can cause low voltage, which in turn causes poor flushing. Check the

voltage across the terminals when the motor is running to see if the required voltage is actually being delivered to the motor. Low voltage can be the result of a loose wire or connection, or an electric cable that is too small for its length.

8. Odors emanating from the head are a more insidious—and more annoying—problem, and one that is often hard to pinpoint. The most common cause is seawater standing in the bowl—pollutants and organic matter in the raw water decompose and give off a foul odor. To avoid this, make sure the bowl is emptied of all water before leaving the boat for any length of time.

9. Sewage odors in the bilge may be due to small leaks in the discharge line, particularly where hoses connect to barbed fittings on through-hulls or valves. However, the most frequent cause of odors in the bilge is using the wrong type of discharge hose. Hose used for a waste line should have a smooth inner wall and should be the type designed for handling waste matter. Otherwise there is a good chance that the hose will allow odors to permeate and seep through the outer walls—even if there is no actual leak. To correct this, replace the hose with a nonpermeable type specifically made for use with marine toilets.

HOW TO KEEP YOUR BILGE CLEAN

A dirty, oily bilge that is cluttered with debris is not only messy and unsafe to work in, it also makes maintenance chores much more difficult to complete. In addition, it greatly increases the difficulty of locating fuel, oil, or water leaks. That's why the wise boat owner tries always to keep his bilge as clean and dry as possible.

The most important step is to constantly check all water

Holding Tank Problems

⚓ If your holding tank emits unpleasant odors, the first thing you should suspect is an obstruction in the line leading from the tank to the outside vent's opening (such vents are required on all holding tanks), or a completely blocked vent opening. This vent is provided to allow sewer gases and odors inside the tank to escape harmlessly to the outside, and if it is blocked, gas pressure inside the tank can build up to the point where the tank may actually rupture—or break some of the connections loose. A similar problem can occur if there is a dip in the vent hose that leads to the vent opening. Water can collect in this dip, completely nullifying the purpose of the vent (the water creates a "trap" in this low point, preventing the tank gases from escaping).

Another possible source of tank odors is a loose connection where the toilet's discharge hose connects to the holding tank, or where the pump-out hose connects to its deck fitting. Make sure that the clamps on all fittings in the system are tight and that there are no cracks or holes visible. Then inspect the tank itself to see if there are cracks or seams where moisture could be seeping out.

You can make a more thorough check for leaks when at a pump-out station. Flush out the tank and all connecting hoses with water, and repeat this flushing several times while watching for signs of leakage. Have someone hold his hand loosely over the vent opening while the tank is being pumped out to determine if he feels a slight suction action as air moves into the tank through this vent opening. At the same time, have someone watch the tank itself. There should be no sign of the tank walls buckling or flexing as it empties—if there is, then the vent is probably clogged or not functioning properly.

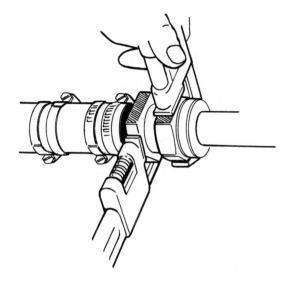

Figure 1.18

hose connections—in the freshwater system and on engine hoses—for leaks. Stuffing boxes should also be periodically tightened or repacked to minimize dripping (Figure 1.18). It's true that bilge pumps can usually get rid of this water as fast as it accumulates, but even when working properly these pumps never get *all* of the water out. The last inch or so of water that is left will spread even small oil spills around when the boat is rolling in rough seas.

Another problem with modern fiberglass boats is that there are always closed-off spaces between stringers where water collects and bilge pumps do not reach. Older wood boats have limber holes that allow water to flow between ribs and stringers, but this is seldom true of fiberglass boats. Extra bilge pumps can be installed in these locations, but this is not always practical. You can mop up accumulated puddles with large sponges or absorbent pads, but it's faster to use a small portable pump to drain these places.

Some boats are set up to allow water from the ice box, the galley sink, and even the shower to run directly into the bilge. This water does get pumped overboard by the bilge pumps eventually, but very often soap, grease, hair, and food particles will tend to accumulate in the bilge, causing noxious odors and sometimes clogging the pump or its float switch. The right way to correct such a problem is to install a separate sump to catch all this "gray" waste water. Then install a small automatic bilge pump inside this sump to pump the waste water directly overboard as it accumulates.

Oil spillage in the bilge when changing engine filters and when draining and changing the lubricating oil is probably the most frequent cause of a greasy or oily bilge. Although this is inherently a messy job, there are various methods for preventing accidents and spills while draining the oil.

1. Before unscrewing an oil filter cartridge, slide a plastic bag over the filter, then hold the bag in place while removing the cartridge as shown in Figure 1.19. The plastic bag will catch all drips and spills and, along with the old cartridge that falls loose inside the bag, can then be neatly disposed of outside the boat.

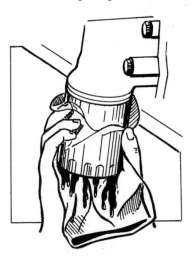

Figure 1.19

2. When draining oil from a crankcase or engine pan through the drain plug at the bottom of the pan, you can catch the oil in a shallow pan that you can make yourself. Cut one side out of a plastic gallon-size antifreeze container (you want the side with the spout) and lay it on its side under the drain opening with its cutout side facing up. When full of

the waste oil, carefully slide the pan out and pour the oil out through the original spout.

3. Another method for draining oil is to use a funnel with a length of hose attached to it. The funnel is supported in a vertical position under the drain opening by a "tripod" bent out of a wire hanger. The engine oil flows into the funnel and then through the hose into a separate container for safe disposal onshore.

Unfortunately, no matter how careful you are, accidents will happen and leaks will occur. Here are some suggestions for minimizing such accidents, as well as for simplifying cleaning up any mess that does occur:

• Wipe up oil spills up immediately to keep them from spreading, and to keep them from soaking into the fiberglass or wood. Use the special oil absorbent pads (widely available in marine supply outlets) to help clean up the mess. They will absorb oil but not water, so they're ideal for picking up oil that is floating on top of bilgewater.

• Line the bottom of the engine pan and other places where spills are most likely to occur with disposable baby diapers. They are highly absorbent and will soak up oil, water, and spilled fuel. The saturated materials can then be picked up and dropped into plastic garbage bags for safe disposal in an approved location. You can also use a thick layer of kitty litter or similar absorbent granules in the engine pans to absorb oil spills.

• Use absorbent granules (the kind sold in home centers and auto supply outlets for soaking up spilled oil) to absorb oil from wood, fiberglass, or other porous surfaces. Spread a thick layer of the granules over the oil-stained area and allow it to remain in place for several days. Then sweep up the granules and scrub the area with a strong detergent or a bilge cleaner mixed with only one or two parts of water.

• Try using baking soda to get rid of remaining diesel odors. Scatter this over the fuel-saturated area in a thick layer and allow it to soak for several days. If the bilge is wet, place the baking soda in shallow pans to keep it from being washed away, then set the pans as close as possible to the source of the diesel odors. Another trick that sometimes works to get rid of diesel odor is to spray cider vinegar over the area, using a pump-type plastic spray bottle.

• To locate a small but persistent oil or fuel leak, clean the area thoroughly, then spread some newspapers or clean paper towels around and under the suspected lines or fittings. Let the engines run for a while, then check these papers for stains—they will quickly show you where any leaks or drips have occurred.

• Remove rust stains and dirt stains, which make it harder to keep the bilge clean and to find leaks. Most rust stains can be removed with a commercial rust stain remover available in hardware stores. Dirt and grease stains should be scrubbed off with a stiff brush and a strong detergent. Don't use any acid for cleaning the engine room, and don't use any of those powerful hull cleaners that contain acid (many contain phosphoric acid).

• Put scrap pieces of carpet under each battery to absorb water when you accidentally overfill it. The carpet will also catch spilled battery acid before it can damage nearby hardware.

• Make sure you have safe footing in the engine room. Pay particular attention to places where you step when climbing down into the bilge, especially if that surface is not level and apt to be slippery at times. Nonskid plastic grids or teak grating can be put down where needed. If the bilge is deep, you can install wood steps or small raised platforms to provide safer (and cleaner) footing when climbing in and out of the bilge.

KEEPING SEAGULLS AWAY

Seagulls can wreak havoc on glossy varnish and polished gel coat when a boat is sitting at its mooring. However, here is an inexpensive solution that will end most seagull problems forever:

Set up a tall pole near the center of the boat, then tie six or eight lengths of light line to the top of this pole so that the lines radiate out and down to form a "Christmas tree" of string as shown in Figure 1.20. The lower end of each line is tied to a pad eye, railing, or other convenient point along the sides of the boat. Instead of tying the lines in place around the boat, you can tie a brass S-hook to the bottom end of each line, then hook this into the pad eye (make sure there is a slight amount of tension on each line).

The tricky part is setting up the tall pole (a telescoping pole is easier to store). I used a fishing rod holder attached to the front of the console as a supporting socket that holds the pole up while the lines are being secured, but you will have to rig up the setup that will best fit your particular boat. Obviously a sailboat or a powerboat with a tall mast near the center will not need a separate pole. Label each line with a colored piece of tape so you can quickly set up the lines in the same pattern next time.

This will keep gulls away because they will not fly under a structure that looks like it might be a trap, and they are

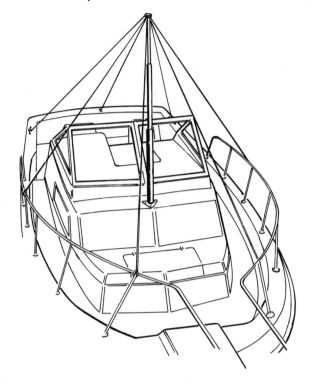

Figure 1.20

afraid to come close to wires or strings that might snag their wings. If you normally cover your boat when it is at its mooring, you will have to make a reinforced hole in the center of the cover for the pole to fit through.

GIVE YOUR BOAT A MIDSUMMER SPRUCE UP

During spring commissioning there never seems to be enough time really to do a proper job of sprucing up and renewing the appearance of the boat. Although summer is the time to enjoy your boat, some forget that midsummer maintenance is almost as important as the spring commissioning routine—if you want to keep your boat from "growing old" before its time. This doesn't mean you have to give up a lot of your cruising time—

it just means that you should make good use of some of those days when the weather is not ideal for taking the boat out, or some of those "lay-up" days when you are just sitting around while tied to a dock in the middle of a cruise, waiting for the weather to break.

Exterior Fiberglass

You probably gave your boat a coat of wax as part of its regular spring commissioning, but in most cases this wax doesn't maintain its original gloss for more than a couple of months. Restoring that gloss is not only desirable for esthetic reasons, it also helps shed dirt more effectively, thus making the job of washing and cleaning the boat a lot easier. Most professionals feel that a paste wax is best, but many of the better-quality liquid waxes and polishes do a surprisingly good job of restoring the gloss to dulled gel coat without requiring any rubbing or buffing—which is why many will opt for using one of these when trying to spruce up the boat.

It's generally best to apply wax sparingly when rubbing it on (two thin coats are almost always better than one heavy coat) and to follow the manufacturer's directions exactly. Wax or polish that is applied too heavily, or wax that is not thoroughly buffed, will stay soft and will attract and hold dirt. It is best to stay away from a wax or polish that has silicone in it if you think you may want to paint that surface at some time in the future because silicones are very difficult to remove. Also, before applying any wax or polish, make sure the surface is absolutely clean and dry.

Sometimes waxing or polishing is not enough to restore the shine because the gel coat is badly oxidized. In such cases you may have to use an abrasive-type fiberglass polishing compound or fiberglass cleaner to remove the oxidized layer before any wax is applied. This actually removes a thin film of the gel coat, so try not to let things get that bad before applying a fresh coat of wax to the finish.

Teak and Brightwork

The two secrets to maintaining any clear finish—varnish or sealer—is not to let them go too long between applications, and to touch up defects promptly. In other words, apply a fresh coat as soon as the finish starts to dull or to show signs of wear, and touch up nicks and scratches as soon as you notice them.

This is particularly important when dealing with varnished finishes because water that seeps through and into the wood is certain to cause cracking and peeling of the varnish. Varnished teak will usually turn white if water gets under the varnish, but in most cases sanding and touching up will remove these blemishes. Mahogany, on the other hand, will usually turn dark; the only way to lighten this wood is to strip off all of the old varnish, then use a wood bleach to get rid of the discoloration.

To touch up scratches and nicks in varnish, first sand these spots with a small folded piece of #220 paper, being careful to avoid sanding outside the damaged area if possible. Sand deep enough to get rid of any discoloration (if the wood is dark and the stain won't come out, you may have to use a wood bleach). Clean off sanding dust by wiping with a rag moistened with paint thinner, then apply a thin coat of varnish with a small brush, feathering the varnish out so it blends in with the surrounding surface. When this dries, sand again with #400 paper, then apply one or two more coats in the same fashion.

When varnish starts to lose its gloss in the middle of the summer, it's time to apply a fresh coat—don't wait till all the varnish is dull or starting to crack or peel. Sand carefully as described above, then apply fresh varnish on a day when there is low humidity and little wind. If possible, don't varnish in direct sunlight, and don't varnish when temperatures are likely to climb above 85 degrees while the varnish is still wet.

Teak that has been coated with an oil or sealer, rather than a varnish, will need to be refinished more often because all these finishes tend to wear and get dull rapidly. In most cases they need to be redone once every sixty to ninety days to maintain the original finish. Hosing down frequently with fresh water is a must if you boat in a salt water area, but be prepared to give the teak a more thorough scrubbing at least once a month during the summer. When recoating, it is usually best to stick with the same brand; be sure you follow directions on the can regarding how to apply it and how many coats to apply.

Chrome and Stainless Steel

Good-quality deck hardware of stainless steel or chrome is highly resistant to corrosion and the marine environment, but it still needs *some* maintenance if you want to keep it looking bright, shiny, and like new. Small streaks of surface corrosion can develop due to corrosion and oxidation of fasteners or due to slight amounts of surface corrosion where metal tools or abrasive pads (used by the manufacturer or boat builder) left microscopic particles of ferrous metal in the pores of the metal.

This type of oxidation can usually be removed with a good metal polish, but avoid using abrasive pads or steel wool on highly polished stainless steel and chrome. After polishing, protect the metal with a light coat of marine wax, or with one of the clear metal protective coatings that are sold in marine outlets. You can also wipe on a light film of a moisture-displacing and corrosion-resistant lubricant, but this will have to be renewed more frequently.

While cleaning and polishing the deck hardware, take time to test each bolt, nut, and screw for tightness, and try each fastener to see if it is loose (Figure 1.21). If the fastener is

Figure 1.21

corroded, replace it with a new one. If a screw won't tighten completely, take it out and fill the hole with wood toothpicks or matchsticks before reinserting the screw and tightening it again. Or replace the original screw with a slightly larger one.

Canvas and Curtains

Canvas tops, covers, and roll-up curtains should be kept clean not only for appearance sake, but also to minimize rot and mildew. It is essential to hose them off with fresh water to remove salt spray at the end of each day, and you should never roll up curtains while they are wet—allow them to dry thoroughly first, or wipe carefully with a soft chamois to dry. Use a vinyl cleaner or shampoo to remove embedded dirt and streaks in the canvas or vinyl, but don't scrub any more than you have to. Never use a brush to scrub clear vinyl "windows" in roll-up curtains. When washing is necessary, use a soft sponge or a cloth with mild soap and water, or use one of the special cleaners that are made for use on plastic windshields and vinyl curtains. These help remove fine scratches and cloudiness, as well as stubborn stains, from clear plastic and vinyl.

Interiors

Wood paneling and trim can go for years without the need for refinishing, but the finish will look better and last longer if you clean it regularly. An all-purpose spray-on household cleaner can be used for wiping off fingerprints and mild soil. Heavy soil that won't come off easily can be cleaned by wiping down with a rag moistened with paint thinner (make sure there is plenty of ventilation while doing this). Turn the rag frequently as it gets dirty, and dispose of the rag on shore when you are done. If the finish looks dull after it is cleaned, wipe down with a wood polish or apply a coat of an oil-type finish such as Watco's Danish Oil or Minwax Antique Oil finish.

Small nicks and scratches in the wood can be touched up by using one of the crayon-type wax sticks or touch-up pencils that are sold for this purpose in paint and hardware stores. They come in a range of wood-tone colors, so you should be able to find one that will match closely. Run the wax stick or pencil back and forth across the scratch or nick until it is filled in, then smooth off any excess with a plastic scraper. To restore the gloss, wipe on a little wax or polish, and buff with a cloth when dry.

Clean all upholstered cushions and furniture using a vinyl cleaner on vinyl-covered cushions and a regular foam-type upholstery cleaner on fabric-covered cushions. Use a commercial spot remover first to get rid of noticeable stains. After cleaning vinyl cushions, wipe on a protective vinyl coating (those sold in marine supply stores). Conventional fabric-covered upholstery can be cleaned by first using a vacuum and then using a foam-type upholstery cleaner to give the entire piece a thorough cleaning.

Many modern cruisers make extensive use of carpeting on the interior—both as a floor covering and as a decorative wall covering for bulkheads and exposed fiberglass on the inside. This also serves as an acoustical and thermal insulation, but it does have one drawback—it tends to attract and hold dust and dirt. That's why it is essential to clean thoroughly this carpet at least once a year by vacuuming and by using a foam-type carpet cleaner.

If the cabin soles (floors) are covered with sheet vinyl

rather than carpet, then a good scrubbing is all that is required to get it clean. Use one of the cleaners made for use on vinyl floors, then apply a vinyl dressing—don't use a floor wax or polish that will leave the floor slippery. If the vinyl is drab-looking or worn, you may want to put down new vinyl floor-ing. If there is only one layer of vinyl on the floor, you can put a second layer down right on top of it. However, if the old vinyl has a cushion backing, then it's not a good idea to put new flooring over it—the old material should be ripped off first.

Countertops and cabinets that are covered with plastic lam-inate should be cleaned and polished with one of the various polishes that are sold for this purpose in supermarkets and hardware stores. Wood drawers should be pulled and cleaned, then the exposed wood on the inside and outside should be sprayed with shellac or a similar sealant to keep the wood from absorbing moisture that could cause swelling. Interior trim that has been finished with a clear varnish or sealer of some kind usually needs cleaning at least once a year to get rid of finger marks and soil (Murphy's Oil Soap works fine for this).

Protecting Clear Plastic Curtains

The clear plastic curtains used on flying bridges and deck or cockpit enclosures quickly will begin to discolor and scorch during the summer months wherever the clear plastic is al-lowed to come in contact with the hot metal pipes and other fittings that form the framework for that enclosure. To keep this from happening after new curtains have been installed, buy some flexible, white corrugated plastic hose—the kind sold for use with bilge pumps. Cut this into the lengths needed to cover each piece of metal pipe where the vinyl lays against it. Slit each piece of hose lengthwise, then slip it over the pipe supports without taking the framework apart. The plastic hose will keep the vinyl from touching the hot metal pipes, yet each piece can be easily pulled off when not needed or when you wash or polish the metal.

FINDING AND FIXING TROUBLESOME LEAKS

Boat owners normally expect to encounter some dampness inside their boat, but a leak that allows water to drip down into the cabin or a locker is not only frustrating and annoying, it can also cause quite a bit of damage. The most frequently encountered troublesome leaks are those in which water finds its way in around window frames or portholes that have not been properly installed, or when water seeps in around bolts and screws that hold stanchions, cleats, and other deck hardware in place.

Before you can fix any of these leaks, you must first pinpoint the place where water is entering. Unfortunately, this is not always easy. Water can seep in through tiny, sometimes invisible, openings, and it can show up on the interior some distance away from where it actually entered. Water will not normally flow uphill, but it can flow along horizontal surfaces, and since boats roll and pitch, these horizontal surfaces can change their slope—and thus the direction in which the water will run.

The best time to pinpoint the source of any leak is while water is actually coming in—in other words, while it is raining. Unfortunately, this is not often possible; you have to be on board at just the right time to watch from the inside. The best option, then, is to use a hose on the outside to simulate rain (or flying spray) when trying to track down the source of a leak.

This strategy works in most cases, but it does take time and patience. You have to direct the stream of water against the surface at an angle that closely simulates the angle at which rain or spray normally strikes that area, and you have to hold the hose in one spot for some time in order to test thoroughly for a possible leak in that area (some leaks don't show up until after it has been raining for thirty minutes or more—and then only if the wind is blowing from a certain direction). Therefore, it's usually best to tie the hose nozzle to a stanchion or other support so that the hose will be aimed at one area for as long as it takes for the water to show up while you watch from inside to see where the moisture is first visible. Do not adjust the nozzle for a strong jetlike stream—try to simulate natural rain by setting the nozzle for a wide spray, or even by using the hose without a nozzle in some cases.

You may also have to direct the water over the suspected location from several different directions, each time for at least fifteen to twenty minutes. Then shut the water off for about ten minutes before turning it on again from another direction. Position the nozzle at different heights if the first setup doesn't cause the leak to show up, but make sure someone is watching from below all the time. If you are not sure where to start, begin wetting the outside at the lowest point near the suspected location, then gradually move the hose higher a foot or so at a time. If necessary, you may also have to move the stream of water from one side of the suspected area to the other until you see water coming through on the inside.

Once the leak shows up on the inside, the next step is tracking it back to its source. Start at the spot inside the boat where you first see water dripping or signs of dampness, then backtrack until you get to the spot where water seems to be entering. This is seldom easy, and it often requires removing some interior moldings or even a section of paneling or head-liner in order to follow the path of the water back to its source. One trick that helps is first to dry off all surfaces so that there is no visible water or dampness, then watch patiently (while it is still raining or while a hose is flooding the outside) to see where the first sign of dampness shows up. It usually helps to shine a flashlight around in dark corners or enclosed spaces such as the inside of lockers or cabinets, and it's a good idea to place strips of dry paper toweling on the various surfaces after you dry them so that you can see which piece of paper towel first shows signs of moisture.

Carefully examine the areas that are directly above and to each side of the place where the leak first showed up on the inside. Inspect every joint and seam on the outside as well as the inside, and inspect all of the deck-mounted hardware above and next to this area. Look for signs of cracked or dried out sealant, or for places where water could be working its way in under the base of a stanchion, chock, cleat, or other piece of deck hardware.

When searching for the source of the leak, don't take for granted that the source will necessarily be directly above or next to the place where you first spotted the water on the inside—the actual point of entry could be several feet away. For example, a damp spot on interior wood paneling directly under a porthole does not necessarily mean that there is a leak around that port. As illustrated in Figure 1.22, water could be seeping in through one of the bolts used to secure a hatch installed on the deck above this port—even it is several feet

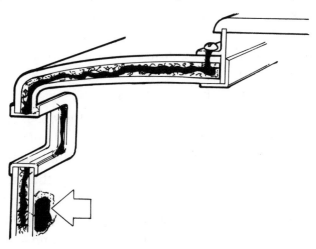

Figure 1.22

off to one side of the port's frame. Water would then drip down through the bolt hole onto the sloping headliner below, and then run horizontally along the headliner until it drops off into the space behind the interior wood paneling. The water might then flow down onto the top of the porthole's frame and run along the outside of this frame until it dripped down to the wood blocking that supports the interior paneling. A puddle would then accumulate until it soaked into the wood panel from behind—creating a damp spot that would show up on the inside.

Of course, in some cases you will be able to spot the source of a leak fairly quickly. For example, if you see a bead of caulking that is cracked, or if you spot an open joint or seam. Deck-mounted hardware (cleats, chocks, stanchions, grab rails, and railings) are other common sources of hard-to-find leaks. To locate these, first test each of the screws or bolts that hold the hardware in place to make certain they are tight.

Stanchion bases are frequent offenders because they are subject to considerable stress when people lean against them or pull on them while climbing on board. Pull on the top of each one to see if its base moves or lifts slightly under stress. If they wiggle or move the slightest amount when tugged on, there is a good chance that water could be finding its way in under the base and seeping down into and through the deck. Don't forget to also check fasteners for hand grips, railings, and other brackets that are mounted on the cabin sides and decks. Even when fastened to a vertical surface, these can still be a possible source of leaks.

Trying to fix a leak under a piece of deck-mounted hardware by running a bead of compound around the outside of its base is usually a waste of time. The only way to do the job right is to remove the fixture completely, then reinstall it properly. Scrape away all of the old bedding compound—from the base of the hardware, as well as from the surface on which it was mounted—then inspect the fiberglass to see if it has been cracked or stressed out of shape. If so, this must be repaired before remounting the hardware.

After spreading a layer of marine-grade bedding compound, force some of the same compound into each of the mounting holes. Replace the hardware in its original position, pressing down only hard enough to squeeze out excess sealant on all sides, but not so hard as to squeeze out *all* of the compound. Spread additional compound under the head of the bolt and around its body before you insert it, then apply a little more compound to the threaded portion of the bolt that comes out at the other end. Tighten by turning the nut rather than by turning the bolt; this lessens the chance of creating voids in the sealant when the bolt is turned. Tighten the nut by hand and give it about one more half turn with a wrench, then wait about twenty minutes before tightening it the rest of the way. This will allow the silicone to cure sufficiently to form a water-tight gasket that won't squeeze out.

In addition to poorly bedded stanchions and other deck hardware, another common source of leaks is a window or porthole whose frame was not bedded properly. Here again, efforts to stop the leak by merely running a bead of sealant around the outside will seldom solve the problem for long. The only sure cure is to remove the window or port frame completely, then rebed it properly using a marine-grade sealant under the flange or rim. When you do this, make certain all bolt holes or screw holes are sealed by forcing compound into each one before replacing and tightening the fasteners.

If there is a leak in a deck joint or a seam where molded sections meet, the first thing you should try is to dig out all of the old sealant and then reseal that seam by forcing in a new bead of fresh compound. If the leak seems to be along a rub rail or toe rail, chances are you will have to take that rail off completely and then rebed it to solve the problem. In extreme

Condensation: Often Mistaken for a Leak

⚓ Moisture that forms inside the boat due to condensation can be just as annoying—and sometimes just as damaging—as an actual leak. Eliminating this problem is easier than finding and fixing a leak in most cases, but first you have to understand the causes of condensation.

Warm air can hold more moisture vapor than cold air, so if warm air is chilled by coming in contact with a cold surface, the excess moisture condenses to form drops of water on the colder surface—just as a glass of ice water "sweats" on a hot summer day. The warmer inside air gets chilled by the cold glass, and some of its moisture condenses, forming beads of water on the inside of the window and its metal frame.

The best way to combat this problem is to increase ventilation and air circulation inside the boat. The circulation of air not only serves to dry off damp surfaces by helping moisture evaporate, but the added ventilation also brings in drier and colder air from the outside. One way to accomplish this is to install vents that will let air circulate through the inside even when the boat is closed up. Another way is to leave some ports or hatches open slightly—especially when the boat is closed up for several days. To keep windshields from fogging on rainy days or chilly nights, install one or two small 12-volt fans under the windshield so that they blow upward and across the inside at an angle (such fans are sold in auto supply stores for use in trucks and vans).

Some form of insulation is usually not necessary to prevent condensation from forming on the inside of the fiberglass hull mold in boats that are made with a separate interior liner or those of "sandwich" construction. However, condensation can be a problem if the hull consists of a single layer of laminate that is uncovered on the inside. In such cases carpet is often glued to the inside to keep the warm, humid inside air from coming in contact with the cold fiberglass.

Insulating windows or portholes is usually not as simple, at least not during the boating season when you want to be able to open windows. However, those who live aboard during cold weather can prevent condensation forming on the glass and on the metal frames by taping sheets of clear plastic over the inside of the window and its frame to create a kind of interior "storm window" that will keep warm inside air away from the cold surfaces. The sheet of plastic should not touch the metal or the glass.

Most condensation problems in lockers and cabinets can be eliminated by adding louvered vents that will allow air to circulate. An even more effective method is to add a mild source of heat to the inside of such spaces. One popular solution is to install one or more GoldenRods (from Buenger Enterprises, 800-451-6797). These tubular low temperature "heating rods" are sold in marine supply outlets and are normally placed along the bottom of the cold wall inside lockers or cabinets. When plugged into a 110-volt AC outlet, they give off enough mild heat to prevent condensation and to help increase air circulation.

cases where disassembly and rebedding doesn't stop the leak, it may be necessary to cover that entire seam or joint with a built-up layer of fiberglass laminate, or with some type of metal or plastic molding. This must be suitably fastened in place with mechanical fasteners after making certain it has been properly sealed with bedding compound.

SECTION 2

TOOLS AND EQUIPMENT

BILGE PUMP PRIMER

The number of bilge pumps required for any boat will depend not only on the size of that boat, but also on how the bilge area is divided up or partitioned into compartments. If there are places where bilgewater cannot flow freely from one space to another, then a separate pump may be required in each compartment.

Electric bilge pumps come in two basic types: diaphragm pumps that must be mounted above the water level, and submersible pumps that sit in the bilgewater right against the bottom of the hull. All pumps approved for marine use are self-priming; they should be unaffected by the oil and grease often present in bilgewater, without damaging the pump's impeller or other internal components.

As a rule, submersible bilge pumps are more compact and easier to install since you don't have to run a separate intake hose from the pump down to where the water is. Those that are not submersible must be mounted above the water level—

which means you then have to run an intake hose from the pump to the lowest point in the bilge. To avoid clogging, the intake end of this hose should be protected with a strainer of some kind. Submersible pumps should be installed in the lowest part of the bilge where they will draw water in through screened or slotted openings around the base—no separate intake hose is required. All bilge pumps, regardless of type, still require a discharge hose to carry the water overboard by means of a through-hull fitting located high enough to be above the outside waterline at all times.

Submersible pumps come with electric wire leads that are at least 12 to 18 inches in length, so you should be able to make all electrical connections high enough to keep these splices out of the water. Use insulated crimp fittings and wrap these with waterproof electrical tape or seal with "heat shrink" insulation. Some submersible pumps have built-in float switches, but many require the installation of a separate float switch to provide fully automatic operation.

Float switches—built-in or separate—are the most frequent source of trouble with any bilge pump. That's because floating trash sometimes accumulates around the float arm, preventing it from riding up and down freely. This results in the float arm or lever getting stuck in the raised or "on" position, causing the pump to run continuously.

One simple way to prevent such problems is to enclose the float switch and the submersible pump with a wire mesh "cage" as shown in Figure 2.1. The mesh will act as a strainer to keep floating trash away from the switch. It can be in the form of a small cage that fits only over the float switch, or it can be in the form of a larger, boxlike enclosure that fits over both the switch and the submersible pump. This will also keep foreign objects from being dropped on the pump or switch from above.

The newest way to eliminate float switch problems is to

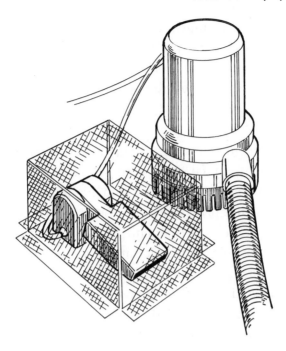

Figure 2.1

install a computerized bilge pump that needs no float switch. It has a built-in microcomputer in the base of the pump that checks to see if water is present every couple of minutes. If water is present, the pump comes on and stays on till the water is gone. If no water is present, the pump stays off. There are also electronic detectors that have no moving parts yet serve the same function as a float switch. They consist of a small plastic box that lays in the bilge and has a conductive metal button on the bottom that senses when water is present and then turns the pump on. A twelve-second delay keeps the pump from coming on unnecessarily when there is only a small amount of water sloshing around in the bilge.

Electric bilge pumps are very dependable and normally will last for many years, but they do require a source of electric power. Unfortunately, there are times when electric power fails—for example, when batteries lose their charge, or when a boat takes on so much water that the batteries are submerged. For these and other safety reasons, every boat should also be equipped with at least one good manual bilge pump—preferably a permanently installed model which has a vertical handle that you pump back and forth to remove water from the bilge.

These come in two types: single-action models that draw water into the pump chamber with one stroke, then discharge the water on the return stroke; and higher-capacity double-action models that discharge water on both strokes. On some models this handle is permanently attached, but on most the handle is removable so that it can be stored out of the way when not needed. A suction hose is attached to the intake side of the pump and should be placed where its end will reach down to the lowest part of the bilge. There should also be a strainer of some kind attached to the intake end.

Even if a boat is equipped with both electric and manual bilge pumps, in a serious emergency the boat could start taking on water so rapidly that all of the pumps cannot keep up with the water coming in. That's when a high-capacity, engine-driven bilge pump can be a lifesaver. Available from marine supply outlets and engine dealers, these pumps are usually belt-driven by the engine's flywheel or a drive pulley mounted on the engine. A remotely controlled electric clutch or a manual clutch serves to activate the pump.

Even if your boat is not equipped with such an engine-driven pump, in an emergency you can use the engine's cooling system as a high-capacity pump to suck water out of the bilge. Here's how: Shut down the engine; then close the engine's intake seacock (cut it off if you have to) for the cooling system, pull the hose off this seacock, and wrap screen mesh around the end of this hose. Drop this screened end into the bilgewater and start the engine again. This will cause the engine to draw its cooling water out of the bilge instead of

Having Two Float Switches Eliminates Frequent Cycling

⚓ Float-type bilge pump switches frequently turn the pump on for many unnecessary short cycles when the boat rocks at a dock or mooring. This can shorten the life of the pump and switch, as well as drain the battery.

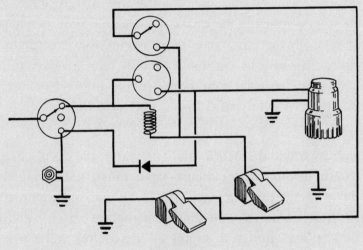

Figure 2.2

To solve this problem you can "piggyback" a second float switch a little higher than the original one, wiring them as shown in Figure 2.2. Both switches are in the same circuit, with a double-pole, double-throw switch (center position off) that enables you to select which of the two float switches will control the bilge pump. In one position the lower float switch is used to activate the pump; in the other position it turns control of the bilge pump over to the upper float switch. When under way, the three-way switch is in position to activate the lower float switch position; when the boat is at a dock or mooring, the three-way switch is set to activate the higher float switch.

The lower switch keeps the water level as low as possible

because, when under way, frequent cycling is no problem. When the switch is set to activate the higher float switch (when at dock or mooring), the pump will come on less frequently even if the boat rocks; it won't be as much of a drain on the battery.

In addition to the double-pole switch, a relay is needed in the circuit to keep the pump operating when the water level is between the upper and lower limits of the two switches. Another toggle switch in the circuit allows you to turn the pump on manually at any time, regardless of the float-control switches. The parts needed can be obtained from any electronics supply store, but make sure the switches and the relays match the voltage on your boat (12 volts or 24 volts DC).

through its original seacock, and the water will be discharged overboard through the exhaust—at a much faster rate than any bilge pump can manage. This technique is, of course, to be used only in an extreme emergency when water is pouring in at a rate fast enough to supply all the cooling water needed by the engine.

You can create a permanent setup that will permit you to use the engine in this manner quickly, without having to disconnect the intake hose from its seacock. All you have to do is install a permanent Y-fitting in the existing intake water-line of the cooling system. One opening in the Y is attached to a shut-off valve, while the other opening in the Y connects to the intake seacock in the usual manner. During normal operation the shut-off valve attached to the extra opening in the Y-valve is closed, so water will then be drawn in through the seacock in the usual manner. When there is an emergency and you want to use the engine to pump out the bilge, all you have to do is close the seacock and open this extra valve, allowing water to be drawn in from the bilge rather than through the seacock.

ROPES AND LINES

Anchor lines, mooring lines, docking lines, and all other lines used on a boat must meet certain requirements to ensure maximum strength and security, so the boat owner must take care to buy the right type of rope for each use.

Manila rope and other ropes made of natural fiber have just about disappeared from the pleasure-boating scene so that it is now almost impossible to find a marine dealer who still stocks them. Synthetic rope is not only a lot stronger and more durable, it is also a lot more resistant to attack by sunlight, rot, or mildew. It comes in many different varieties that differ in the type of fiber used and in how that particular type of rope is manufactured or put together.

The three most common types of rope used on pleasure boats are those made of nylon, polypropylene, or polyester (commonly referred to as Dacron, although this is actually Du-Pont's brand name for its polyester fiber). A newer synthetic fiber, Kevlar, has also been used in making rope, but this high-tech rope, as well as some specialized ropes that are made with a blend of this and other fibers, is mostly used on sophisticated racing sailboats.

Nylon rope is generally considered the strongest rope fiber, while polyester (Dacron) is a close second. Both are highly resistant to attack by most organic solvents and, like all rope made with synthetic fiber (including polypropylene), both can be stowed wet without worrying about rot. However, both will degrade after long exposure to ultraviolet rays (sunlight), but here Dacron has the edge on nylon—it is a little more resistant to attack by ultraviolet rays.

The big difference between nylon and Dacron is that a nylon rope will stretch, while Dacron rope hardly stretches at all. This ability to stretch under load is a useful and very desirable feature in dock lines and anchor lines because the ability to stretch and recover under sudden loads and surges means that a nylon line can absorb considerable shock without breaking and without exerting sudden stress on the boat's cleats, mooring bitts, and chocks. A dock line that stretches and springs back when the boat is being pushed around by the wind or by surging wave action will act like a shock absorber without transferring the full force of each surge to the boat, and by the same token an anchor line that stretches will absorb shocks more easily and thus will be less likely to pull the anchor loose when you have to ride out a storm.

On the other hand, Dacron's resistance to stretching makes it ideal for running rigging on a sailboat—sheets, halyards, etc. It is also useful for lifelines and for lashing things down on a powerboat or sailboat where you obviously do *not* want the lines to stretch when under load.

Polypropylene rope has limited use on most pleasure boats because it will not stretch or absorb shocks the way nylon will, and it is much more susceptible to damage by long exposure to sunlight. In addition, polypropylene isn't nearly as strong as nylon or Dacron, and it is much more susceptible to damage from chafe and abrasion. Another drawback is that it is so "slippery" that knots often do not hold well. However, polypropylene does have two big advantages—it is very lightweight, and it floats. As a result, polypropylene is often used for towing a dinghy or tender—the towline will float when it goes slack and thus will not foul the propeller, and it is also widely used as a towrope for hauling water-skiers.

In addition to varying in the type of fiber used, ropes also vary in how they are "constructed" or manufactured. The two types most often used on pleasure boats are three-strand laid rope and braided rope. Three-strand laid rope (also referred to as twisted rope) is the oldest type. This manufacturing method has been around for thousands of years; the individual fibers are first twisted together to form strands, then three of these finished strands are twisted together to form the actual rope.

When the fibers are twisted to form each strand, they are most often twisted in a counterclockwise direction—which is technically known as a left-hand lay. Then when the separate strands are twisted together to form the finished rope, they are twisted in a clockwise direction—technically referred to as a right-hand lay. These opposing twists, plus the fact that the rope is manufactured under carefully controlled tension, keep the rope from untwisting or "unlaying" when in use.

Braided rope is not made of strands that are twisted together in this manner; instead, it consists of multiple strands that are plaited or "laid up" to form the braided rope. The simplest form is single-braid, but the type most often used around boats is double-braid. Small-diameter single-braided rope has only limited marine use—it is seldom if ever used for dock lines or anything for which the safety or the security of the boat is at stake. Double-braided rope, on the other hand, is often used for dock lines. It is much stronger than single-braid, and actually consists of two ropes in one—a solid braided core in the center surrounded by a hollow braided cover on the outside.

Braided lines are more flexible and "softer" to handle than equivalent-size laid or twisted line—and they can be coiled in either direction without kinking. On the other hand, braided rope does not have the shock-absorbing qualities of an equivalent size three-strand twisted line, an important point to consider when selecting an anchor line. This is not an absolute and may vary when comparing different brands of rope in each category. Also, splicing braided rope is a bit more difficult than twisted rope and special tools are required that will vary with the diameter of the rope being spliced.

Most experienced boat owners agree that a braided line is easier to coil and to handle than an equivalent-size three-

Taking Care of Your Lines

⚓ Abrasion damages rope severely, so inspect chocks, cleats, and mooring bitts frequently to eliminate rough spots, burrs, and sharp corners. Use chafing gear to protect dock and mooring lines where they pass through or around these items, or wherever the line may be subject to any abrasion. Also, rotate your "permanent" dock lines periodically so that the same line is not always under maximum strain. Keep bitter ends from unraveling by whipping or dipping into one of those liquid plastic compounds that are sold for this purpose.

If lines are dirty or covered with salt, hose them off with fresh water to wash out particles that could cause internal damage to fibers. Better yet, put each line in a net laundry bag, then drop the whole bag in a washing machine. Use lukewarm water with one cup of mild detergent for the washing, then rinse with two caps full of fabric softener added to the water. After spin drying, your lines will come out clean and fresh, and should be a lot softer to handle.

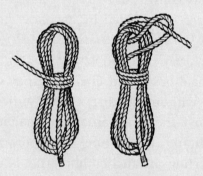

Figure 2.3

Coil each line neatly before storing it, and don't just throw it into a locker or lazarette with other gear. There are many methods for coiling, but one simple method is to first form a coil by winding the line around your hand and bent elbow, coiling it in a clockwise direction. Slip the coil off your arm and wrap the free end two or three times around the middle of the coil as shown Figure 2.3. Then finish by pulling a loop through the center and pass the free end of the line through this loop as indicated. The protruding end then forms a handy tail that simplifies carrying the coil around, as well as tying that coil to a railing or cleat.

Store lines out of direct sunlight when possible, and never drag lines over a rough dock or deck surface, or over dirt, stones, and sand. Particles can work their way into the rope and damage the fibers on the inside. When this is unavoidable, hose off the dirt or sand before using the line again.

strand laid line, but there is considerable difference of opinion (among manufacturers as well as boat owners) as to which type of line is more resistant to chafing. Many feel that braided lines tend to chafe easier, but some experts point out that this is only because the outside cover on a braided rope will snag more easily—on splinters, rough pilings, etc. These snags pull out some fibers and can weaken the outer cover, but only in extreme cases will it affect the actual strength of the line itself.

Manufacturers of braided rope point out that size for size, braided line usually has a higher breaking strength than three-strand twisted line, so that even if the outer braided cover does show signs of chafe, that line will still be as strong as most stranded lines of equivalent size. Chafing damage takes place only on the outer cover; the solid inner core is still fully protected. In addition, the inner core is also completely protected from ultraviolet damage.

When shopping for rope, bear in mind that qualities vary—

not only the quality of the materials used, but also the quality of the manufacturing process. A rope should be flexible and have a nice feel, but it should also be relatively firm when handled. When you flex a three-strand rope and try to separate the strands, it should take some effort to open the strands and pull them apart, especially in sizes larger than ½ inch. It should take some pulling or prying with a fid to separate the strands. If you can pull the strands apart easily with your fingers, the rope is too soft.

Braided rope should look smooth on the outside, with no tufts or snags sticking out. If you bend the rope sharply in your fingers, the outer braid should not separate to expose the inner core. The rope should feel firm when coiled and flexed. If it feels very soft, it will snag easily and will be more susceptible to chafing.

SIX ESSENTIAL KNOTS

Every boat owner should have at least a rudimentary knowledge of the most basic—and most useful—knots, bends, and hitches. Some are used for tying one rope to another, but most are for tying one end of a rope to something else. Fortunately, most boat owners can get by with a knowledge of only six frequently used knots and bends, each of which are illustrated here.

A few simple definitions will make it easier to follow the instructions that go along with each drawing: The main part of the rope is called the *standing part*. The free end of the line, the part you are actually manipulating or working with as you move it around and over the standing part, is the *bitter end*, or *working end*. When you turn or fold the line back on itself to change its direction by 180 degrees, the curved section is called a *bight*, and when the bight is fully closed by bringing the bitter end across or over the standing part, then you have formed a *loop*.

The Bowline

This knot is used to form a loop on the end of a line and is probably one of the most useful of all marine knots. It is quick and easy to tie, and once formed, the knot has a high breaking strength almost equal to the rope itself. The knot will not slip or jam, and it is easy to untie when the loop is no longer needed. The most frequent use of the bowline is to create a large, fixed loop on the end of a dock line that has no eye splice at the end, or when you need a loop that is larger than the eye splice—for example, when you need a large "lasso" to throw over a piling or a group of pilings. The bowline is also used for hoisting heavy loads and can be tied in the line after it is wrapped around a ring or other fixed object.

Start by forming a large bight near the end of the line, making it about the size of the fixed loop you want to create, making a small loop in the standing part of the line as shown in Figure 2.4. While holding the small loop in your left hand, use your right hand to pass the bitter end of the line up through the small loop (from behind), and around in back of the standing part as shown. Curl this same end around the standing part and bring it back down through the small loop as illustrated. Then, while holding the standing part (above the little loop) in your left hand, hold the bitter end and the side of the big loop together with your right hand and pull the knot tight.

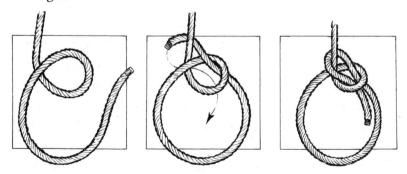

Figure 2.4

The Clove Hitch

The clove hitch is an easy hitch that can be quickly made and adjusted—either as it is being made up, or after it has been tied. Most often used to secure a docking line to a piling or large dock ring, the clove hitch is really *not safe to use when leaving a boat unattended* because it tends to slip easily when there is no tension on either end of the line. However, you can make it more secure after the hitch is complete by tying an extra half hitch over the standing part of the line (not illustrated) to keep the clove hitch from slipping or coming undone.

The clove hitch is the most frequently used method of tying the end of a dock line to a piling when pulling in to a dock because it is so easy for the person on the dock to pay out more line or take in slack as the boat is maneuvered closer to the dock or marina float. It is also very easy to adjust the line after the boat has been tied up—for example, if the wind or current changes, or if there is considerable variation in tide level.

There are really two ways to tie a clove hitch around a piling—depending on whether or not you can easily reach over the top of that piling. When you can reach over the top of the piling then you can quickly throw two loops over the piling as shown in Figure 2.5. If the piling is too high for you to reach over it, or if the top of the piling is closed off, then you can use the method shown in Figure 2.6.

In the first case you throw two counterclockwise preformed loops over the top of the piling, then pull tight on the working or bitter end. In the second case you pass the working end counterclockwise around the piling twice, each time passing this end under the standing part of the line and under the bight just made. In both cases you end up with the same hitch—two turns that go around the piling with the bitter end always passing *under* the loops. For added security it is always a good

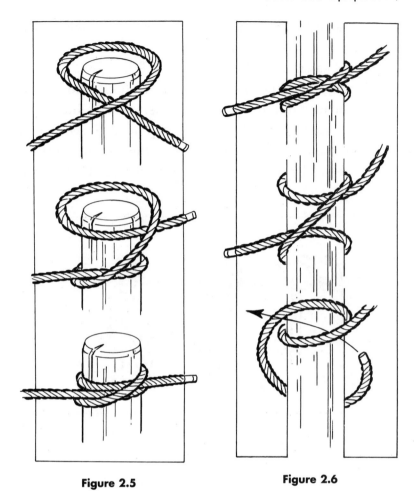

Figure 2.5   **Figure 2.6**

idea to then use the bitter end to tie an extra half hitch over the standing part.

Round Turn with Two Half Hitches

Half hitches are temporary knots that are quickly and easily tied or untied. Added strength and security against slipping is provided by combining two half hitches with a round turn as shown in Figure 2.7. This hitch is widely used for securing a line to a spar or ring, as well as for fastening fender lines to a railing, for securing a painter (towline) to the towing eye, or for tying up to a mooring ring.

Begin by passing the bitter end of the line twice around the railing or ring, then use this as the working end to take two half hitches around the standing part of the line. Make certain that in each case the end of the line is passed behind the standing part and through the eye of the loop just formed, as indicated in Figure 2.7. When finished, pull the two half hitches up tight.

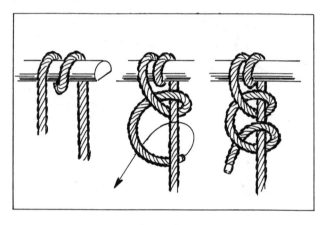

Figure 2.7

Anchor Bend

Also called the fisherman's bend, this useful knot is similar to the round turn with two half hitches, but it is a lot more secure. It is also a little harder to do, and is harder to untie when in a hurry. As its name indicates, it is most often used by mariners for securing an anchor line to the anchor's ring and is thus an excellent way to make up a spare anchor with its line. It can also be used for tying up to a mooring ring when the boat is to be left unattended for some time.

This bend is made by first passing the end of the line two or three times loosely through the ring (Figure 2.8 shows the line going through just twice because that is most common),

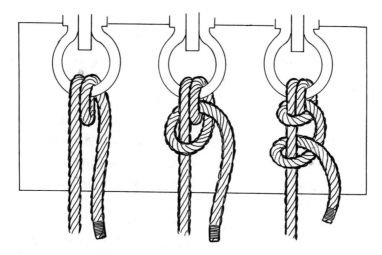

Figure 2.8

then passing the bitter end around the standing part and through the two turns (close to the ring) as shown. This forms the basic anchor bend, but for additional security an extra half hitch is almost always taken around the standing part of the line as illustrated here. When this knot is used to make up a permanent anchor rode, the bitter end is then further secured by seizing this end against the standing part of the line with whipping thread.

Sheet Bend

This knot is used to tie two different ropes together, end to end, when dealing with ropes of different diameters, or of completely different textures—for example, when joining a small braided line to a laid nylon line. On pleasure boats it is most often used to join a flag halyard to a larger line or to a corner of the flag. It is also used when tying a dinghy painter to the end of a larger-diameter docking line or anchor line. When this same bend is used to tie a smaller line to a closed eye splice at the end of a larger line, it is called a becket bend rather than a sheet bend.

Easily tied, the sheet bend increases in holding power as the strain on the knot is increased—the harder you pull the tighter the knot gets. Yet it can be untied as quickly as it was originally tied after the strain is released.

To make the knot, start by forming a bight in the end of the heavier line. Pass the end of the smaller line through this bight or loop, coming in from the back as shown in Figure 2.9. Pass the working end of this small line around the back of the loop in the heavier line, then bring it across the front of the loop while also threading it under the standing part of the smaller line as the drawing indicates. Finish by grasping the standing part of each line and then pulling both loops or bights away from each other to draw the knot tight.

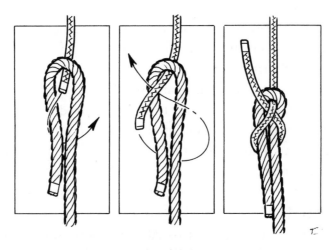

Figure 2.9

Double Carrick Bend

This is the traditional and most effective way of tying two lines of the same size together end to end, particularly when they are relatively heavy lines. It is often used when you have to make up an extra-long anchor line, or when a long docking line is needed. It's also the best way to tie two relatively stiff or coarse lines together. It is a bit more difficult to tie than the sheet bend, but is also much more stable and will not slip. However, it can be more difficult to untie after it has been subjected to lots of strain, or if the lines are wet.

Start by making a loop in one line. Hold this in your left hand. Then make a loop in the end of the second line after passing its end under the eye of the first loop and over the standing part of the first line. Continue forming the second loop by weaving this end under the working end of the first line and then coming down into the first loop and up behind its own standing part as shown in Figure 2.10. The knot is then tightened by pulling on both standing parts. You will find that when this knot is tightened it will tend to capsize and bunch up (not shown) with the two ends drawn close together and parallel to each other.

Figure 2.10

....
WINDSHIELD WIPER CARE

Although most boat owners don't use the boat's windshield wipers very often, it is important that they do the job properly when they are needed. However, even when wipers are not used, the sun's rays do considerable damage to the rubber blades. Protecting them from the sun will greatly lengthen their life.

The simplest way to accomplish this is to remove the blades and keep them stored out of the weather. This will keep them in "like new" condition and ready for use when needed. When rain threatens, the blades can be quickly snapped back into place to do their job. While the blades are stored away, keep the metal arm from scratching the windshield (if it should get moved around) by placing a small plastic bottle cap under the end of the arm. Also, spray the metal arm regularly with a rust preventative to protect against corrosion.

FENDERS

Fenders are used to protect pleasure boats from damage when they are tied against a dock, bulkhead, or pier—or when rafting up alongside another boat. Years ago boat owners used burlap sacks filled with rags or seaweed, or old automobile tires, but nowadays pleasure boat owners use molded plastic fenders that come in a wide assortment of styles, shapes, and sizes (Figure 2.11). They are not only neater looking and easier to handle, they are also tougher and longer-lasting. They come in two basic categories: those that are hollow and filled with air, and those that are solid or filled with a resilient compound of some kind.

Air-filled models are the most popular. They are filled under slight pressure (two or three pounds is typical) so that when combined with the flexibility of the outer casing of molded vinyl or similar plastic, they provide the resiliency required for proper cushioning. Air-filled fenders can be further divided into two separate classifications: those that are permanently sealed after having been pumped up at the factory, and

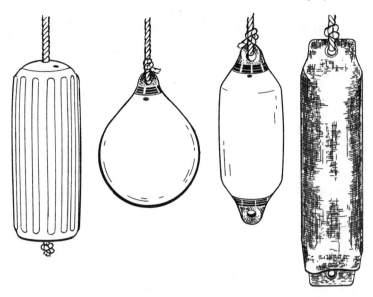

Figure 2.11

those that include a built-in inflation valve similar to the kind found in footballs or basketballs. The inflation valve makes it possible for the boat owner to inflate the fender with a needle-type pump.

Some fenders have flattened ends with a heavy ring or eye molded into each end for tying a line to them. Others have a continuous hole or tube running lengthwise through the center to accommodate a ⅜-inch or ½-inch line. A stopper knot is tied at each end of this line to keep it from being pulled all the way out.

Most fenders can be hung over the side in either a horizontal or vertical position. To hang an eyelet-type fender horizontally, two lengths of line would be required, one tied to each end of the fender. However, when this fender is hung vertically, you have to contend with one line hanging down— possibly into the water. To hang the type with a hole through the middle horizontally, only the one line is needed. But if you also want to be able to hang that fender horizontally, then the line should be about twice as long so that there will be enough line to permit hanging from each end.

Another style of air-filled fender that has become increasingly popular in recent years is the round, ball-shaped fender that looks like a floating buoy (some manufacturers refer to them as inflatable buoys, rather than as fenders). These spherical fenders have only one molded, reinforced rope eye at the top. In many cases, especially when tying up to a floating dock, these fenders are most effective—they are less likely to ride up onto the dock, especially if hung low enough to actually float on the water.

Several companies have introduced solid fenders that are not hollow or filled with air. They are filled with a highly resilient, closed-cell plastic foam or inner cushion that is covered with a tough polyester fabric on the outside. These solid, shock-absorbing fenders will withstand many years of hard wear and abuse. Manufacturers claim that, since solid fenders cannot burst they will actually outlast air-filled fenders. They also claim that, since they are denser than air-filled fenders, they will not compress as much in most cases, so boat owners can get by safely with fenders of a smaller diameter.

SEACOCKS

Although not all through-hull fittings are equipped with a seacock, because those located above the waterline may not need a shut-off valve, any through-hull located below the waterline must have one so that, if a hose or pipe connected to this fitting breaks, there will be a quick way to shut off the water that would otherwise come pouring into the boat. In addition, don't forget that even a through-hull fitting that is normally well above the waterline can still be a hazard if not equipped with a seacock. If the boat heels severely, or sinks low in the water due to overloading, that fitting could be submerged—

Fender Maintenance

⚓ Dirty, stained-looking fenders not only detract from a boat's appearance, they also create ugly streaks and stains on the hull as dirt from the fenders gets ground into the gel coat or paint when the fender rolls back and forth against the boat.

Fenders that are only moderately dirty can often be cleaned with a detergent or boat soap, but this is not always adequate if the fender is *really* dirty. One of the special fender cleaners formulated for just this purpose will work much better. They are much more effective in removing stubborn, ground-in stains, and they will also do the job a lot faster and with a lot less hard scrubbing.

Although strong solvents such as acetone or lacquer thinner can also be used for quickly cleaning stains off fenders, this is usually a mistake (and definitely not recommended by manufacturers). More often than not these solvents will tend to attack or degrade the plastic, leaving the surface of the fender sticky or tacky. This shortens the life of that fender and makes it even harder to clean.

and without a valve there would be no way to quickly shut off that opening.

All too often instead of an approved bronze seacock that meets the American Boat and Yacht Council standards and is listed by Underwriters Laboratories (UL) Marine Department, owners who are adding a toilet or other piece of equipment requiring a seacock economize by using a brass gate valve. (Some manufacturers have also been known to cut corners by installing brass gate valves instead of regular seacocks.) If your boat has one or more gate valves below the waterline, this should be replaced with an approved bronze seacock as soon as possible. Here's why:

Brass valves tend to seriously corrode in a marine environment, especially the valve stem. When the stem gets eaten away by corrosion, the valve is inoperable. In most cases the corroded valve stem simply breaks apart under stress (for example, when you're trying to close it in an emergency), so you're stuck with a valve that can't be closed or opened. Another serious drawback to any gate valve is that it requires several turns of the handle to go from fully open to fully closed (no through-hull valve should ever be partly open or closed). A proper seacock, on the other hand, goes from all the way open to all the way closed with only a quarter-turn of the lever handle (moving the handle through a 90-degree arc). When the handle is parallel to the hose, the valve is fully open; when the handle is at a right angle to the hose, the valve is fully closed.

Bronze seacocks that are approved for marine use will normally last the life of the boat and require very little maintenance—but this does not mean they can be ignored entirely. There are two different types in widespread use—the traditional plug-type valve and the ball valve.

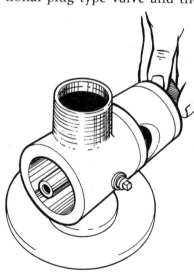

Figure 2.12

Plug-type valves (Figure 2.12) are the oldest. They have a cylindrical, slightly tapered metal plug that rotates inside the body of the valve when the handle is turned. The plug has a hole bored through it at a right angle to the length, and this hole has the same diameter as the valve openings. When the valve is in the open position, the hole that goes through the plug is turned by handle so that the plug's hole is in line with the openings in the body of the valve, allowing water to flow through. When the plug is rotated to close the valve, the hole in the plug is not in line so the flow of water is cut off.

Ball-type seacocks (Figure 2.13) differ in that they have a rotating ball on the inside, also with a hole through the center. The ball may be made of a special plastic, of chrome-plated bronze, or of stainless steel. It is also rotated by the handle so that its hole either lines up with the openings in the valve body (when the valve is open) or is at 90 degrees to the valve opening (when the valve is closed).

Plug valves are heavier and bulkier than ball valves, and they cost more in most cases (one reason why ball-type valves have become more popular in recent years). However, they can be taken apart for cleaning, lubrication, and servicing, while most ball-type valves cannot. Another advantage claimed for plug-type valves is that they have locknuts or wing nuts on the outside that can be tightened to prevent the handle from moving due to vibration. Some ball valves have an inter-

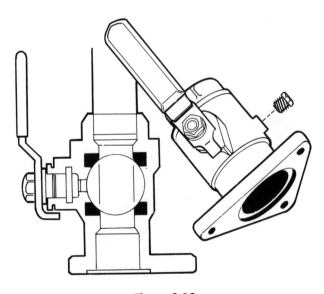

Figure 2.13

nal locking mechanism to accomplish the same thing; others depend only on internal friction to hold the ball in position.

Most ball-type valves have Teflon seats that never require lubrication, but it is still a good idea to lubricate the pivot point on the handle at least once a year by applying a few drops of oil or waterproof grease to the pivot bearing. On some models the seals will also require periodic lubrication with a waterproof grease, but check with the manufacturer if in doubt.

There is also a newer, specialized-type ball-type seacock that provides an added safety feature that boat owners will find useful in an emergency. Called the Groco SBV Safety Series (Figure 2.14), this model has a quick-release plug on the side of the valve body that can be removed by a simple quarter-turn of the plug. With this plug removed, the seacock permits

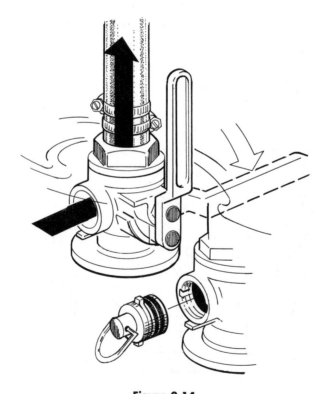

Figure 2.14

you to use the engine's cooling system pump as a high-capacity bilge pump in an emergency. You do this by first closing the seacock, then lifting the pull ring on the plug and giving it a twist so that you can pull the plug out. The engine will then start drawing water out of the bilge instead of through the seacock—assuming, of course, that the water inside the bilge is at least high enough to cover the plug opening in the side of the valve body. This bilgewater is then discharged overboard through the engine's exhaust system.

Plug-type valves are serviced (while the boat is out of the water) by first removing the two nuts on the side opposite the handle (on some models there is a wing nut or T-handle opposite the main handle instead of two nuts). Use a wood mallet, or a hammer and block of wood, to tap on the end of the threaded stud sticking out until the tapered plug comes out on the other side of the valve body. Clean the plug with a solvent to remove any marine growth or other foreign matter, then use a piece of emery cloth to smooth off scratches and rough spots. Smear the outside of the plug and the inside of the valve body with a liberal coat of waterproof grease, then slide the tapered plug back into place and reassemble the valve, tightening the retaining nuts just enough to permit the handle to turn while maintaining enough tension to keep it from moving due to vibration.

No matter what type of seacock you select, make sure you buy one that is a "full flow" design—one in which the opening in the rotating ball or plug is the same size as the pipe to be used with that seacock so that there will be no restriction when in the fully open position.

All seacocks, regardless of size or type, should be tested at least twice a year to make sure that they are still working properly. Open and close each one several times to make certain it is not "frozen" in either the open or the closed position. If your seacock has a wing nut or T-handle instead of retaining

Installing Seacocks

⚓ Making certain that your boat is equipped with approved bronze seacocks is only the half the battle. The other half is making sure that they are properly installed in accordance with the recommendations of the ABYC and the Coast Guard, and the listing requirements of UL's Marine Department.

Each seacock should have a mounting flange that allows it to be fastened solidly in place against the hull with bolts or screws that go into a backing block that is permanently bonded in place as shown in Figure 2.15. A seacock should never depend only on its through-hull fitting to hold it in place. The interior end of the through-hull fitting is normally a threaded length of pipe that screws into the base of the seacock so that when the pipe is tightened down it will clamp the seacock firmly in place. However, this alone is not enough for permanent mounting according to approved standards.

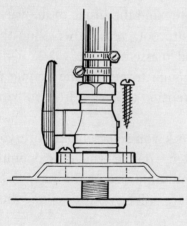

As Figure 2.15 shows, a solid backing block of wood or hard plastic is first bonded to the hull, then the seacock is fastened to this with screws or bolts. In a fiberglass boat the backing block should be bonded with epoxy resin, then the through-hull fitting and the seacock thoroughly bedded with a marine sealant suitable for underwater use before it is secured to the backing block and the hull material. Each fastener should be thoroughly bedded in marine sealant before it's tightened.

Figure 2.15

The body of the valve should be electrically connected to the boat's bonding system after it has been installed.

In metal hulls, a solid backing plate is needed to add extra strength to the relatively thin hull material, as well as to electrically insulate the metal fitting from the metal hull in order to minimize galvanic corrosion. The wood or metal block should have a shoulder on it that projects through an oversize hole bored through the metal hull so that, on the outside, the metal flange of the through-hull fitting does not come in contact with the metal hull.

nuts, chances are that you will have to loosen it before the valve handle can be turned (a little water may leak in, but this flow will stop as soon as the wing nut is retightened).

While testing each seacock, also inspect the hose clamps attached to it. There should be two clamps on each fitting, and they should be spaced so that the worm screws are on opposite sides. Most seacocks have one or two removable drain plugs in the body of the valve, so remember to remove these when the boat is being laid up for the winter.

MARINE PLUMBING

Delivering water to each sink or plumbing fixture inside the boat requires a plumbing system not unlike the one in your home, and this system is something the boat owner should be familiar with and know how to repair or replace when necessary; it's not as easy to get a plumber to work on your boat as it is to get a plumber to come to your house. Fortunately, with modern-day plastic pipe and fittings, marine plumbing work is usually a simple, do-it-yourself project that anyone can tackle safely. No special skills are required, and the only tools needed are those that most likely are already in your tool kit.

Clear, flexible vinyl tubing that is approved for use with potable water is still used in some boats, but all of the newer boats use opaque plastic pipe and fittings. This type of plastic plumbing is also used by most boat owners who have occasion to replace vinyl tubing when upgrading or repairing their existing water lines. These plastic pipes and fittings are now widely available in most home centers and plumbing supply outlets.

Although the clear vinyl tubing is easier to work with, it does have some serious drawbacks. It tends to discolor as it ages and often develops algae on the inside because it is transparent (algae needs light to thrive). When this happens, the water can develop an unpleasant taste. Also, it is very susceptible to annoying leaks, especially when the hose clamps are overtightened.

Opaque plastic pipe is not only stronger and more permanent than clear vinyl tubing, it also costs less. Unlike metal pipe or tubing, it will not rust or corrode, and it is not susceptible to attack by electrolysis. In addition, it does not build up scale on the inside the way some metal pipes do, and it weighs considerably less than metal.

There are about half a dozen different types of plastic pipe on the market, but only two are of interest to boat owners— CPVC (chlorinated polyvinyl chloride) pipe and PEX (cross-linked polyethylene) pipe or tubing. CPVC pipe is semirigid and is normally sold in straight lengths of ten or twenty feet. PEX pipe (also referred to as tubing) is flexible and comes in coils, although you can often buy it by the foot in local stores. Both CPVC and PEX are approved for use with either hot or cold water, and both are approved by the National Sanitation Foundation for carrying potable water.

Since CPVC is almost rigid (although it can be bent in a

slight curve) it has to run in an almost straight line. Elbows or tees must be inserted when the pipe has to go around obstructions or make sharp turns. PEX pipe or tubing, on the other hand, is flexible and can be bent around corners and obstructions, so fewer fittings are needed. Its flexibility also makes it easier to snake the tubing through bulkheads and openings. Another difference is that semirigid CPVC pipe needs less support on long runs, and it looks neater where the pipe is visible.

The two types also differ as to the type of fittings used to assemble them. With flexible PEX pipe you use compression-type plastic fittings that slip on over the pipe and are then screwed in place and tightened with pliers or a wrench. A full range of tees, elbows, and straight unions are available. All these fittings are like unions because they can be taken apart and reassembled without having to cut the pipe or destroy the fitting. Most compression-type plastic fittings can also be used to join plastic pipe to copper pipe or tubing, or to join copper to copper—which means that in many cases no transition fittings are necessary when connecting to existing water lines.

For rigid CPVC pipe, the fittings most often used are one-piece molded plastic fittings that are "welded" to the pipe with a special cement sold for just this purpose. These fittings cost considerably less than compression-type fittings, which is one reason why they are much more popular with professionals and boat builders. They are more permanent and less likely to develop leaks when properly installed, but they do require more care during assembly. Once a fitting has been cemented in place, it cannot be shifted or taken apart; the only way a joint can be disassembled is to cut the pipe or cut apart the fitting. Everything must be measured and precisely aligned before assembling with the cement—there is no time to make adjustments or to realign fittings after they have been assembled with the adhesive.

Nevertheless, assembling CPVC pipe and fittings is not really difficult if you take your time to line up and then dry-fit all connections before applying any cement. Line all fittings up, then use a pencil or felt pen to mark the outside of the fitting and the pipe to indicate proper alignment. Take each joint apart and clean the outside of the pipe and the inside of the fitting carefully with a small piece of fine abrasive paper, then wipe off dust and dirt. Don't touch the cleaned areas with your fingers, and use a clean cloth to wipe the special primer onto both the outside of the pipe and the inside of the fitting. Immediately apply the cement by smearing it on around the outside of the pipe and the inside of the fitting and push the pipe into its fitting. Give it about a quarter-turn to spread the cement around, then line up the fitting properly and hold it in place for a few seconds until the cement sets. Don't try to shift or realign the parts after they are in position—moving the parts will ruin the joint so that it will no longer be watertight.

Threaded compression-type fittings that are used with flexible PEX pipe and tubing can also be used with rigid CPVC plastic pipe. Made in several different styles, all are designed to screw together without cementing, and all can be loosened and realigned if necessary. They can be taken apart after they are in place without cutting the pipe or ruining the connection.

One widely sold type of plastic compression fitting is the kind pictured in Figure 2.16 (made by U.S. Brass under the brand name Qest). It has a threaded collar that is slipped over the end of the tubing first, after which you slide on a serrated metal ring that will lock onto the tubing when the threaded collar is tightened around the outside of the tubing. There is also a tapered plastic compression ring that slips on over the tubing right after the metal ring, as shown, so that when the threaded collar is tightened, this tapered plastic ring compresses

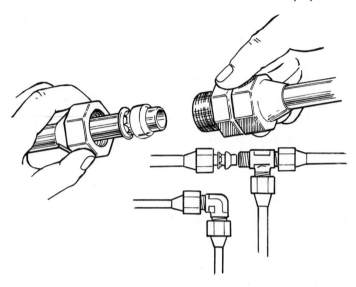

Figure 2.16

to ensure a watertight connection. The serrated metal ring keeps the pipe from pulling out when under tension.

Another type of screw-on CPVC plastic compression fitting (made by Genova) does not have to be taken apart when connecting it to a length of pipe. To connect this version, you simply loosen the threaded collar, then push the end of the plastic pipe all the way into the fitting. An O-ring and compression ring on the inside grips the pipe to form a watertight seal after the collar has been firmly tightened. These plastic compression fittings can also be taken apart and reassembled without cutting the pipe or fitting, and they can be used with CPVC, PEX or copper tubing.

CAULKING, SEALING, AND BEDDING COMPOUNDS

Most of the caulking, sealing, and bedding compounds found in marine stores fall into one of four major categories: silicone, polyurethane, polysulfide, and elastomeric compounds (a ge-

Freshwater Cockpit Shower

⚓ A simple plumbing improvement that can be added to almost any boat with a pressurized water system is a freshwater shower in the cockpit. Handy for use by swimmers and divers when they climb back on board the boat, the shower will also be a welcome luxury on boats that do not have a regular shower.

Using the same pump that supplies fresh water to the galley and head, this project involves cutting one of the existing water supply lines on the discharge side of the water pump (Figure 2.17). A compression-type plastic tee is inserted here, then a new length of plastic pipe leading out to the cockpit is connected to this tee as illustrated. A standard garden spigot is attached to the end of this in the cockpit, after which you can connect a regular "telephone type" hand shower and hose to this spigot or faucet.

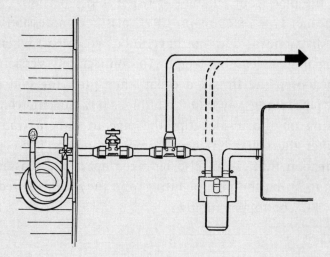

Figure 2.17

There should also be a shut-off valve in this water line located somewhere inside the boat. That way you can close off the line each time you leave the boat, thus preventing someone from climbing on board and draining your tank when you are not there. The valve is also an important safety measure that prevents your tank from draining if the spigot leaks or if someone forgets to shut it off.

neric group based on one or more elastic synthetic rubber compounds, perhaps with an acrylic or similar binder added).

The three most widely recommended products, and the ones most often used by experienced owners and boatyards, are the silicones, the polyurethanes, and the polysulfides. A few manufacturers combine two or more of these polymers in a single compound, and all three can be correctly classified as being adhesive sealants—that is, they serve as both an adhesive and a sealant in many applications.

Silicones: These are widely used as bedding compounds— for installing stanchions, cleats, and other deck hardware, as well as for sealing around screw holes and bolt holes when attaching equipment with bolts or screws. They dry to a tough, rubbery consistency that retains its gasketlike resiliency for years without drying, cracking, or shrinking to any measurable degree. They are also very resistant to high temperatures, as well as to attack by most solvents and fuel spills. However, silicones have lower adhesive qualities than the other three, and they do not form as strong a bond in most cases.

On the other hand, silicones do have very high *cohesive* qualities—meaning that once they are cured they form a tough, resilient "gasket" that is hard to tear apart (that's why a cured bead of silicone can often pulled out of its seam in one long, rubbery "rope"). This combination of low adhesion, combined with its cohesion, is a definite plus when silicone is used as a bedding material for installing hardware and fittings.

In those applications adhesion is not needed and the hardware will be easier to remove when necessary.

Polysulfides: Still often referred to as "Thiokol" (the name of a large corporation that produces this polymer) this sealant is available in both one-part and two-part formulations. Most retail dealers stock only the one-part material; the two-part versions are sold mostly to boatyards and boatbuilders who prefer it because its curing time is much faster.

Polysulfides were first widely used for bonding and sealing joints in wood planking on lapstrake boats, as well as for bedding teak planks and filling in the seams on teak decks. This compound has a very high bonding strength with excellent resistance to teak cleaners and most solvents, and it forms a highly flexible, strong joint that lasts for many years.

Unlike most silicones, polysulfides can be sanded after they are fully cured (although this may take days) and they take paint well (some brands require you to wait until the material is fully cured). They are also excellent for use in many bedding applications, particularly for bedding through-hull fittings and underwater fittings. This is also the compound most often chosen for bedding teak rails and teak trim because the bond formed is stronger than that formed with a silicone.

Thiokol sealants do have at least one limitation—they should not be used for bedding when installing fittings that are made of some plastics such as Plexiglas, Lexan, PVC, or ABS. Although the material will bond to these plastics, in time the solvents may cause the plastic to harden, crack, or split. (Polysulfides can be used with many high-quality plastic fittings made of Delrin, nylon, and epoxy because these are not affected by the solvents.)

Polyurethanes: These have the strongest adhesion of all—in fact, polyurethanes bond so well that the joint is almost impossible to pull apart. The bond formed is considered virtually permanent, yet it is also resilient—which is why polyurethanes are widely used by boat manufacturers for assembling deck and hull sections. This sealant is also sometimes used for bedding teak deck planks, but it is not good for filling in the seams between those planks because the compound tends to soften when certain teak cleaners are used.

Polyurethanes form such a strong, practically permanent, bond that they are not often used for routine maintenance or repair. They should not be used as a bedding compound for fittings that may have to be removed some day, and never in a joint or seam where there is any likelihood that the joint will have to be taken apart in the foreseeable future. Polyurethanes can be painted over and sanded, although not quite as easily (or as smoothly) as the polysulfides.

CHOOSING AND USING ELECTRIC SANDERS

The sanding projects boat owners most often face generally fall into one of three categories:

1. Removing stock and/or reshaping of rough surfaces and large fiberglass patches.
2. Removing rust, varnish, paint, and other finishes, especially when there are many layers to be stripped off.
3. Smoothing and fairing wood and fiberglass, and sanding between coats of paint or varnish to ensure the smoothest possible finish.

The fastest-working sanders are *belt sanders* (Figure 2.19), although professionals often use industrial-type, right-angle-drive disk sanders when making major fiberglass repairs and structural modifications. (These are more accurately called portable grinders, rather than sanders.) Although a belt sander may occasionally come in handy when sanding large areas such as decks and hulls, they are pretty much limited to use

Application Tips

⚓ Laying down a neat, uniformly shaped "bead" of caulking compound is not as easy as it looks, and if not done properly you could end up with a poorly filled seam that will not seal out water properly. To help avoid such mishaps, here are some tricks of the trade that will help ensure better results on most caulking and bedding jobs.

• Cut off the plastic tip on the caulking cartridge at approximately a 45-degree angle. For small beads, cut near the end of the nozzle to create a small opening; for larger or thicker beads, cut farther away from the tip (to provide a larger opening).

• To achieve a smooth, even bead, maintain steady pressure on the caulking gun trigger and keep the tip moving steadily without sudden starts and stops. Push the cartridge away from you, rather than pulling it toward you to pack the compound into the joint more firmly without "stretching" it and with less chance of leaving voids.

• For the neatest seams, use masking tape on each side of the joint (Figure 2.18). Peel the tape off before the compound dries.

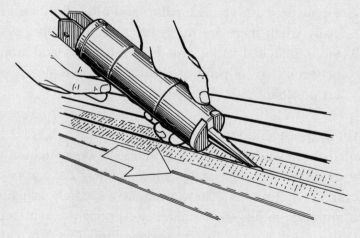

Figure 2.18

- To ensure a secure, form-fitting "gasket" when using silicone to bed hardware, don't tighten screws or bolts all the way. Tighten fasteners about three-quarters of the way, then wait about thirty minutes to allow the compound to almost cure. Then finishing tightening the rest of the way.

- When bedding fittings, make sure you also seal the bolt holes by forcing some compound into each hole and around each bolt. Hold the bolts in place while you spread compound under the base of the fitting and, if possible, tighten the bolts by turning the nuts on the other end, rather than by turning the bolts. Turning the bolts to tighten them is likely to twirl some of the compound out and leave voids through which water can enter.

on fairly flat sections. They are heavier and harder to handle than most other do-it-yourself sanders, and therefore more tiring to work with, especially on vertical and overhead surfaces. For most boat owners, these sanders are not the tool of choice when doing finish work.

Finishing sanders are far more popular. They have flat pads (rectangular, square, or circular) and use sheets or disks of

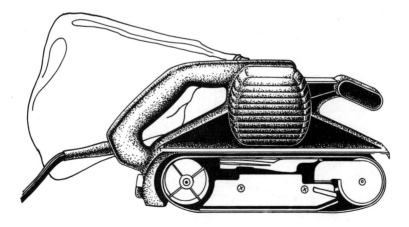

Figure 2.19

abrasive paper, rather than belts. Most will fall into one of the following categories:

• The oldest type is the orbital action sander (Figure 2.20) which has a rectangular-shaped flat pad that accepts one-half or one-third of a standard sheet of sandpaper. Most are two-handed machines that require you to grip with both hands to control them properly.

• Palm-grip, orbital action sanders (also called block sanders) are the "next generation" (Figure 2.21). These are smaller and lighter machines that have square sanding pads that accept one-quarter of a sheet of sandpaper; they have become the sanders of choice for many boat owners. They can be held easily and controlled with one hand, and they run at a higher speed, which produces a smoother finish with less scratching, especially when sanding across the grain. They also make flush sanding easier when working into corners, and their compact size makes sanding in tight places or awkward positions a lot easier.

• Random orbit disk sanders (Figure 2.22) have round pads and use circular sanding disks that are attached to the pad with

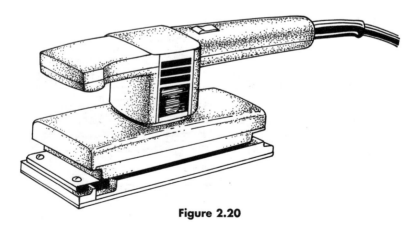

Figure 2.20

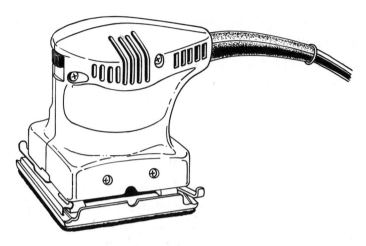

Figure 2.21

a pressure-sensitive adhesive or with some type of hook-and-loop system. As the pad rotates, its axle simultaneously moves in a random oscillating pattern, moving the pad randomly at the same time. These versatile machines are powerful and aggressive enough for heavy sanding and shaping—yet when properly handled they leave a smooth finish that is equal to that of any other finishing sander. In addition, most random

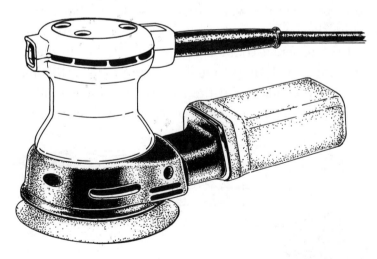

Figure 2.22

orbit sanders have semiflexible pads that make them ideal for sanding lightly curved contours. They come in two versions: models that have a vertical, direct-drive motor mounted right over the sanding pad, and models that have the motor mounted horizontally with a right-angle drive. On these, power is transmitted to the rotating pad through a set of bevel gears.

• Detail sanders, also called "corner sanders," are the newest addition (Figure 2.23). These compact little machines have small, triangular-shaped sanding pads that vibrate or oscillate in an orbital pattern with very short strokes. They can reach into places no other sander can fit—such as between louvers and into grooves and moldings. They've become quite popular in just a short time because they can reach into tight corners and narrow crevices where hand sanding used to be the only way to get the job done.

When using any finishing sander, it's important that you do not make the common mistake of pressing down hard in an effort to make the work go faster—pressing hard will actually slow the sanding action and cause overheating and clogging of the paper. It could also result in damage to the motor. So bear down with only enough pressure to keep the abrasive paper in firm contact with the surface. Move the sander back and forth in straight lines, and be careful when going past an

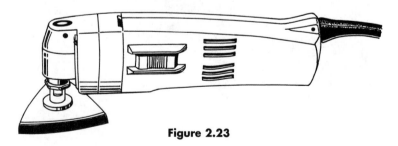

Figure 2.23

edge or end that you don't allow the machine to dip. This could result in rounding off edges or cutting too deep on corners.

Almost all of today's portable electric sanders are available with or without a dust-catching system—either built-in or attached to the machine by means of a vacuum hose that is attached to a shop vacuum. The most efficient systems are those that provide "through-the-pad" dust collection—both the pad and its abrasive sheet have holes punched in them so that dust is drawn through the paper and pad, then sucked through into the dust-collection bag on the sander.

TOOLS FOR WORKING IN CLOSE QUARTERS

When working inside a boat, it's not unusual to have to reach into tight, crowded corners where you can't even see the screw or bolt you are trying to tighten. In fact, sometimes you have to work almost entirely by feel. Space in an engine room is often so cramped that there is no room to swing a conventional wrench, and some places even the shortest "stubby" screwdriver will not fit.

Experienced professional mechanics have learned how to tackle awkward jobs of this kind successfully because many have acquired an assortment of specialized tools and accessories that are designed for working in close quarters. Some of these tools are sold in hardware stores and by dealers that specialize in sales to automobile mechanics, while others are primarily sold through mail order catalogs.

For example, when it is necessary to work where a conventional drop light would be hard to position properly (without the light shining in your eyes) you can use one of various compact "miner's lamp"-type flashlights that are attached to an elastic band that wraps around your head. By moving your head you can then aim the light where needed, leaving your

Choosing and Using Abrasive Papers

⚓ Although we call them *sandpaper*, none of the abrasive papers used are actually made with sand. The name comes from the fact that flint paper, the oldest and least-expensive type of sandpaper, is coated with flint—a natural abrasive that looks like sand. Unfortunately, flint dulls quickly and the paper tears easily, so it is never used with an electric sander. In fact, it also has limited use for hand sanding and is seldom sold anymore.

The most widely used type of abrasive paper, especially with most electric sanders, is aluminum oxide paper. Aluminum oxide is a synthetic abrasive that is much sharper and longer-lasting than flint, and the backing paper used is much stronger and more resistant to tearing. In addition, this abrasive can be used on wood, fiberglass, plastic, and even on nonferrous metals.

Aluminum oxide papers come in a variety of grits, from very fine to very coarse, with numbers stamped on the back to indicate the grade—the higher the number, the finer the grit. A #50 paper, for example, is called very coarse and is primarily used for rough shaping and fast stock removal. A #80 or #100 (medium) paper is used to remove scratches and for moderate smoothing, while a #180 or #220 (fine) is used for removing the scratches left by the coarser grades for final smoothing before applying paint or varnish. Smoothing between coats of paint or varnish calls for the use of very fine grits, ending up with #400 or even #600 paper if you wanted a super-smooth finish.

There are two other types of abrasive paper that are of much use to the average boat owner—silicone carbide papers and emery cloth.

Silicon carbide is a black, synthetic abrasive that is sharper and harder than aluminum oxide, but it doesn't wear as well or last as long. These are black, water-resistant papers that are most often referred to as wet-or-dry papers because they can be used for wet or dry sanding. Dipping the paper in water lubricates the abrasive for finer smoothing, and it also helps to flush away gritty particles that could cause tiny scratches. In the finer grades (#220 to #600), silicone carbide is used wet for final polishing of fiberglass and gel coat finishes, as well as for ultrafine polishing of a final coat of varnish.

Emery cloth is a natural abrasive that is also black, but it is mounted on a cloth backing, rather than paper. It is not as sharp as either of the synthetic abrasives mentioned above, so it is less likely to scratch. It also doesn't wear well or cut very fast and really is used around a boat only for polishing metals or removing rust. It is seldom used with an electric sander.

hands free. These are available from many hardware stores and mail order catalogues and can be a useful addition to any boat owner's tool kit.

There are also magnetic and spring-clamp flashlight holders that can be used with almost any regular flashlight to direct its light beam where needed, again while leaving your hands free. And for really flexible pinpoint lighting in very close quarters, there is also a compact little penlight that has a five-inch-long flexible arm sticking out at one end. A tiny high-intensity bulb at the far end will direct its bright, concentrated beam exactly where needed. Once bent, the shaft will remain in that position until you bend it to a different angle. Called Bend-A-Light, it is distributed by Leading Edge Tool Company (P.O. Box 16088, Newport Beach, CA 92659; 714-549-7027).

Another handy lighting accessory that is available in many tool outlets is a small inspection mirror that can be used to reflect light into dark corners, or that enables you to see around corners in tight places. Some have a small pocket-size mirror attached to the end of a flexible shaft or telescoping rod, while others come with a tiny built-in flashlight that also throws light on the work.

For driving or removing screws in very narrow places where even the shortest "stubby" screwdriver will not fit, you can buy right-angle screwdrivers that require less than one inch of clearance above the screw head. Sold in most hardware stores and home centers, some of these have a short ratchet-operated blade sticking out at one end, while others are one-piece tools that have been bent to a right angle at each end (Figure 2.24). A more sophisticated model (called the Skewdriver and also available from Leading Edge) has a right-angle ratchet-and-gear mechanism at the blade end (Figure 2.25). Turning the screwdriver's handle rotates the right-angled blade. The blade is interchangeable with various size Philips-type and flat blades.

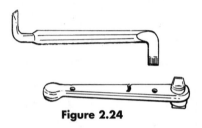

Figure 2.24

Special wrenches are also available for reaching into tight, awkward places where there is not enough room to swing a

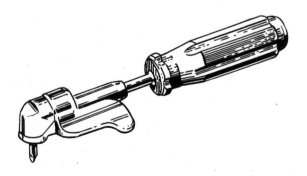

Figure 2.25

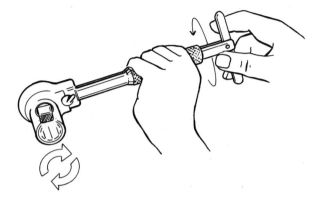

Figure 2.26

conventional wrench—or even to fit a wrench onto the bolt or nut to be tightened or loosened. One type used by experienced automobile and airplane mechanics is a specialized wrench called the Sidewinder (Figure 2.26) made by Sidewinder Products (320 Second Ave. N., Birmingham, AL 35204). It is a 90-degree ratcheting speed wrench that has a small T-handle at the end of the regular handle. You can either swing its handle in the usual manner, or—when there is no room to swing the handle—simply rotate a small T-handle at the working end, which will turn the socket wrench in either direction.

Another type of specialized wrench that has long been used widely by automobile mechanics and those who work on heavy machinery is the so-called "crow's-foot" wrench (Figure 2.27). This looks like the working end of a conventional open end wrench that has had its handle cut off so that only the jaws remain. A square hole near the edge of this jaw accepts a square-end extension rod of the kind often used with conventional socket wrench sets. A ratchet-type socket wrench handle can then be fitted to the other end of this extension rod and used to turn the jaws remotely, the distance depending on the length of the extension rod.

A basin wrench—a fairly common tool used by plumbers to install or remove kitchen and bathroom sink faucets—is another

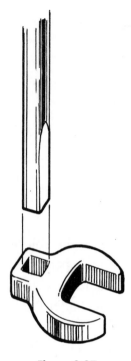

Figure 2.27

useful wrench for working in tight places. As shown in Figure 2.28, this type of wrench will permit you to reach up into a narrow space in which your hands normally will not fit (such as behind a recessed kitchen sink) to firmly grasp and turn a large-diameter nut while working from below. The wrench has one curved jaw that is hinged to the bar-type handle so that the jaw can be locked easily around many different sizes of nuts. With the jaw wrapped around the nut you simply rotate the long handle from the lower direction.

A compact and versatile drill attachment that boat owners can use for drilling in really tight corners and narrow places in which even the most compact electric drill will not fit is a right-angle-drive drill attachment. This has a short drive shaft that fits into the existing drill chuck, with a right-angle drive shaft coming out at one side. Another drill chuck is attached to this so that when a bit is inserted and the drill turned on, you are actually drilling at right angles to the drill itself.

For even tighter and narrower places where even one of these right-angle attachments won't fit, there is yet another type of highly specialized drill accessory you can use for drilling holes. Originally developed for

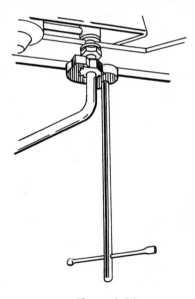

Figure 2.28

use in the aerospace industry and sold under the brand name Tight Fit (also available from Leading Edge) this compact right-angle drill attachment enables you to drill in really narrow spaces where no other drill or accessory would fit. It can be used with any electric drill by inserting the drive end into the drill's existing chuck. However, as shown in Figure 2.29, unlike a conventional right-angle drill drive unit, does not have a regular chuck at the working end of the angled drive unit. It has a threaded hole or recess that accepts a special stub-type drill bit with a threaded end. The bit screws into the working

Figure 2.29

ing end of the right-angle drive. These stub-type drill bits come in various lengths, some as short as ⁹⁄₁₆ inch.

SECTION 3

PAINTING, VARNISHING, AND TEAK MAINTENANCE

PAINTBRUSHES

An inferior-grade paintbrush makes it almost impossible to smooth on paint or varnish properly—regardless of the quality of the finish being applied. A poor-quality brush will leave brush marks, streaks, and uneven areas in the finish, and it will also shed bristles or drip excessively. Cheap brushes also make it almost impossible to "cut in" neatly to a sharp edge.

Paint brushes are made with either natural (animal) bristles or man-made, synthetic bristles. The natural bristle most often used is Chinese hog bristle. This has a natural taper and "split ends," which are "flagged" at the tip as shown in Figure 3.1 on page 130. These split ends not only help the brush pick up and hold more paint, they also spread the paint more smoothly and more uniformly without dripping, running, or spattering.

Synthetic bristles are usually made of either nylon or polyester. Manufacturers have learned how to "flag" the ends of these synthetic bristles to closely simulate the split ends found in natural bristle, and they've learned how to taper the individual filaments as they are being produced so that the best-quality synthetic bristles now closely rival natural bristles in working qualities.

Although some brushes are made with only nylon bristles and some with only polyester, the best synthetic bristle brushes are made with a mixture of the two. This blending of different types of bristle in one brush is done to take advantage of the best features of each and to maximize wear and working qualities—while also keeping costs down. Of course, not all experts agree as to what is best, but it helps if you know something about the principal characteristics—and the advantages and disadvantages—of each type of bristle.

Nylon, which is the oldest type of synthetic bristle, will wear longer than either polyester or natural bristle, especially when used on rough or heavily textured surfaces. Good-quality nylon bristles have a nice springy feel and tend to spread the paint smoothly, but when used in water-thinned paints they tend to get soft and floppy. Nylon also gets soft and floppy when used in very warm, humid weather, and worse yet, brushes made with this bristle tend to lose their springiness and shape when used in any finish that thins with alcohol, acetone, lacquer thinner, or any of the highly volatile solvents that are found in two-part epoxy and polyurethane coatings.

Polyester bristle, on the other hand, is not affected by water-thinned paints or by any of the other strong solvents that affect nylon. Brushes made with this synthetic bristle will retain their stiffness and shape better than nylon when used with these solvents. That is why many companies make their best-quality synthetic brushes with a mixture of nylon and polyester: nylon for its superior working qualities and its ability to pick up and hold more paint without dripping and streaking, and polyester around the outside for its stiffness and ability to retain the original shape of the brush, as well as its resistance to heat, humidity, and most solvents.

There is also another type of modified nylon bristle (from

DuPont) that is called Chinex. Claimed to be superior to the older forms of nylon, this synthetic offers two improvements over conventional nylon:

1. The flagged tips and split ends are more effective than those on traditional nylon bristles and, most important, as the bristle wears, the tips continue to split and form new "flags," similar to the way natural hog bristle wears. With regular nylon or polyester, once the flagged tips wear off only a blunt end, which is no longer efficient at picking up and spreading paint, remains.
2. Chinex does not get as floppy or soft as regular nylon does when used in warm, humid conditions.

In spite of all the improvements made in synthetic-bristle brushes, many experts still feel that the best paintbrush you can buy for fine varnishing and enameling is a brush made of top-quality pure Chinese hog bristle; it will still give you the smoothest finish, and does the best job of picking up, holding, and spreading on the paint or varnish. However, for the ultimate in fine varnishing (when price is no object) there is an even better brush that many pros prefer—a natural-bristle brush made with ox hair, or a mixture of ox hair and Chinese bristle. Ox-hair brushes are softer, finer, and more silky in feel, but they do require more careful cleaning and handling.

Never dip any brush into a can of paint or varnish by more than one-third the length of the bristles. Remove excess paint by tapping the tips of the bristles against the inside rim of the can—never by wiping across the rim. Wiping causes tiny bubbles to form in the paint as it runs back into the can, and this will make smoothing out the finish much harder. To avoid runs and sags, don't load the brush with too much paint, and don't try to flow the paint on too heavily—two thin coats are always better than one heavy coat.

When shopping for a good-quality paintbrush there are certain features you should look for:

- Hold the brush by the handle with the bristles pointing upward and examine the bristle

Figure 3.1

ends carefully. A high percentage of the bristles should have "flagged" or split ends as shown in Figure 3.1. In addition, each bristle should be slightly tapered so it is thicker near the ferrule (the base of the brush) than it is at the end.

- Turn the brush so that you are looking at it from the side to make sure the bristles are not all the same length. They should not look as though they have been cut off to form a square edge at the end of the brush. There should be a mixture of different length bristles with the longest ones in the center of the brush and the shortest ones around the outside so that when viewed from the edge the bristles form a cup-shaped taper with a profile similar to the one shown in Figure 3.2.

Figure 3.2

- Grab a small clump of the longest bristles and bend them out to a 90-degree angle from the ferrule or handle. Then release them. The bristles should snap right back to conform to the original shape of the brush.

• Spread the bristles apart to expose the ferrule at the base of the brush (Figure 3.3). There should be a wood or plastic block in the center that creates a "pocket" in the center of the bristles for holding paint. On cheap brushes this block will be a lot wider than it should be in order to make the brush look thicker, but in a quality brush this block should be no more than about ⅛ inch to ³⁄₁₆ inch in thickness. It should *not* be made of paper or cardboard.

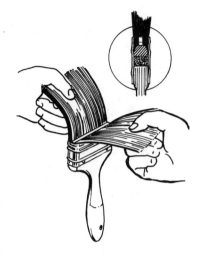

Figure 3.3

Figure 3.4

• Hold the brush by the handle as though you were going to paint with it and press the bristle tips lightly against the back of your hand (Figure 3.4). The bristles should feel springy and should fan out smoothly to form a sharp, chisel-like edge—essential for neat trimming and "cutting in," as well as for smooth application of the finish.

Preserving Varnish Brushes

The best varnish brush is an expensive ox-hair or badger-hair brush, but these must be thoroughly cleaned if you want them to last. Getting the brush perfectly clean at the end of each session, or at the end of each day, can be a chore, but storing the brush for a day or two in the proper thinner will keep it in good shape and ready for use without completely

Cleaning and Caring for Brushes

⚓ A good brush should be properly cleaned and stored after each use. To wash out the bristles you will need a solvent appropriate for the finish you've been using. For most varnishes and marine paints this can be mineral spirits or turpentine and for two-part paints that use stronger solvents you can usually use lacquer thinner or acetone.

Start by first rubbing out as much of the paint (or varnish) as you can by wiping repeatedly across the rim of the can. Then use a stack of old newspaper to rub out as much additional paint as you can. Wipe the bristles back and forth on the top sheet and as this sheet becomes saturated tear it off and discard it. Then start wiping on the next sheet of newspaper. Repeat until no more paint comes out of the brush.

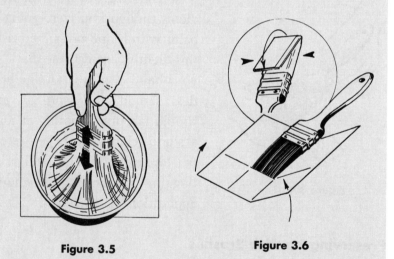

Figure 3.5   **Figure 3.6**

Pour about an inch of solvent into the bottom of a clean container and press the brush down into this, working the bristles up and down vigorously against the bottom of the can (Figure 3.5). Wipe the brush almost dry on some more sheets of

Figure 3.7

old newspaper, then pour the dirty solvent out and pour another inch of clean solvent into the container. Repeat this process two or three times—each time working the bristles up and down in the clean solvent, then wiping the bristles almost dry on the newspaper. Finish by washing the brush in warm water and detergent until the water runs clean. Shake out excess water, then use a comb to smooth out the bristles. Wrap with brown wrapping as shown in Figure 3.6 to help the brush hold its shape, and store flat in a fairly dry location.

A spinner similar to the one shown in Figure 3.7 can help greatly speed up the job of cleaning brushes. It will get excess paint out of the bristles more quickly, and it eliminates the need for wiping the bristles on old newspaper. Spring clips snap on over the handle of the brush, after which you pump up and down on the handle. This twirls the brush back and forth rapidly, spinning all excess paint or solvent out of the bristles. Needless to say, you should hold the bristles down inside a large bucket or other container to contain the spray.

cleaning it each time. However, you must never allow the brush to stand on end or rest on its bristles, so here's a simple way to avoid this by using an empty jar and its lid.

Cut or bore a hole in the lid just large enough to allow the brush handle to come up through it, then drill a hole through the center of the handle. Set the brush inside the jar and push the handle up through the hole in the lid, then push a short length of stiff hanger wire through the hole in the handle so it sticks out at each end. Then let the wire rest of top of the lid to support the brush with its bristles suspended inside the jar of thinner, without allowing them to touch the bottom of the jar.

PAINTING YOUR FIBERGLASS BOAT

Painting a fiberglass boat was once considered a project that only a professional could safely tackle, but this has changed with the introduction of new and improved finishes that can be applied by the average boat owner without spraying. It's still true that a good professional spray job—when done by an experienced pro who is working with the right equipment— will give the finest of all finishes, but today's do-it-yourself marine paints can form a durable and very smooth high-gloss finish that will last for years—if properly and carefully applied. The toughest and longest-lasting are the two-part polyure- thanes, but the one-part polyurethane coatings are easier to apply and will also form a beautiful finish that will satisfy many boat owners.

When preparing for any painting job, keep in mind that 85 percent of the work required to ensure a smooth, professional- looking job is in the preparation of the surface—cleaning and sanding the surface, and careful patching and fairing out of all cracks, holes, and other irregularities. All this must be done *before* the first can of paint is ever opened. If you are painting over old paint, remember that the new paint will be sticking to this old paint, not to the original fiberglass or gel coat. So if the old paint is in poor condition, or is cracking, blistering, or peeling, then the only way to ensure good results with the new paint is to remove *all* of the old paint before you start. If, on the other hand, the old paint is still in fairly good condition, you can paint directly over it—but check directions on the label first. If you will be using a polyurethane, you may have to apply a special primer or a "barrier" coat of some kind as a first coat.

Ideally, painting and varnishing is best done while the boat is in a shed or garage where it will be protected from sun, wind, and dust, but the work can be done outdoors if you limit your painting to calm days when the temperature is between 55 and 85 degrees. Avoid painting on very humid days or when rain is likely to occur within three or four hours after the paint is applied, and always stop painting at least two hours before sunset. Don't start painting very early in the morning when there is still dew on the surface.

With these limiting factors in mind, here are the preparatory steps you will have to take before you actually start to apply any paint:

1. Remove as much deck hardware and trim as possible, including moldings, ladders and brackets, grab rails, chocks, cleats, and light fixtures—not only to make sanding and smoothing easier, but also to make it easier to flow the paint on in straight, parallel strokes without leaving lap marks. Mask items that cannot be removed, using "fine-line" masking tape to keep paint from "bleeding" under the edges and to avoid wrinkling the tape when going around curves.

2. If you are painting over a previously painted surface, remember that if the old paint is badly weathered and cracked, or if it is blistering and peeling, then *all* of that old paint should be removed before you start. If the old paint is still sound you may be able to put new paint on over it, but make sure the new paint is compatible with the old.

3. Patch and fill all holes, cracks, and dents, using a two-part epoxy putty or surfacing compound, or a polyester

patching compound. Fill each depression slightly higher than the surrounding surface; then after this dries, sand it flush, starting with #120 paper and following with #220. When patching fiberglass, do your final sanding with #400 wet-or-dry paper. Dip the paper in water frequently and wipe all grit off the surface periodically to see how the work is going. Dragging your fingertips lightly over the surface is the best way to detect irregularities—you'll be able to feel small bumps or ridges that you can't see.

4. After patching and smoothing, carefully sand the entire surface with #150 paper to dull any remaining gloss, then use a vacuum or brush to remove all grit. Move on to #220 paper for the next sanding, and sand with long strokes to ensure a smoothly faired surface. Pay extra attention near edges and in corners—leaving glossy spots in little areas is probably the most frequent cause of paint peeling. Don't use steel wool for places where sandpaper may be awkward to handle; use bronze wool or stainless steel wool. Steel wool will leave small particles of metal embedded in the surface, and these can cause rust stains to show up later on.

5. After sanding and vacuuming, wipe the surface with a rag dampened with solvent (usually the thinner for the paint you will be using). If you are not going to start painting immediately, you should wipe the surface with solvent again just before you start to paint.

6. If you are painting fiberglass or gel coat that has never been painted before, wipe it down with acetone or the solvent recommended by the paint manufacturer in order to strip off all wax or polish that may have been applied, as well as to remove remnants of any mold release agent that may be left from the original manufacturing process.

Applying the Paint

Before opening the first can of paint, read the directions and follow them carefully. Some paints require a separate primer; others advise merely applying two or three coats of the same paint. Don't shake the can before opening it—this will result in tiny air bubbles that will be difficult to brush out. Stir thoroughly by mixing with a paddle, and do not work out of a full can of paint after it is opened. Instead, pour about half off into another can or bucket, then stir each half separately. Pour all the paint back together into one container, then stir again. Pour the amount you expect to use into a separate can or bucket and work out of this—not out of the original can.

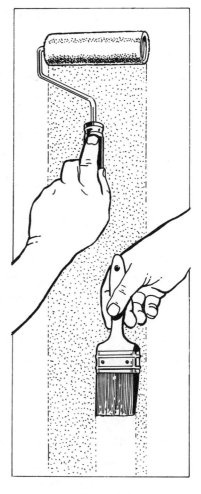

Figure 3.8

Use a brush as wide as practical for large surfaces, and don't *scrub* the paint on. Flow it on smoothly and try to do most of your brushing in one direction. Always brush from a dry area into a wet area so as to maintain a wet edge while you're working. For a really smooth, professional-looking job when applying a brushable polyurethane, use a foam roller to apply the paint, then immediately smooth this over by "tipping off" with a brush as shown in Figure 3.8. The roller cover must be made of a plastic foam or special

Choosing the Right Paint

⚓ Most topside marine paints tend to fall into one of three categories: two-part polyurethanes that must be mixed together just before use, one-part polyurethanes that are formulated for do-it-yourself application and can be applied by brush or roller (or both), and the traditional alkyd-based enamels.

The two-part polyurethanes are the most expensive, but they are also the toughest and most durable finishes. They dry to a harder, glossier coating and will retain their gloss longer. They are also more resistant to fading and chalking. Originally formulated for spray application only, and intended for use only by trained and experienced pros, these paints are now also available in brushable form (the preferred method is by roller and a brush as described on page 137). They are a little trickier and more difficult to apply than the one-part polyurethanes because they tend to run and sag if applied too heavily, especially if the temperature and humidity are not just right.

One-part polyurethanes cost less than the two-part formulations and often contain at least some alkyd resins. They are easier to apply than the two-part coatings because they are less prone to running and dripping, making them easier to brush out smoothly. They are usually more durable than the alkyds, and will tend to retain their gloss longer—but they still won't last as long as a good two-part polyurethane.

Alkyd enamels have been around for years and they are usually the lowest in cost. They are the easiest coatings to apply because they "flow on" more smoothly with less effort, and are less likely to show brush marks or runs, even if laid on a little heavier. In addition, alkyds are not as sensitive to temperature and humidity conditions, and they are generally more "forgiving"—that is, they are less likely to peel or let loose if you were a bit careless when sanding and preparing the old surface.

On the negative side, most alkyds do not form as tough or as glossy a coating as the polyurethanes do, and they will not hold their gloss as long. The finish is not as abrasion-resistant as most polyurethanes, but it is more flexible and thus less likely to crack—especially on wood boats or on wood trim and fittings on a fiberglass boat.

fabric that is resistant to the powerful solvents these paints contain (cheap covers will fall apart).

This method is most effective when two people work together to coat a large surface—one using the roller while the other follows behind with the brush. The paint should be rolled on in a thin, even coat. The brush is then dragged lightly over the same area to smooth out any slight ridges, bubbles, or "stipple" effect that may have been left by the roller. For best results use a top-quality brush that contains a high percentage of natural bristle. The brush should be almost dry and used with just enough pressure to keep the bristle tips in contact with the paint.

Two-part polyurethane finishes are thinner in consistency than most other marine paints and thus will tend to run or drip, so don't try to apply them in a thick coat. If runs or sags do occur, don't try to brush them out or smooth them over once the paint has started to set even slightly—this will only make matters worse. Wait until the paint has dried, then sand out the defects and repaint that area. Sand between coats with #220 paper and remove all dust carefully before putting on the next coat. With some two-part polyurethanes, no sanding will be required between coats if you apply the second coat within a limited period of time (check the directions on the can).

When using only a brush to apply the paint (without a roller) make sure the brush is fully loaded, but never dip the bristles in by more than about one-third their length. Remove excess paint by patting the bristle tips against the inside of the can above the level of the paint, *not* by dragging the bristles across the rim. Brush across the shortest dimension first, then smooth out the finish by cross-stroking parallel to the longest dimension.

Keeping Paint from Skinning Over

When a partially used can of paint or varnish is put away, chances are that the next time you use it the paint or varnish on the inside will have formed a skin over the surface, even if you replaced the lid tightly. This skin forms because the air inside the can causes the surface of the material to dry out. The skin is difficult to remove without leaving lumps, and wastes paint.

You can prevent skin from forming after the can is sealed by pouring a thin film of paint thinner (mineral spirits or turpentine) over the surface in order to keep the surface of the paint from drying out. Very little thinner is required—no more than a spoonful in a gallon can that is half full. The best way to spread this thin film over the surface of the paint is to spray the thinner on with an empty plastic spray bottle. After spraying the thinner over the paint, replace the lid and put the can away without shaking or agitating it so as not to mix the thinner in with the paint.

SECRETS OF A SMOOTH FINISH

Nine times out of ten, a poor finish is not the fault of the paint or varnish used but of one of two common causes: either the surface was not properly prepared beforehand, or the user did not follow instructions as to proper mixing or application techniques. No finish can ever be any smoother than the surface over which it is applied, and that is why it is essential that everything possible be done to smooth over rough and uneven areas and to fill in gouges, scratches, dents, or other blemishes. Marine finishes dry with a high gloss, and a shiny finish always accentuates every dust speck, brush mark, and rough spot.

If the old finish is relatively smooth and still bonding firmly, sanding and patching the existing surface may be all that is required. However, where the old paint or varnish is alligatored and rough, or badly cracked and starting to let go in places, the only sure way to achieve a smooth new finish is to completely strip it all off down to the original surface.

When recoating an old finish, sanding is the essential first step—not only to smooth off rough spots and uneven areas, but also to dull down any gloss still remaining on the surface. Never paint over an old finish that is still glossy. If the existing finish is fairly rough, start with a medium-grit paper such as #80. If it does not need such heavy sanding, start with #100 or #120—this will leave fewer scratches to be removed. Sand parallel to the grain when smoothing varnished finishes, and sand along the longest dimension when smoothing painted surfaces. Be careful not to skip inside corners and places that are hard to reach because glossy spots left on the old finish are probably one of the most common causes of paint or varnish lifting later on.

After sanding, dust thoroughly, then sand again with fine (#220) grit paper. If you are sanding by hand, use a sanding block as a backing to avoid creating hollows or dips. The block should have a resilient facing of some kind—a piece of carpet stapled to one side works fine. When sanding on curved surfaces, use a kitchen sponge as a backing or buy one of those foam-backed "sanding sponges" that are widely available in hardware stores and marine supply outlets. To make sure the surface is smooth and properly faired, shine a bright light across it from an acute (very low) angle. Also, feel the surface periodically by dragging your fingertips lightly over the finish to feel dust specks and slight bumps or irregularities that are almost invisible.

When patching and filling holes or depressions, spread the compound on as smoothly as possible to minimize the amount of sanding that will be required later on. A trick that often works for the final smoothing with many epoxy patching compounds is to dip your spreader into soapy water before you use it—the compound will not stick to the wet spreader or putty knife and will smooth it to a really slick finish that will need little or no sanding after it cures.

If you are patching wood that will be finished with a clear varnish you obviously cannot use an opaque white or gray patching compound. If you can't actually sand out the defect you will have to use one of the colored wood patching compounds that are often referred to as a "wood dough" or wood plastic. Available in a choice of wood tones, these can be tinted if necessary by mixing in tinting colors (sold in paint departments) to achieve a more accurate match. Just remember that the match will never be perfect, so keep your patches as small as possible and avoid smearing the compound onto adjacent areas.

To achieve a really smooth paint or varnish finish on raw wood that has an open grain (teak, mahogany, or oak), you will have to first fill in the open pores with a paste wood filler. This is not the same material used for filling screw holes, scratches, etc. It comes in paste form and must be thinned to about the consistency of heavy cream with mineral spirits before brushing it on to fill in the open pores in the wood. It is not for filling in larger defects.

Brush the thinned paste filler on across the grain, covering only a few square feet at a time. Wait a few minutes until it just starts to lose its shiny, wet look and starts to dull, then immediately start rubbing the excess off with burlap or other coarse cloth. Rub in a circular motion, the idea being to rub off only the surface layer of filler without also scrubbing it out of the pores. Timing is important here. If you start rubbing too soon you will rub the filler out of the pores; if you wait too long the filler will start to dry and be almost impossible to rub off.

Paste wood fillers come in a "natural" or neutral grayish-tan color, or in a choice of wood tones (mahogany, teak, etc.). Colored fillers act as a stain as well as a filler and thus are often used to ensure uniform coloring on mahogany and other dark woods. As a rule, paste wood filler, if required, is usually applied after all other patching is done. Allow the filler to dry overnight before sanding smooth—first with #120 paper, then with #220.

For best results, especially with varnish, use a top-quality bristle brush. Badger hair is probably the best—and also the most expensive—but good results can also be achieved with a top-grade synthetic bristle (a mixture of polyester and nylon is probably the best). The varnish should be applied with a fully loaded brush and with only a moderate amount of pressure applied to the handle (never try to "scrub" the varnish on). Brush across the grain first and then smooth it out by cross-stroking with an almost dry brush and with long, steady strokes parallel to the grain. At the end of each stroke lift the brush in a gradual arc up and away from the surface, as shown in Figure 3.9, rather than lifting it straight off. On large areas that are too long to finish with a single stroke, go past the midpoint from each direction, allowing these strokes to overlap in the center before you draw the brush up and away from the surface.

BOTTOM PAINTING

The most widely sold antifouling paints for use on pleasure boats contain cuprous oxide, a biocide that is not as harmful to the environment as the older formulations were. Most are

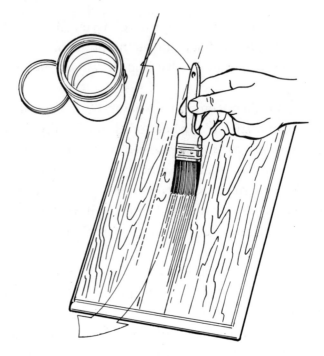

Figure 3.9

copolymers—ablative-type coatings that wear off evenly to leave a constantly smooth, relatively slick surface, much in the way that a bar of soap wears down as it is used. The biocides in the paint leach out gradually and at a relatively constant rate so that the antifouling qualities of the paints are almost as effective at the end as they were when the paint was first applied.

Generally speaking, the rules and procedures that govern any good paint job will also apply to the application of bottom paint—that is, making certain that surfaces are clean, dry, and as smooth as possible before you start; not applying paint on days that are very hot, very cold, or very humid; and using a special primer where necessary (as specified in the directions on the can).

However, bottom painting does differ in two important respects: First, antifouling paint must be applied in a relatively heavy, thick film of uniform thickness in order to provide the antifouling qualities needed. Second, smoothing the surface beforehand is actually more important than when painting above the waterline because here it is not merely for aesthetic reasons—a smooth bottom creates less friction and thus increases speed while also lowering fuel consumption. If the bottom was properly cleaned after the boat was hauled, only a minimum amount of preparatory work will be required. Scrape off any paint that is loose or flaking (wear goggles and a protective face mask) and sand rough spots smooth. Finish by sanding the entire bottom with #100 paper to smooth it, then remove all dust and wipe down with a suitable solvent/cleaner. Depressions should be patched and filled in, using a two-part epoxy patching compound rather than a polyester (epoxy will stand up better under water).

If you are switching to a different type of bottom paint that is not compatible with the old one (for example, you cannot apply a hard-drying vinyl or copolymer bottom paint over a soft, sloughing type that rubs off easily), or if the old paint is very rough, pockmarked, and peeling or flaking off in places, then the only way to ensure that the new coating will bond properly is to remove all of the old paint before you start. This can be done by sandblasting, by sanding with an electric sander, or by using a chemical paint remover.

As a rule, sandblasting is the fastest way to strip off all of the old bottom paint, but it must be done by an experienced operator who knows how to control and use the right type of abrasive. Otherwise sandblasting can damage and partially destroy the gel coat or fiberglass, thus increasing the porosity of both the gel coat and the underlying fiberglass (often leading to eventual blistering of both the laminate and the gel coat).

Removing the old paint by sanding it off with an electric

sander is slower and more time consuming and creates clouds of hazardous dust, so you *must* wear a protective face mask made for this purpose. Either a belt sander or a disk sander can be used. A belt sander is heavier and thus harder to hold against the surface when working overhead, and it may not work on curved areas or in tight corners. A disk sander is easier to handle in this respect, but only the larger, professional or industrial models are of any use—a small disk sander chucked into an electric drill is almost useless.

The safest way for the do-it-yourself boat owner to remove all of the old bottom paint is to use a chemical, semipaste paint remover that is made for use on fiberglass. Be sure you wear goggles to protect your eyes, and wear a long-sleeve shirt and a hat while working.

The fastest and easiest way to apply bottom paint is with a 9-inch paint roller equipped with a long extension handle. There will be corners and crevices where the roller won't fit, so in those places a brush will still be needed. Spread the paint on liberally, following manufacturer's recommendations on how much area each gallon should cover in order to ensure a film of proper thickness. Usually two or three coats will be required. With multiseason copolymer antifouling paints, the life of the coating is almost always directly proportional to the number of coats applied—the more coats you apply the longer the coating will last.

When painting the boot stripe, make sure you also use an anti-fouling formula, although you will probably want a hard-drying type with a bit of gloss. Use "thin-line" masking tape to get a neat line when painting this stripe, and to separate it from the regular bottom paint (Figure 3.10).

When painting the bottom, don't forget struts, rudders, shafts, trim tabs, and other underwater metal parts of the running gear. While it is true that friction through the water will wear most of this paint off in less than one season, the anti-

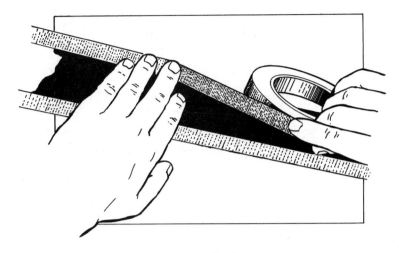

Figure 3.10

fouling paint will last a while and will help protect against underwater growth for at least part of the season.

TEAK CARE AND MAINTENANCE

Teak is a durable, weather-resistant wood that is also highly resistant to rot (although, contrary to popular opinion, teak will rot under some conditions). This does not mean that teak is maintenance-free—at least not for those who take pride in the appearance of their boats. Some feel teak looks best when it is protected by frequent applications of a teak oil or sealer; others insist that teak looks best when it is varnished. A third opinion favors the "natural" look—leaving the wood unfinished and simply scrubbing it clean at frequent intervals so that the teak weathers to a silvery-gray color that will eventually look something like sun-bleached driftwood.

Fortunately, teak is a very "forgiving" wood. Even badly weathered teak can be fully restored with a thorough cleaning. Most experts advise against using harsh teak cleaners that contain acids or caustics (an ingredient contained in most, but not

Blistering Problems

⚓ If the bottom shows signs of blistering, steps should be taken to correct this problem before any paint is applied. Most major paint companies sell complete systems with detailed directions for application. Basically, the procedure consists of first cutting open and gouging out all the blisters with a small grinder or sharp tool, then allowing these cavities, as well as the entire hull, to dry out completely. This can take anywhere from a few days to several months—which is why it is best to do this part of the job in the fall after the boat is hauled. It will then have the whole winter to dry out, as long as it is indoors or sheltered from the elements (in some cases a plastic tent is erected over and around the hull to keep out moisture during this drying-out period).

After the laminate is completely dry, each cavity is filled in and faired with a two-part epoxy resin, then the entire hull is coated with several coats of the special epoxy primer recommended by that manufacturer. Apply enough to build up the film to the thickness recommended (usually 8 to 10 mils), which may require as many as four coats in some cases. It is best not to skimp on this if you want permanent protection against future blistering. After the last coat is dry, two or three coats of the bottom paint is applied.

all, of the two-part liquid teak cleaners sold in marine stores). These tend to eat out the soft grain in the teak, leaving the surface with a rough, uneven finish that is more likely to attract and hold dirt. Sanding is often the only way to restore surface smoothness after one of these harsh cleaners has been used.

Another problem with some of these cleansers is that, when used on teak decks, they may soften the caulking compound or sealant that was used between the planks. However, these products do a terrific job of cleaning and brightening badly discolored and stained teak, so if the wood has been badly neglected, using one of these harsh cleaners may be the only satisfactory solution.

It is generally safer to first try using a powdered household cleaner or detergent of some kind, or one of the specialized one-part teak cleaners that are sold in marine stores (these come in both liquid and powder form). When unfinished teak is properly cleaned it should be light tan in color. If the teak still looks even slightly gray, then the wood needs more cleaning. Remember that even the slightest amount of dirt or soil left in the grain will be sealed in when a coating of any kind is applied, so it is important that the wood be perfectly clean (and dry) before any finish is applied.

Scrubbing is best done with a bristle brush, never with a wire brush. Some like to use bronze wool—in fact, some labels recommend this—but many pros advise against using either bronze or stainless steel wool (*never* use steel wool) because these will tend scour away the softer grain and leave you with a rough surface.

If you do find it necessary to use one of the strong two-part caustic cleaners, make sure you follow the directions on the package explicitly. All caution you to wear rubber gloves to protect your hands, but remember that your feet also need protection, so don't do this work in your bare feet. The same holds true for exposed skin on your arms and legs. Wear long-sleeve shirts and full-length jeans or trousers rather than shorts. It's also wise to wear safety goggles to protect your eyes against splashing or dripping, especially when working on surfaces above eye level.

Many two-part caustic cleaners will damage or discolor gel coat, paint, and varnish; therefore, you should avoid runoff onto adjacent surfaces whenever possible, especially onto fiberglass, aluminum moldings, and other polished metal hardware. The best way to prevent this kind of damage to adjacent surfaces is to wet everything down thoroughly with a hose before you start, then keep flushing these surfaces with water while you are working. Keep wetting everything below where you are working, and everywhere runoff is a possibility. The surest way to accomplish this is to have someone help by standing by with a water hose to keep adjacent surfaces wet and to flush away runs and drips as soon as they occur.

Although freshly cleaned teak dries to a pleasant, light tan color that looks as if it has been just sanded, it won't stay that way for long. Teak will start to oxidize and turn gray within an hour or two if it is not promptly treated or coated with some kind of protective finish. Most teak finishes will fall into one of two broad categories: penetrating sealers and oils that soak into the pores of the wood and leave only a slight amount of surface film, and surface coatings such as varnish that are designed to build up a thick, glossy film on the surface. Opinions differ as to which is preferable, but one point that all professionals agree on is that teak decks should never be varnished—varnish is too slippery underfoot, especially when wet. Teak oils and sealers dry with a nonskid, matte finish that provides much safer footing.

Applying a teak oil or sealer is a lot easier than applying varnish—you can brush these on with inexpensive throwaway-type foam "brushes" or with a sponge mop or roller (Figure 3.11). There is never a worry about brush strokes spoiling the finish. In many cases, you can even wipe the coating on with a rag or sponge—or, even faster and easier, use a long-handled sponge mop for decks or other large surfaces.

Another advantage of using a penetrating sealer or teak oil

Figure 3.11

is that there is no need for sanding between coats (essential when applying multiple coats of varnish). However, as a rule, a good varnish job will last longer than a sealer or oil—varnish will not need recoating for anywhere from four to six months if an adequate number of coats has been applied. Professionals will put on anywhere from eight to ten coats of varnish, thinning the first coat with about 15 to 20 percent turpentine so it will soak in and help the seal the wood. Most agree that teak oils and sealers must be reapplied at intervals of anywhere from six to eight weeks during the summer.

Regardless of which finish is applied, normal care calls for you to hose it down at the end of each day's run, or at least once a week, even if the boat is not used. If properly renewed at the recommended intervals, an oiled finish should last for anywhere from one to three years without need for stripping back to the bare wood. But this is true only if a fresh coat of oil or sealer is applied as soon as the finish starts to look a little dull or shows the first signs of wear.

Teak Oils vs. Teak Sealers

⚓ There is no industry-wide standard that spells out the difference between a teak "sealer" and a teak "oil," so merely seeing these words in a product's name is not always an accurate indicator of how one product differs from another. Both are penetrating finishes that are designed to soak into the pores of the wood and leave a matte finish. Broadly speaking, a teak sealer is supposed to contain more solids than a teak oil, which leads some manufacturers to claim that the sealer will require fewer coats or will last longer.

However, some products labeled as teak sealers do not last any longer than those that are labeled as teak oils—and some oils actually may last longer than some sealers. All tend to darken the wood somewhat, but the amount of darkening will vary considerably from one brand to another. The only way to tell how much a particular finish will darken your teak is to try it on a small area, or see what it looks like on someone else's boat. Most of these oils and sealers will oxidize and darken over time, so the color may change as the finish ages.

All of these oils and sealers are difficult to remove from fiberglass, gel coat, and painted surfaces after they dry, so be very careful to avoid runs, drips, and smears when applying them. Masking tape helps, but don't trust it too much. Some of the oils have such a low viscosity that they will work their way under the tape. In addition, many will soften the adhesive on the tape. Your best protection is to wipe off smears and drips immediately.

Varnishing Teak

Although varnishing teak involves more work than using one of the teak sealers or oils, it is still preferred by those who like a glossy, mirrorlike finish. However, a really smooth varnish finish calls for a lot more sanding.

Start with #150 paper, always sanding with the grain, then use #220 for the final smoothing. Carefully remove all sanding dust by wiping down with a rag moistened with acetone or lacquer thinners before applying the first coat of varnish. Teak has natural oils in it that often interfere with a good bond, but wiping the wood down with one of these solvents not only will remove any surface oils that can affect the varnish, it also will help draw much of the oil out of the wood's pores.

When working on raw wood, thin the first coat of varnish with about 15 to 20 percent of a brushing liquid such as Penetrol or the one made by Interlux (this is better than using mineral spirits or turpentine). Allow at least an overnight dry, then apply subsequent coats full strength. Don't thin the varnish unless you have to—if brushing or smoothing becomes difficult, or if the varnish starts to feel "gummy." If thinning does become necessary, add only a little at a time, just enough to make brushing easier and to make the varnish flow smoother.

Sand lightly between coats, but make sure you remove all sanding dust before the next coat is applied. Use #220 paper when sanding the first coat of varnish, then sand the second coat—and all subsequent coats—with #400 paper. In each case, wipe with a rag dampened with mineral spirits to remove all dust before applying the next coat. Generally speaking, at least four coats are advisable, although most pros recommend five or six coats on raw wood.

When applying the varnish, brush from a dry area toward the wet area as you finish smoothing off each section. End each brush stroke by arcing the brush up and away from the just-coated section and into a just-finished section. Never lift the brush straight up and away from the surface. When coating large panels, it is best to first brush across the grain, then smooth off by dragging the tip of the almost dry brush lightly along the length of the grain.

....

REMOVING OLD PAINT AND VARNISH

Marine finishes are usually removed or stripped off down to the bare surface in one of four ways—by scraping and sanding, by sandblasting (mainly on hull bottoms), by using a heat gun, or by using a chemical paint and varnish remover.

Scraping and sanding is hard work and time consuming, but it is cheaper and less messy than using a heat gun or chemical remover—which is why many boat owners opt for sanding the finish off with an electric sander (you will still have to use a scraper in tight places where the sander cannot reach).

There are two types of electric sanders in common use: orbital sanders and belt sanders. (Electric drills equipped with a sanding disk should *not* be used on a boat; they almost always result in gouging and swirl marks that are very difficult to remove.) Orbital sanders are most suitable for smoothing and finishing, rather than for removing paint and varnish, but if used with a coarse-grade paper (such as #80) the larger models can be used for stripping off old finishes, but they will be a lot slower than a belt sander.

Belt sanders are faster and more effective for stripping off old finishes, but they can be used only on large, relatively flat surfaces such as transoms, decks, topsides, and cabin sides—and even then on inside corners and curved areas you will still have to sand by hand or use a scraper. They must be handled with care to avoid digging in or gouging the surface. Keep the sander moving continuously all the time the belt is in motion, and don't release the trigger while the belt is still in contact with the surface. At the beginning of each stroke press the trigger and start the belt moving before you bring the abrasive into contact with the surface.

When using any electric sander do not press down hard

because you think this will make the machine cut faster. Bearing down too hard will only slow the machine down and possibly cause the motor to overheat. It will also cause the abrasive to overheat and clog more rapidly. So with any sanding machine, use only enough pressure to ensure firm contact with the surface.

Sandblasting is probably the quickest method for removing multiple layers of paint from a large area, especially when removing bottom paint. However, this technique requires the use of special equipment and a considerable amount of experience because it poses the very real danger of damaging the gel coat or fiberglass if the operator is not *very* careful or if the wrong type of abrasive is used. It is generally not recommended for the do-it-yourself boat owner.

Heat guns apply concentrated heat to a small area, causing the paint or varnish to soften and bubble up so that it can be easily scraped off with a dull putty knife or very coarse steel wool (useful on curved or molded surfaces where a putty knife or scraper won't work). This is usually the slowest method, but it eliminates the problem of contending with great clouds of sanding dust. However, it can be messy as sometimes melted or scorched paint and varnish will drip down onto adjoining surfaces—and there is the danger of scorching wood. When using a heat gun, it is a good idea to keep a fire extinguisher or bucket of water handy, and you should wear gloves to protect your hands. It is not a good idea to use a heat gun on fiberglass or gel coat because the high heat (up to 1,000 degrees on some models) could damage these materials.

Using a chemical paint remover is usually the quickest and easiest method for most boat owners to strip off multiple layers of paint or varnish—but it is also probably the most expensive. Brands vary in consistency, in whether or not they are flammable, in the types of finishes on which they will work effectively, and in the substrata over which they can be used safely (fiberglass, metal, wood, etc.). Some are also more hazardous or toxic than others. As a rule, the semipaste removers (sometimes referred to as "heavy-bodied" removers) will be more powerful than the liquid removers and usually will be more effective on marine finishes, especially when there are several layers to be removed.

Liquid removers tend to run and drip more, especially on vertical surfaces, so they may not soak in enough to soften completely the old paint. They will also tend to dry out more quickly, and since removers only work when still wet, they will not continue to soften the coating for as long. The semipaste removers have inhibitors that float to the surface to keep out air, thus helping them to stay wet longer.

Although most boat owners would naturally choose to use a remover that is nonflammable (not all are) this could be a problem if the remover is to be used over fiberglass or gel coat. Many nonflammable (and more powerful) removers contain a high percentage of methylene chloride, the most aggressive and most potent of all remover solvents, but this powerful solvent will also attack gel coat and fiberglass if left in contact with it for a few minutes. As a result, the labels on many of these nonflammable methylene chloride removers will carry a caution that warns they are not safe for use on fiberglass.

However, labels can be confusing. On some heavy-duty, industrial-grade removers the label states that they are formulated for marine use and are excellent for removing tough "marine finishes" such as epoxies and two-part polyurethanes. It's true that these *will* work better than many other removers on those tough finishes, but if you read the fine print carefully you may find that the company warns that this remover is *not safe* for use over fiberglass or gel coat.

Your safest bet is to choose a remover that is formulated for use over fiberglass when used according to its directions. The job will probably take longer because the ones that are formulated for use over fiberglass contain less potent and less aggressive solvents. Unfortunately, these solvents are also highly flammable, so the removers that contain them are also highly flammable. In addition, they are also slower-acting and may have to be applied more than once—especially when there are many heavy coats of paint to be stripped.

Removers that are based on methylene chloride—or at least a high percentage of this solvent—are hazardous to the environment and are a definite skin irritant, so gloves and protective clothing are always essential. Their fumes can be toxic, especially when used indoors without lots of ventilation, and most experts recommend wearing a safety respirator or mask, in addition to gloves and protective clothing. Eye goggles or a face mask should also be worn when working at eye level or higher in order to protect against spatters.

Several manufacturers have introduced newly formulated removers that are claimed to be much less hazardous to health and safety, as well as being "environmentally safe." These contain no methylene chloride and they contain no volatile compounds that are dangerous to the environment. Most can also be washed off with water.

These environmentally "safe" removers are less powerful and usually slower working—especially when multiple layers of old paint have to be removed. Where a traditional methylene chloride remover might take anywhere from five to fifteen minutes to soften up several layers of paint with a single application, some of these "environmentally safe" removers can take as long as several hours—or even up to a full day—to do the same job. All of them also cost more than conventional removers—anywhere from two to three times as much per gallon in some cases.

Always brush the remover on liberally, covering only about three or four square feet at a time, and avoid working in direct sunlight or on hot surfaces. Apply in thick layers, slapping it on with a single brush stroke—as though you were spreading icing on a cake. Don't brush back and forth if you can avoid it because the less the film is disturbed, the longer the solvents will take to evaporate—and the longer they stay wet, the more effective the removing action will be.

Allow the remover to soak into the finish for about fifteen or twenty minutes, or until the old finish bubbles up (this will vary with different brands and with the ambient temperature). Scrape off the sludge with a dull putty knife, taking care not to scratch or gouge the surface (Figure 3.12). A stiff toothbrush is handy for scrubbing the softened residue out of crevices and tight corners where you cannot reach with a scraper or with coarse steel wool.

Ideally, the remover should be put on heavy enough, and left on long enough, to remove all of the old finish down to

Figure 3.12

the bare surface in one application. However, very often a second, or even a third, application will be required to remove all the finish. If, after waiting the normal length of time, you find that when you start scraping the finish is not soft all the way through, it may be best to brush a second coat of remover on right over the original application, then wait for another fifteen to twenty minutes before scraping again.

Let Others Do the Stripping

Stripping old layers of paint or varnish from a boat's paneled doors, drawer fronts, railings, and other small areas of wood trim around the inside or outside of the boat is a labor-intensive, tedious, and time-consuming chore that most boat owners dread. However, many do not realize that if the pieces to be stripped can be taken off and removed from the boat, there is a quick and easy way to have someone else do all the work—although it will cost a bit more than doing the job yourself. Bring the doors, drawer fronts, or other items in to a commercial furniture-stripping service. These companies have enormous vats full of special solvents that will remove most finishes easily. They are to be found in almost all communities these days and can be located by looking in the Yellow Pages under Furniture Strippers.

SECTION 4

PROJECTS AND IMPROVEMENTS

Rigid plastic laminates (such as Formica, Micarta, Wilsonart, etc.) can be applied over most smooth, hard materials, although the most frequently used core materials are plywood and particleboard. You can also apply new plastic laminate over an old layer of the same material—for example, when you want to re-cover an existing countertop or bulkhead that is already covered with a plastic laminate. This requires thoroughly sanding the old surface until it is uniformly dull, then cleaning with lacquer thinner.

One caution: when applying a second layer of laminate over a door or panel that is not rigidly braced on the back side, you may have a problem with warping—unless you also apply an additional layer of laminate to the back of that door or panel.

The material is available in sheets that range from two by five feet to five by twelve feet in size, although four-by-eight-foot sheets are probably the most popular. They come in two thicknesses, $\frac{1}{32}$ inch and $\frac{1}{16}$ inch. The thinner material is intended primarily for vertical installations; the thicker for covering horizontal surfaces such as countertops and tabletops. The adhesive most often used for installing them is contact cement. This must be applied to both surfaces—the back of the laminate as well as the surface of the core material to which it will be bonded.

Epoxy cement is sometimes used for laminating commercially built cabinets that will be installed in a cockpit, on an aft deck, or in other locations where it will be exposed to the weather. However, unlike contact cement, which bonds instantly and requires no clamping pressure, epoxies do require clamping while the adhesive cures. This not only makes these adhesives more difficult to use, it also requires more specialized equipment (for clamping).

Plastic laminates can be cut to size with a handsaw or power saw, or by scoring with a plastic scribing tool. For cutting by hand, use a hacksaw or fine-tooth woodworking saw, and when using a portable saber saw or circular saw, select a blade with very fine teeth to ensure the smoothest cut. With a handsaw always cut with the pattern side facing *up* because these blades cut on the down stroke—any chipping that does occur will be on the back side. (Just be careful not to drag the blade against the edge on the up stroke).

With a portable power saw, always cut from the back side with the pattern side facing *down* because these blades cut on the *up* stroke. Regardless of what type saw you use (hand or power) make sure the sheet of laminate is firmly supported so it does not vibrate excessively while cutting. If possible, clamp the sheet between two pieces of wood laid along the line of cut. These will not only hold the laminate firmly, the strips will also act as a guide for the saw blade.

Scoring instead of sawing can be done with a special plastic scoring tool that is sold for this purpose. Use a metal straight-edge as a guide and press the blade of the tool down hard while dragging it across the sheet to score the line of cut. Repeat this scoring four or five times, then snap the sheet in two along the line of cut. Cut sheets about ¼ inch wider and longer than needed to allow for about a ⅛ inch overhang on all sides. This excess will be trimmed off with a file or router after the sheet is in place. Make paper or cardboard patterns where necessary to guide you in cutting curved or irregular shapes—also allowing for the ⅛-inch overhang on all sides.

The plywood or particleboard must be clean and smooth, and free of all paint or varnish. If the surface has been painted or varnished, then the finish must be completely stripped off— by sanding and scraping or by using a chemical paint remover. If you use a chemical remover, be sure you rinse off all traces of the remover before applying the contact cement. Fill in holes, cracks, and other defects with a suitable filler, then smooth off bumps and high spots by sanding. Also, make sure there are no nails or screw heads sticking up.

Contact cement should not be applied when the temperature is below 65 degrees or during periods of high humidity. The cement can be applied with either a paintbrush, a roller with a mohair-type cover, or a special notched spreader. Apply the adhesive in a thin, uniform coat with no missed spots or "holidays." In most cases one coat will be enough; if the adhesive dries dull, this indicates that either not enough was applied, or the surface was too porous for one coat, so a second coat is needed. Wait for the first coat to dry, then apply a second coat right over it. The contact cement must be applied to both surfaces—the back of the laminate and the surface of the core material—then allowed to dry for the time specified on the can (usually about thirty minutes) before bringing the cement-coated surfaces together for bonding. To make sure the adhesive is dry before bonding, test by pressing a piece of brown wrapping paper against the coated surface, then pull it away. If none of the adhesive sticks to it, the surface is ready. If some adhesive comes off on the paper, more drying time is needed.

After two cement-coated surfaces are brought into contact with each other, they cannot be shifted, moved, or even realigned. This means you must be careful not to allow the two surfaces to touch each other until they are exactly positioned and properly aligned. When dealing with small pieces you can usually line them up properly by just holding the piece of laminate close to or next to the surface before bringing the two together.

However, when dealing with sizable sheets of laminate, it is best to use spacers of some kind to keep the cement-coated faces from touching each other while you line them up or move the sheet around to the correct position. Since the adhesive will stick only to another surface that is coated with the same kind of adhesive, you don't have to worry about the cement sticking to the spacers—or to anything else that comes in contact with it. On a horizontal surface such as a countertop, the easiest method is to first place a row of dowels on top of the counter surface as shown in Figure 4.1, spacing these no

Figure 4.1

more than about 18 inches apart. Carefully place the sheet of laminate on top of the dowels and shift it around as necessary until you have it in exactly the right position for bonding (the dowels will not stick to the cement above or below them).

When the alignment is precise, you start pulling the dowels out one at a time, while making certain the sheet of laminate does not move. As each dowel or strip is removed, press the sheet down to make firm contact with its cement-coated core material. After all dowels are out, use a hard-rubber roller or a wood rolling pin to press down and remove all air bubbles and to apply proper bonding pressure over the entire surface of the panel. In lieu of a roller, you can also use a block of wood and a hammer, pounding repeatedly as you move the block around over the surface.

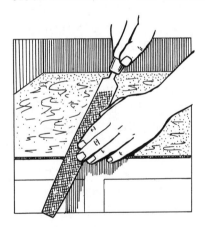

Figure 4.2

Trim off the excess laminate that sticks out around the edges by using either a portable router equipped with a special laminate-trimming bit or a coarse, flat file. When using a file, work carefully to avoid chipping. Hold the file almost vertical as shown in Figure 4.2, and stroke in a downward direction only (away from the pattern side) and apply steady pressure during the full length of the stroke. File until the finished edge is flush with the core material or with the face of the laminate on the edge (if the edge was covered as described below). This edge should have a very slight bevel that slopes slightly inward.

If the countertop or other surface being covered is also to have the edges covered with laminate, then it is best to cover the edges first. Cut a strip of the laminate that is about ⅛ inch

Maintenance Pointers

⚓ Plastic laminates need only occasional washing with mild soap and water, but if they start to get dull you can restore the luster with a wax or polish that is sold for use on these surfaces.

However, there may be problems when the laminate is applied where it will be exposed constantly to the weather—for example, on cabinets, locker doors, and drawers in open cockpits and flying bridges. Colors tend to fade under such exposure, and the surface may cloud up and acquire a hazy look due to microscopic crazing or cracking. The plastic may even start to peel or delaminate in some places.

To help protect against such weathering, it is a good idea to coat the plastic laminate with a light coat of good-quality marine wax once or twice a year. Even a liquid furniture wax such as Pledge or Jubilee will help—not only for shedding water and dirt or soil, but also for restoring the gloss and color to partially faded laminates. Two useful products for this purpose are Penetrol (a paint and varnish additive that is sold in paint stores) or a penetrating teak sealer such as Deks Olje No. 1 (both made by the Flood Co., 1-800-321-3444).

Start by first washing the plastic down with a mild detergent, then allow the surface to dry thoroughly for at least eight hours. Wipe on a light coat of sealer or oil with a lint-free rag, then wait about fifteen or twenty minutes. Wipe on a second light coat and after another fifteen or twenty minutes, rub off the excess and buff vigorously with a clean, dry cloth.

wider than necessary, making certain its pattern is running in the desired direction. Apply this to the edge of the plywood or particleboard with the excess projecting up over the top. After bonding, trim this excess off with a router or file until the laminate edge is flush with the top surface of the core material.

Then cover the top with its sheet of laminate as described above, allowing its excess to stick out or overlap the edge of the strip just applied. Be careful when trimming excess off the top sheet not to mar the laminate on the edge.

The last step is smoothing off all exposed edges and corners on the laminate. For this final dressing use a sanding block with medium-fine sandpaper, or a 10-inch mill bastard file. Stroke downward with steady pressure and lift the file off the surface without dragging it across the edge when you bring it back up. When the edge is flush with the edge of the surface you are working on, tilt the file inward slightly at the handle end so as to create a slight vertical bevel.

AIR-CONDITIONING YOUR BOAT

Marine air conditioners come in two basic types. The first is the central system that uses a remote condensing unit that is usually installed in the bilge or engine room, with separate evaporator/blower units located in the various staterooms or other areas to be cooled. The second is the self-contained console type that is very simple to install. These compact units include the condenser, evaporator, precharged refrigerant coils, and everything else needed to form a complete cooling system—except for a separate seawater pump to supply cooling water to the condenser.

Factory-installed air-conditioning systems are most often a central system with one or more remote condensing units and separate evaporator/blowers in the various areas throughout the boat where cooling is desired. Insulated copper tubing, along with a wiring harness, connects each condenser to the compressor and evaporator unit so that the refrigerant can flow back and forth in a continuous cycle. Seawater that is circulated through the condensing coils by a separate pump cools the condensing coils.

Installing this type of system in an existing boat is a difficult and complex job that calls for the services of a professional installer—tubing and wires must be snaked through bulkheads and decks, and after all the tubing has been connected, the entire system has to be charged with the proper amount of refrigerant under the right amount of pressure. However, installing one of the self-contained air-conditioning units is another matter entirely. The condenser and its compressor, the evaporator and its cooling coils, and an integral electrical box are all contained in a single unit. The compressor and refrigerant lines come fully charged so the machine is ready to go as soon as you get it installed. The only separate installation required is a seawater pump for supplying a continuous stream of cooling water to the condenser.

The most popular type comes with a built-in squirrel cage blower for circulating the cooled air. Some of the larger models are available with a separately mounted blower assembly, which makes it easier to run the flexible ducts off in different directions, allowing you to use a single unit for cooling more than one stateroom (Figure 4.3). It also permits much more flexibility when locating air grilles or outlets. For example, it is always more efficient to locate the outlet grilles as high as

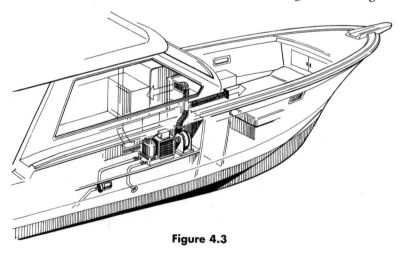

Figure 4.3

possible in the area being cooled—and installing a unit with a separate blower makes this simpler.

Air-conditioning units vary in size depending on the number of BTUs of cooling power needed, and many are available with optional reverse-cycle heating capability so that they can be used for heating as well as cooling.

Self-contained air-conditioning units are often installed under a bunk or settee, under a dinette seat, in the bottom of a hanging locker, or under a chest of drawers (after removing the bottom drawer). They can also be installed inside a locker that is close to the area being cooled, or in the under-deck space located behind or alongside a stateroom wall. Some come completely set up inside a finished wood cabinet, so they look like a piece of furniture and can be installed wherever there is room—for example, next to a settee where it may also be used as an end table. The smaller units can be mounted on top of a counter, built-in chest, or even on a shelf. They come complete with grilles, control panels, and wiring; and they are fully charged so that all you have to do is hook up the water lines to a remotely installed seawater pump and then plug the unit into a 110-volt outlet.

Before buying any air conditioner, measure the overall size carefully to make sure it will fit the space available. Factors to be considered when choosing a location for the air conditioner include the ease of running ducts from that location, where the air-intake grille can be located, and how you will run wires and hoses from the seawater pump in the bilge up to the unit.

You will also need a 110-volt AC outlet nearby to power the unit. This outlet should preferably be on its own circuit since even the smallest units draw at least 8 amperes, especially on start up. If the boat only has one 30-amp shore power line coming aboard, it is a good idea to add a second line. Without it, you won't be able to run the hot-water heater or many other appliances while the air conditioner is in use.

As mentioned previously, all units need a remotely installed seawater pump to bring a continuous flow of cooling water to the compressor and its condensing coils. There are two types of pumps you can use: centrifugal pumps and positive displacement pumps that have a rubber impeller. Centrifugal pumps are not self-priming, so they must be located well below the waterline (Figure 4.4). They are quieter, longer-lasting, and require much less servicing than impeller-type pumps—so most marine mechanics recommend using this type of pump whenever possible. Impeller-type displacement pumps should be used only where it is impossible to install properly a centrifugal pump below the waterline.

The pump should be installed as close as practical to its through-hull fitting, using the recommended size valve for the seacock. A high-speed scoop-type fitting should be installed on the outside of the hull, and an inboard strainer of adequate size should be installed between the pump and the seacock. All the seawater lines, from the pump to the strainer and from the strainer to the seacock, should run in as straight a line as possible without dips or loops. And since these water lines will be below the waterline, don't use lightweight plastic hoses;

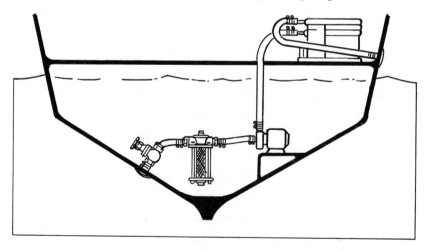

Figure 4.4

use only reinforced hose similar to the kind used on engine cooling systems.

When trying to fit the air-conditioning unit into a tight space, remember that some units allow you to remove the electrical control box on the top or side of the unit so that you can mount this separately. Also, the blower assembly often can be turned or even removed for remote mounting when necessary. When making the necessary connections, be sure you allow enough slack on all lines to permit lifting the unit in or out after it is hooked up.

Most boat owners install insulated flexible plastic air ducts—when ducts are needed. You can run the ducts through hanging lockers and behind cabinets, or you can run them between the inside lining and the fiberglass hull in many cases. When planning for the location of discharge grilles, remember that while most small cabins can be adequately cooled with a single discharge grille, it's best to put in more than one when you can—more grilles in a given space provide more uniform cooling for that space.

Make sure the seawater pump in the bilge is mounted higher than the inboard strainer, but it should still be well below the waterline. Run the hoses and the power cable leading from the pump to the electrical box on the unit, then connect up the water lines. The through-hull fitting for the discharge line should be *above* the waterline. You will also have to install a small-diameter piece of tubing connected to the unit to carry away condensation water that forms when the unit is running. The usual method is to run this condensate drain into the bilge and then count on the bilge pumps to get rid of it, but you can also direct these drains directly overboard where feasible.

The final step is installing the switch plate and control panel, as well as the thermostat or temperature-sensing tube that fits near the air-intake grille. The grilles are available in either aluminum or teak. Although most people choose grilles on the basis of appearance and cost, keep in mind that metal grilles will sometimes "sweat" in humid weather when the unit is running; wood grilles will not.

ONBOARD HEATING FOR CRUISING BOATS

During chilly weather, many boat owners use compact portable electric heaters to warm the inside of the cabins. The use of such heaters is limited to those times when you are tied to the dock with an electric shore cord plugged in, or to boats that have an AC generator running onboard. Unfortunately these electric heaters can pose a fire and safety hazard if not carefully located away from flammable materials, and if not constantly monitored (especially if there are pets or small children on board).

For those who want more dependable heat, especially when living aboard, or those who desire to make greater use of their boats during cold weather, there are different types of marine heaters and heating systems that can be installed which may not require 120-volt AC current. These vary from small bulkhead-mounted fireplaces and stoves to automated central heating systems that have small furnaces or boilers similar to those found in a home heating system. The central heating systems are designed to provide a safe, steady, and thermostatically controlled source of heat any time it is needed—while under way, while anchored out on the water, or while tied up at the dock.

Bulkhead-mounted fireplaces have been around the longest and are still popular, especially in sailboats and smaller powerboats. They usually burn charcoal or wood and need a chimney or vent pipe that goes up through the cabin top to the outside. Many modern versions are compact and efficient cabin heaters that burn propane gas and must be vented directly to the outside for safety reasons, usually by means of a 3-inch-diameter flue pipe that goes up through the ceiling. The newer units have built-in spark ignition, so there is no potentially dangerous pilot light burning all the time, and no need for matches to light them each time. Additional safety features include a sensor that will automatically shut off the burner if the oxygen content of the air inside the cabin drops below a safe level, plus a separate thermocouple that will cut off the flow of gas from the tank if the flame should accidentally go out while the heater is turned on.

Although a good bulkhead-mounted cabin heater will do a great job of warming the stateroom in which it is installed, it is not always effective for heating other areas throughout the boat. Its heat is circulated only by radiation and air convection—there are no blowers or air ducts to carry the heated air to different parts of the boat. Therefore, owners of multi-cabin cruising boats with more than one stateroom (plus an enclosed head) may not find these heaters adequate for comfort in really cold weather.

A fully automatic central heating system, similar to the kind used at home, will provide effective and comfortable heating for the entire inside of the boat, and there are a number of different boat-heating systems available. Especially designed for marine use, as well as for use in trucks and motor homes, these usually burn kerosene or diesel oil and will fall into one of two categories: forced-air systems with a built-in blower or fan that sends heated air from the furnace through ducts to all different parts of the boat, and hot-water systems that circulate hot water from a small boiler unit through rubber hoses connected to small radiators or radiator/convectors mounted in various locations throughout the boat (Figure 4.5). Convector-type radiators are much smaller than conventional radiators, making them ideal for locations where there is not enough wall space to mount a standard radiator. They are designed to

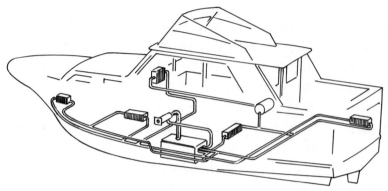

Figure 4.5

be recessed into the "kick space" under a bunk, settee, or galley counter since they are horizontal units about 12 to 15
inches wide and only about 2 or 3 inches high. They contain
snaked coils of copper tubing with fins around them, plus a
small blower that forces air over the heated coils and out into
the room.

Hot-air systems are generally more popular than hot-water
systems—especially in small- to medium-sized boats. They are
usually simpler to install, especially for the do-it-yourselfer,
because on most boats a hot-air system will require two or
three air ducts branching off to various parts of the boat to
warm the entire inside (Figure 4.6). A circulating hot-water
system uses ¾-inch or 1-inch-diameter rubber hoses to carry

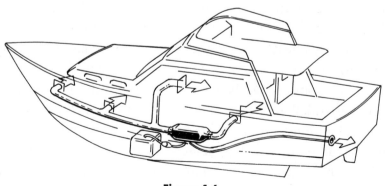

Figure 4.6

heated water to radiators or convectors throughout the boat—so the hoses are obviously a lot easier to snake through bulkheads and around obstructions—but two hoses are connected to each radiator, one bringing hot water in to the radiator and another continuing on to the next radiator to form the continuous loop required by this type of system. In addition, the boiler needed for a hot-water system is usually more complex and requires the installation of a number of sophisticated valves and other controls that are more complicated than those needed for a typical hot-air system.

Another factor that should be considered when trying to choose between hot air or hot water is how much wall space is available for mounting the baseboard radiators—finding this space may be a problem in some boats. Although convector-type radiators are much smaller than the regular baseboard radiators, they still take up more space than the simple air vent openings needed for a hot-air system. In addition, radiators/convector also require wiring to supply the electric power for the built-in blower that is contained in each unit.

There is also another entirely different type of boat heater that is mainly suitable for smaller boats—or those that may not need full-time heating. These heaters are similar to the type found in automobiles—they draw their heat from the engine's cooling system and thus do not burn any fuel at all. In other words, they circulate hot water from the engine to a built-in heat exchanger (a set of hot-water coils inside the unit). A blower then forces the heated air out into the cabin or cockpit through one or more ducts as shown in Figure 4.7.

Because this type of heater depends on engine heat, it is effective only while the engine is running, although most models will continue to give off heat for a limited amount of time after the engine stops—that is, until the heat in the coolant is all used up. They come in different styles and sizes to suit different size boats and different layouts. Some are designed to

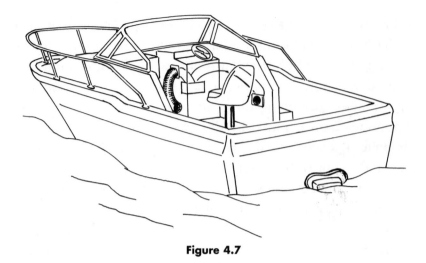

Figure 4.7

send heat out through ducts, while others are installed as flush-mounted units that can be set into a bulkhead or floor. An option available with some ducted units is a special extension that can be extended or pulled out to a length of six feet to direct heat precisely where it's wanted. When not needed, this duct can be collapsed into a short tube that fits inside the cabinet where the heater is mounted.

ON TAP—CLEANER, BETTER-TASTING WATER

When fresh water is stored in a boat's tank, it often develops an objectionable taste or odor, especially if the dockside water source is questionable. That is why owners of many cruising boats have been in the habit of carrying bottled water onboard for drinking and cooking. However, keeping a supply of bottled water on hand is really a nuisance—the bottles are heavy to carry and load, bulky to store, and relatively expensive to buy on a continuing basis.

To solve this problem, many boat owners have installed filter units in their freshwater system—similar to the kind many homeowners have installed. A good-quality filter will ensure a steady supply of clean, good-tasting water that will be free of objectionable odors, sediment, and other contaminants—without the hassle and expense of constantly having to buy bottled water.

Most water filters sold for home use can also be used on boats, but one thing is true for all of them: Water filters do *not* "purify" the water by removing harmful bacteria; they will only filter out dirt, sediment, objectionable odors, and some chemical pollutants, including chlorine and other contaminants that make the water taste bad, smell bad, or even look bad. (There are treatment systems that can purify water and remove harmful bacteria, but these are much more expensive than ordinary water filters.)

Water filters vary in size and style—from small portable "pour-through" units to large "whole-house" units that are used to treat all the water that goes through the boat's system. The small pour-through units (you pour water through the filter and catch it in a glass or bottle) are used to filter water only as needed. They are actually too slow and too small for most family-size cruising boats. Larger whole-house units, on the other hand, can be wasteful if installed to treat all the water coming into the boat because the life of the filter cartridge is greatly shortened when it filters water that doesn't need it—for example, the fresh water used for washing dishes, taking showers, etc.

The most widely sold type of water filters use disposable cartridges. The cartridges are usually of two types: those made for removing objectionable tastes and odors, and those made for removing dirt and sediment. Taste and odor cartridges normally contain some form of activated carbon, while dirt and sediment cartridges are made of cellulose or spun plastic that will filter out particles. Most water-filtering units will accept either type of cartridge, but they are not always interchangeable, so be sure the cartridge desired will fit the size and shape of the unit you buy.

If you want a filter to do both jobs—remove taste and odors as well as sediment—then you have two options. You can buy combination cartridges that have an outer covering of spun cellulose (for removing sediment), plus an inner core of activated carbon (for removing tastes and odors). Or you can install two separate filtering units in line with each other so that water goes through both of them before going on to the galley faucet. Combination cartridges will have a shorter life than separate units, so for best results in a cruising boat, install two filters in series as previously described. Install them so the water goes through the sediment filter first, then through the taste and odor filter.

Although activated carbon filters or cartridges will remove most tastes and odors, the effectiveness of any of these filters will vary with how long the water actually remains in contact with the carbon. As a rule, the larger the cartridge, the more effective that filter will be; the slower the flow rate, the better a job it will do in removing contaminants. That's why those small disposable units that screw onto the end of the galley faucet cannot really do much of a job—because of their size and the short amount of time water is in contact with the filtering medium.

Not all filters use replaceable cartridges; some are designed so that the whole canister has to be replaced when it becomes saturated with contaminants—usually indicated by the fact that flow rate drops considerably. These filters are claimed to last a lot longer than those with disposable cartridges, but their longevity will depend on the quality of the water coming into them, as well as on the quantity of water flowing through them. For example, if the water coming into the filter is loaded with rust and sediment, the filter will clog up a lot faster than it would if it only had to treat relatively clean water.

The most logical place to install a water filter, and the location most often selected, is directly under the galley sink in the cold-water line leading to the sink. The location must allow for enough room under the filter housing to permit dropping it when necessary to change cartridges. The filter can be connected in one of two ways: by cutting into the cold-water line and hooking it up so that all water going to the galley faucet goes through this filter, or by tapping into the cold-water line so that the filtered water coming out of the filter goes to a separate spigot installed on or near the galley sink as illustrated in Figure 4.8. By adding a separate faucet, you ensure that only the water needed for drinking or cooking will be filtered—so the cartridge will last much longer.

If water is not run through an activated carbon filter for days or weeks at a time, the carbon can serve as a breeding ground for some of the bacteria that has been brought in with the water supply. So, to play safe, it is best to let the water run for a minute or two the first time you use it after having been away from the boat for more than a week or so.

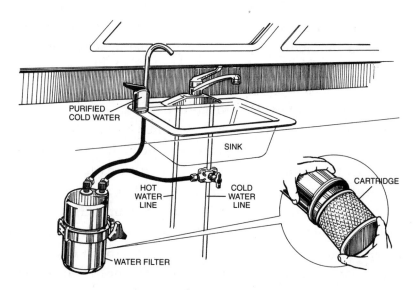

PURIFIED COLD WATER

SINK

HOT WATER LINE

COLD WATER LINE

CARTRIDGE

WATER FILTER

Figure 4.8

To help prevent bacteria from thriving in the carbon filter when it is not in use, some manufacturers have added silver or other heavy-metal compounds to the activated carbon. Manufacturers claim that the silver inhibits the growth of bacteria and thus prevents their multiplication inside the filter. Usually referred to as bacteriostatic filters (bacteria will not multiply or increase inside the filter media), these are quite a bit higher in cost than standard carbon filters. They do not actually *kill* any bacteria that comes in with the water; the silver is merely supposed to ensure that bacteria will not thrive or grow inside the filter. (Tests run by the EPA some years ago confirmed bacteria buildup in activated charcoal that did not contain silver, but did not confirm that adding silver was uniformly effective in slowing the growth of this bacteria—at least in the products they tested.)

Improving Your Fresh Water System

The freshwater pump in most pressurized freshwater systems cycles on and off frequently to keep water flowing steadily when a faucet is opened. This frequent cycling is not only noisy but also causes the water to pulse as it flows and shortens the life of the pump. There are two simple modifications you can make to solve both these problems—add an accumulator tank and a separate pressure control switch as shown in the before and after drawings in Figure 4.9.

The original pump usually has a built-in pressure-control switch that senses a drop in pressure (when a faucet is opened) and turns the pump on. This switch also turns the pump off when the pressure reaches a preset level—but provides no way to vary or adjust the cut-in and cut-out pressures. The solution is to disconnect this switch and install a separate household pressure switch that *can* be adjusted. Set this to cut in at about 10 psi and cut out when the pressure reaches about 30 psi. This will greatly reduce the frequency of cycling—especially

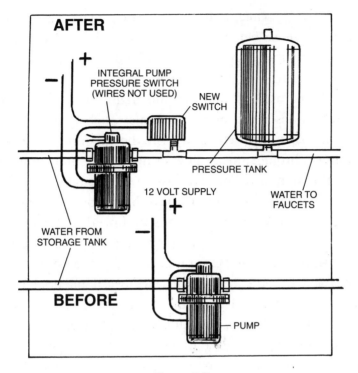

Figure 4.9

when combined with the installation of a two-gallon accumulator tank as shown in Figure 4.9. These tanks store water under pressure so that water is fed into the system without activating the pump immediately. The tank has an air bladder on the inside and pressure is built up inside this with a bicycle pump (it has to be renewed only occasionally). The tank is cut into the water line just past the water pump and the new pressure switch.

LOWERING ENGINE NOISE

There are two methods one can use to lower the level of the engine noise inside the boat: reduce the amount of noise at its source where possible, and use acoustical materials to absorb or block the noise before it gets into the cabin or cockpit.

There is really not much that can be done to reduce engine noise at its source—except to make certain that the engine has good mufflers installed, and that the engine sits on good-quality vibration-absorbing engine mounts. Such mounts (if not already in place) will cut down on the amount of vibration transmitted through the engine stringers and hull, thus minimizing the amount of noise transmitted through the hull.

Assuming these precautions have been observed, the most practical and most effective means of lowering engine noise levels inside the boat is to install acoustical insulation to block out or absorb the noise before it gets into the cabin or cockpit. The heavier and the bulkier this acoustical material is, and the denser the material used, the more effective its acoustical insulation will be. That is why, for example, sheet lead is much better for blocking out noise than wood or fiberglass, and why ¾-inch plywood is a better sound barrier than ¼-inch plywood.

The most widely used types of marine acoustical insulation are made of acoustical plastic foam or fiberglass, combined with a layer of either sheet lead or a dense type of heavy-weight "loaded" vinyl that is just as dense as lead (each weighs 1 pound per square foot). This "loaded" vinyl is claimed to be just as effective as lead when used as a sound barrier, but it is easier to work with and less hazardous to dispose of. It is also thicker than lead of the same weight. A sheet of lead that weighs 1 pound per square foot is about ⅟₃₂ inch thick, while a sheet of "loaded" vinyl of the same weight is about ⅛ inch thick. The best sound insulation consists of at least two layers of foam or fiberglass, with a layer of lead or loaded vinyl laminated between them.

Fiberglass and plastic foam materials used for this insulation are fire-retardant, but not necessarily fireproof. In other words, the material could burn if subjected to a flame or high enough temperature, but it will not burn or support flame by itself—it will self-extinguish if the flame is taken away. This meets or exceeds the requirements of Underwriters Laboratories UL-94HF-1, and is acceptable to the U.S. Coast Guard for pleasure vessels.

The sheets of soundproofing material should be attached with both cement and special mechanical fasteners sold for this purpose. The fasteners are necessary because cement alone is not enough to hold the material in place when there is a lot of vibration. When installing the acoustical insulation, make certain it does not block off any air vents, and seal all seams with tape. Cover all exposed edges with the reflective tape recommended by that manufacturer.

The effectiveness of any of these soundproofing materials will vary with the thickness of the material (the thicker the better), but this increase in effectiveness tends to diminish rapidly beyond a certain point. As a rule, sheets 1 inch thick are generally considered the minimum; sheets 1½ inch to 2 inches thick are preferable. Material thicker than this, even if there is space for it, generally will produce only a slight additional reduction in decibel levels—often too little to be detected by the human ear.

Keep in mind that even the thickest layers of insulation can reduce only the amount of noise coming through it—insulation has no effect on sound waves that filter out around the perimeter of the hatch or that escape through vents and other openings that are never completely sealed off. That is why effective soundproofing also requires the installation of resilient rubber or plastic gaskets around engine room hatches and doors.

In boats that have the engine under the cockpit floor, or in a raised box that sticks up in the center of the cockpit, the soundproofing material is applied to the underside of that box or enclosure as shown in Figure 4.10. In cruisers that have

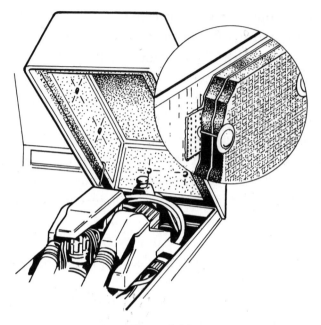

Figure 4.10

engines under the salon, the soundproofing material is applied to the bulkheads in front of and aft of each engine, and on the sides of the hull near the engine, as well as under the hatches and decks immediately over the engine(s). If there is no bulkhead forward or aft of the engine, it's a good idea to erect one of plywood covered with fiberglass, then cover this with the same soundproofing material. Make certain that when you enclose, or partially enclose, the engine you don't obstruct air vents that are required for proper ventilation. Openings for air vents should be baffled so that sound waves will not have a straight path to the outside—such baffles will deflect and at least partially absorb some of the noise as it escapes.

HATCHES AND VENTS PROVIDE LIGHT AND AIR BELOW

The most effective way to provide more light and air in staterooms and cabins is to install an extra deck hatch in that location—one that not only opens and closes, but that also is translucent so that it lets light in even when closed.

Deck hatches come in a wide variety of sizes and styles, most of which are square or rectangular in shape and made of either heavily anodized cast or extruded aluminum, or of heavy-duty injection-molded plastic. As a rule, the plastic hatches usually will cost less than those made of aluminum, but on all good-quality hatches the hardware—hinges, locking dogs, adjusting struts, etc.—should be made of marine-quality, corrosion-resistant stainless steel that is designed to stand up to the marine environment.

The lid on many hatches is made of a translucent acrylic plastic or Lexan with a "smoked" or tinted color—dark enough to keep out much of the sun's heat and provide a fair amount of privacy, yet transparent enough to let in plenty of daylight. Although Lexan is almost unbreakable, it is thinner than acrylic and flexes more if stepped on, so supporting bars are usually installed under this plastic to reinforce it. Most deck hatches sit on top of the deck when installed and stick up anywhere from 1½ to 3 inches above the surface. However, for those who prefer, there also low-profile hatches that project up only about ¾ inch above the deck.

Most hatches come with one or two struts that serve to hold them open in a choice of three or four positions. Others come with special hinges that eliminate the need for these supporting bars or struts. These hinges have built-in notches, or friction-controlled stops, that enable you to set the hatch at different open positions simply by moving the lid up or down. All hatches have some type of locking "dogs" or levers that can be secured (or unlocked) from below, and some also permit you to lock the hatch in a slightly open position for ventilation even when the boat is otherwise closed and locked.

On some boats, installing an additional hatch may not be practical because there may not be enough deck room, or there may be interior lights, bulkheads, or other structures on the inside that prevent installing a new hatch where it is needed. In such cases, some other type of deck vent can still be installed to provide more ventilation.

On sailboats, the traditional way to provide such ventilation has been to install cowl-type vents that stick up above the deck or cabin top. These can be turned to face into the wind to scoop air in and direct it below. In most cases these either snap into, or thread into, a plate cut into and installed in the deck (usually 3 or 4 inches in diameter). To keep water from entering, this cowl vent is often mounted on top of a Dorade-type box that has a built-in water trap, but some companies also make cowl-type vents that have water traps in the base, thus eliminating the need for a separate Dorade box (water that does enter the ventilator gets caught in the base, then runs outside through openings around the bottom of the vent housing).

On powerboats mushroom-shaped, low-profile circular deck vents similar to the ones shown in Figure 4.11 are far more popular than cowl-type vents. They stick up only about 2 inches above the surface of the deck and can be used either to draw fresh air into the boat or to exhaust stale air out—even when the boat is completely closed up. There are three basic types: passive models that have no motor or fan and

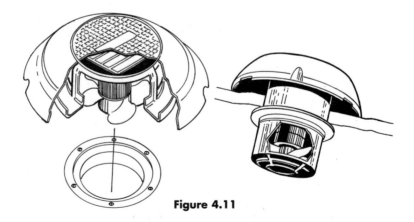

Figure 4.11

Tips on Installing Hatches

⚓ When selecting a location for your hatch, make certain there are no wires, tubing, or structural members that will be damaged by cutting through the deck or cabin top at that location. The surface on which the hatch will be mounted must be flat, so if your deck is curved or cambered, you will have to fashion a teak mounting pad of some kind.

Place the hatch on the surface where the hatch is to be installed, then trace the outline of the hatch onto the fiberglass surface. Use a jigsaw equipped with a fine-tooth blade to cut out the required opening, cutting just inside the lines traced on the surface. Mark where mounting holes for the bolts or screws will be drilled, again using the hatch frame as a template, then drill these holes with the proper-size bits. It is generally advisable to use bolts in the corners and along the hinge edge, even if there are screws in other places. If the deck is of sandwich construction with a balsa or plywood core, then backing plates should be installed on the inside where bolts are used.

Before slipping the hatch into place, cover the exposed edges of the deck where the cutout was made with a layer of marine-grade silicone bedding compound. Then apply a layer of the same compound to the underside of the hatch's deck flange and the outside of the plastic or metal "horn" that projects down into the opening. To finish off the inside of the cabin ceiling, and to cover up any ragged edges that may be visible, install a trim ring from below.

depend only on natural air movement across the outside, electric models that have a small fan built in which is powered by a 12-volt electric motor, and those that have fans that run on solar power.

Passive vents are lowest in cost and are the most popular.

They are designed to help ventilate the boat when it is closed up and often are installed on top of an existing hatch so that even when the hatch is closed air can flow in or out without fear of rain entering—and without having to leave the hatch slightly open. These vents are aerodynamically designed on the outside so that when there is a breeze blowing across the top a suction or "vacuum" effect is created on the inside to draw stale air out while other vents let fresh air in, thus helping to keep the interior ventilated even when the boat is closed up.

FOLDING CHART TABLE

In an open cockpit there is seldom enough space to spread navigation charts out while under way without their blowing around. Usually charts are jammed under a cushion or in a corner, then have to be unfolded and spread out on the deck or on a seat cushion when you need them.

The drop-down folding chart table shown in Figure 4.12 can solve that problem for most boat owners. It is attached to the coaming or side of the cockpit near the helm in an open boat, or to the side of the enclosure on a boat that has a flying bridge. The clear plastic cover will keep the chart flat, yet visible and ready for instant use while preventing it from blowing around. A folding leg under the table holds it horizontal when the table is in use, yet allows it to be dropped down out of the way when not needed. Courses can be plotted right on the clear plastic cover using a marking pencil, or you can lift the plastic lid and work directly on the chart with a pencil and protractor.

The table consists of a sheet of ½-inch-thick marine plywood about 18 inches by 24 inches in size, although this can be varied to suit the space available. The clear plastic cover is cut from a sheet of ⅛-inch-thick Plexiglas or Lucite, and is

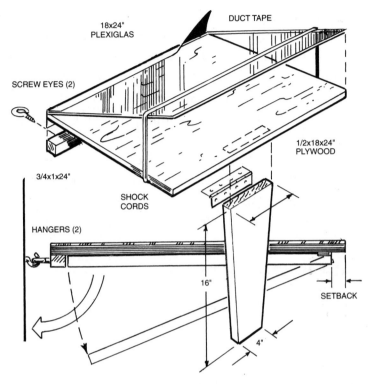

Figure 4.12

hinged to the back edge of the plywood with a strip of wide duct tape as shown. Using tape for a hinge is less expensive than a piano hinge and enables the cover to lie flat against the charts under it.

The plywood table is attached to the side of the boat or coaming with two hooks and screw eyes as indicated. Before screwing the hooks into the fiberglass, you will first have drill a ¼-inch hole for each and insert plastic expansion anchors. The hooks are then screwed into these. A strip of ¾-inch-thick solid wood is glued under the back edge of the plywood so that you can drive the screw eyes at the back edge of the table into this. The screw eyes will slip over the hooks when you want to attach or mount the table, while also permitting you to lift the table off when it is not needed.

The folding leg that supports the table is attached to the underside of the plywood with a brass hinge so that the table can be folded up against the bulkhead when not needed. Two bands of elastic shock cord snapped around the outside serve to keep the plastic cover tight against the plywood and to keep the charts from sliding out when the table is dropped down.

All edges and corners—on the plywood and the plastic—should be sanded and rounded off to eliminate sharp edges. Then apply two coats of paint or varnish to the wood and plywood, covering all sides and all edges to help prevent warping.

....
MARINE BURGLAR ALARMS

Marine security alarm systems, which are available from marine supply outlets and electronics dealers, are similar to the systems that are sold for use in homes, but they do differ in at least two important respects: All components, including the control panel and computerized console, are weather-resistant and corrosion-resistant; and the sensors, switches, and other devices sold for use with these systems are more shock-resistant and thus less subject to damage from vibration.

Home security systems are usually powered by 120-volt AC power (although some have built-in standby batteries in case of a power failure), but those designed primarily for marine use are powered by DC battery current because a system that depends on AC power could be easily disabled by simply pulling out the shore cord plug on the dock before venturing onboard.

Alarm systems make use of different kinds of sensors and detection devices to detect the presence of a thief or would-be "pirate" who wants to steal your boat. The most widely used type of sensor is the two-part magnetic switch that is normally used to protect windows, doors, and hatches (Figure 4.13). One half of this unit is a "normally open" proximity switch

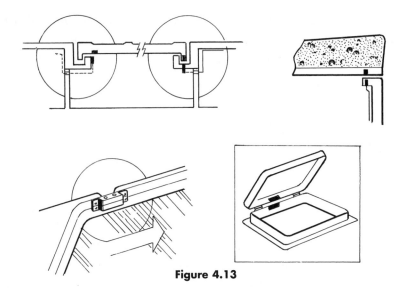

Figure 4.13

that is mounted on the frame of the door, window, or hatch. It is wired into a continuous circuit or series loop that connects all sensors to the main control panel. The other half of the switch or sensor is actually a small permanent magnet; it is mounted on the movable part of the hatch, door, or window in such a location that it will be right next to the proximity switch when that door or window is closed.

As long as the magnet half is next to the other half, the switch remains closed and the circuit is unbroken. However, when the magnet is pulled away from the switch (by opening the window or door) that proximity switch opens, breaking the continuous circuit and causing the alarm to sound.

In addition to these magnetic switches, there are also other types of sensors that are used to sense an intrusion, including the following:

• Pressure mats that sound the alarm when stepped on. They can be placed on the deck or under the carpet inside or outside the cabin.

• Photoelectric eyes that can be strategically located to sound the alarm when anyone breaks the beam by walking between its source and the sensing cell.

• Canvas snap sensors that can be installed in place of existing canvas snaps on boat and cockpit covers or curtains. If anyone unsnaps that fastener while the system is activated the alarm will go off—unless that person has the key or code to disarm the system beforehand.

• Security cables that can be looped around or through outboard motor brackets, dinghies, and other equipment to be protected. If the cable is cut or otherwise damaged, the alarm will sound. These are also used to tie the boat (or the dinghy) to a dock or piling so that if someone tries to steal the boat, the alarm will go off.

• Equipment sensors that are installed to protect radar and loran units, or other electronic pieces of equipment. One end of a special cable is attached to the equipment and the other end is plugged into a sensing device that sounds the alarm as soon as anyone tries to move or disconnect that equipment.

• Vibration and tilt sensors for protecting trailers and boats. These sense movement when someone tries to unhook a trailer, or when someone tries to lift the trailer tongue in order to haul it away.

• Motion detectors that use infrared or microwaves to detect movement. Unlike conventional motion detectors that are used in homes, these are much less subject to false alarms (otherwise they would be liable to go off when the boat rocks). The most reliable marine versions use both infrared and motion detection, making them even less likely to generate false alarms.

• Engine-disabling devices that prevent a would-be thief from starting the engine(s) while the system is armed. These devices will not allow the engine to be started even if the thief tries to hot-wire the ignition.

Most systems activate the alarm by sounding a loud horn or siren, but many systems can also be set up to start navigation lights blinking, to start a strobe light flashing on top of the mast or radar arch, or to cause the ship's horn to sound intermittent blasts. Another option offered by many systems is an automatic telephone dialer—it will dial any phone number programmed into it to alert whoever answers that an intruder is trying to board your boat.

The most trouble-free and dependable alarm systems are those that are "hard-wired"—that is, where all sensors and switches are connected by wires to the central control panel in one continuous loop (Figure 4.14). If any of these wires are cut, or if one of the sensing switches opens, the alarm goes off.

However, there are also "wireless" systems that eliminate the need for running wires from each sensor back to the central control panel. These use the same magnetic switches and other sensing devices that the wired systems use, but instead of requiring wires that run from each one to the main panel, their wires extend only a few inches to a tiny radio transmitter

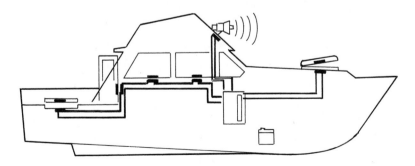

Figure 4.14

Other Steps You Can Take to Discourage Burglars

⚓1. Make sure you have good locks on all doors, windows, and hatches, even if you have to add padlocks to the flimsy units originally installed by the builder. Also, make sure you have good, weatherproof padlocks on all cockpit cabinets and lockers.

2. Use bicycle-type chains and locks to secure onboard dinghies, outboard motors, fishing poles, water skis, and other sports equipment left in open cockpits or on deck.

3. If your boat is plugged into shore power, install one or more timers to turn on lights each night, and to turn them off late at night. Don't leave lights on all the time—it's a sure indication that no one is onboard.

4. Cover up or hide radios, TVs, stereos, and other valuable equipment that can be seen through windows or doors. These easily sold items serve as a temptation to thieves.

5. Make a record of serial numbers on all equipment; if there is a break-in and anything is stolen, you will be able to identify it later on.

6. Install a hidden ignition-disabling switch under the helm or inside the engine compartment. This must be turned on before you can actually start the engine, so even if a thief tries to hot-wire the ignition switch he still will not be able to start the engine.

mounted next to the window or door (Figure 4.15). The transmitter has its own battery and sends its signal to a receiver inside the control unit, sounding the alarm just as the hardwired systems do. These wireless systems are much easier to

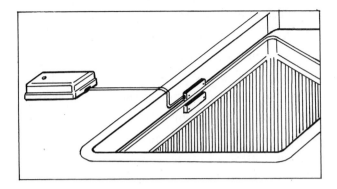

Figure 4.15

install than a wired system, but they are more prone to false alarms due to conditions often encountered in the marine environment, and due to interference from other electronic equipment that may be operating in the area.

AC POWER WITHOUT A GENERATOR

Cruising families often want to be able to use their TV sets, VCRs, electric razors, blenders, toasters, and other electrical tools and appliances when onboard, but many are limited to doing this only when tied to a dock with shore power available because they do not have a generator. However, even without a generator, most boat owners can have a quiet, steady supply of 120-volt AC power onboard—all they need is a solid state inverter that will convert the boat's DC battery current (12, 24, or 32 volts) to 120-volt AC. The current put out by these inverters can be used to safely power all standard 120-volt appliances and tools, including computers, television sets, and other electrical conveniences, without interfering with onboard electronics.

Inverters come in all sizes, from small portable units that can be plugged into a boat's cigarette lighter and will deliver anywhere from 70 to 100 watts of AC power, to larger, permanently installed inverters that are permanently connected to the boat's batteries and will deliver as much as 2,500 watts of AC current—enough to run a microwave, refrigerator, or hair dryer. Although smaller units may work only with 12-volt battery systems, some of the larger-capacity models may require 24-volt or 32-volt systems—or a bank of series-connected 12-volt batteries that will provide the voltage required.

The wattage rating of an inverter refers to the load that it can handle on a steady basis, but the better-quality units will handle starting surges of up to three or four times the rated output for a few seconds—necessary for starting refrigerators and similar motor-driven appliances. Many models can also be used to monitor and automatically recharge the batteries as soon as another source of AC current is available (for example, when the shore cord is plugged in or when an onboard generator is turned on).

Although inverters are most often thought of as a source of 120-volt AC power for boats that don't have generators, many cruising boats that do have generators also install them. Here's why: Besides converting DC current from the ship's batteries into AC current, inverters can also convert DC current from the engine's alternators into AC current. This means that when under way it can eliminate the need to run the auxiliary generator in order to merely keep the refrigerator and freezer going—probably the most frequent reason for turning on the generator while cruising. This not only saves fuel, it also helps lengthen the life of the generator.

Normally, an inverter is wired into the electrical system so that it draws DC power from either the engine's alternator or the batteries, but the most frequent source of power will be the battery system. For maximum efficiency there should be a separate "deep-cycle" battery (or bank of batteries) to run the inverter, thus eliminating the danger of draining the engine's starting battery. Ordinary starting batteries are not really adequate because they are designed to deliver a high amperage for a short period of time only (while starting). They are not designed to withstand repeated cycles of deep discharging and recharging—the conditions most often encountered when an inverter is used. Deep-cycle batteries will last many times as long under these conditions.

The question most often asked about using an inverter is how long it can run various appliances before drawing down the batteries. The answer depends on how many watts the appliance draws, and on how much battery capacity is available. Batteries are rated in "ampere hours" (a battery rated at 100 ampere hours, for example, should deliver 5 amperes for a period of twenty hours). Therefore, if you have two 100 amp/hour batteries you theoretically have a total of 200 amp hours available.

However, this rating of 200 amp hours is really just theoretical because it applies only if the power is consumed at a slow, steady rate—usually over a twenty-hour period. If you tried to draw a continuous load of say 10 or 20 amps, the battery's capacity will be considerably reduced and you will get only about 75 amp hours out of that battery. That is why all experts recommend counting on only about 65 to 75 percent of the battery system's maximum rating when estimating battery capacity.

All inverters come with one or two AC outlets on them so you can plug appliances directly into the control panel, but most boat owners prefer to install them on a permanent basis so that they are hard-wired directly into one or more AC circuits in the boat—or even directly into the main AC breaker panel. The trouble with this setup is that it would be easy to accidentally overload the inverter, unless the boat owner makes certain that circuit breakers that control high-wattage appliances (such as an air conditioner) are always turned off when the inverter is the only source of AC power.

Adding a Third Battery to a Two-Battery System

Many twin-engine cruising boats are delivered with just two batteries—one for each engine. Usually there are also one or two selector switches that permit temporarily putting the batteries in parallel when necessary (for example, when one battery is too weak to start its engine). As shown in Figure 4.16a, each battery is normally charged when under way by the alternator connected to that engine. Power for the ship's service (lights, electronics, etc.) is drawn off either one or both batteries.

There are several drawbacks and limitations to this setup. The first is that because the starting batteries are used for powering lights, radio, and other parts of the ship's service when the engines are not running, there is always the risk of running one or both batteries down to the point where there will not be enough energy left to start the engine(s).

It's true that in such an emergency the selector switches

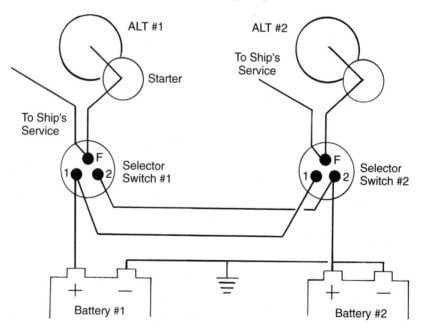

Figure 4.16a

can be set to the "Both" position so as to parallel the batteries for extra power, but in this position power could also be draining from the stronger battery into the weaker one. And if you accidentally forget and leave the switch in the "Both" position while running, there is another danger: If one alternator is stronger than the other, current could feed from the stronger alternator into the weaker one, causing damage to the diodes in the weaker alternator.

Another limitation of this basic system is that in most cases each alternator charges only its own battery, and then only for as long as it takes to fully charge that battery. The flow of current from that alternator then ceases—even if the other battery still needs charging and even if the selector switch is set in the "Both" position.

To get around these limitations, and to make certain there will always be a fully charged battery available for starting each engine, most experts strongly recommend adding a third battery to the system, as well as a battery isolator to control and direct the flow of current to each battery. The isolator serves to automatically charge the lowest battery first, after which current will continue to flow to each of the other batteries until all are fully charged. The isolator also directs current from the alternators—or from a built-in battery charger—first to the battery that needs it most, after which it will continue to charge the other batteries until they too are fully charged. Another function of the isolator is to act as an electrical "check valve" that allows current to flow only in one direction—thus preventing a weak battery from drawing down a stronger one, and preventing current from one alternator from flowing into the other.

Figure 4.16b shows how the original system can be updated to include a third battery and an isolator, while still using the original selector switches. Note that the third battery (which should be a deep-discharge type) is now used only for supply-

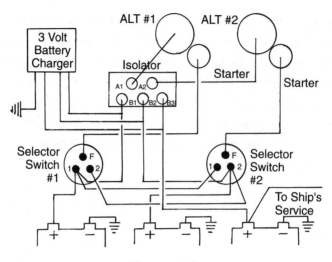

Figure 4.16b

ing the ship's electrical service—not for starting—and does not draw power from either of the engine-starting batteries. The original starting batteries are still connected to the same selector switches.

INSTALLING SEARCHLIGHTS AND FLOODLIGHTS

For navigating through a crowded harbor or looking for an unlighted navigational aid on a dark night—or even for pulling into an unlighted marina at night—a searchlight or floodlight of some kind is invaluable. Owners of smaller boats often use handheld portable spotlights—some of which have their own batteries—but the most powerful models are those that are connected to the boat's internal 12-volt or 24-volt DC electric system. Some have power cords that merely plug into a cigarette lighter, but the most useful type for most cruising boats is a permanently mounted searchlight or spotlight, which may range from about 5 inches in diameter to as much as 15 or 16 inches in diameter.

The difference between a searchlight and a spotlight is in

the type of beam it projects. Searchlight beams are broader and less focused, while spotlight beams are more concentrated and brighter. The more concentrated beam of a spotlight is also more effective for penetrating fog and rain because the broader searchlight beam tends to get reflected back into your eyes under those conditions.

Some of the smaller searchlights (5 or 7 inches in diameter) can be used as either a spotlight or a floodlight because they use double-filament sealed beam lamps that can be switched from flood to spot—much as an automobile headlight can be switched from high to low beam. Some larger searchlights also allow you to focus the light beam to some extent by turning a knob that moves the bulb in or out with relation to its reflector. This enables you to change the beam from floodlight to spotlight, but only within a limited range.

In most cases the larger the size (diameter) of the light, the more powerful the candlepower of the light. For a small boat, a marine searchlight or spotlight that is mounted near the bow should have at least 100,000 candlepower to be really useful. For most medium-size cruisers a 200,000 to 300,000 candlepower light will be more suitable, especially for night vision in fog and rain.

Unlike an automobile, which has fixed headlights, most marine searchlights can swivel to either side, or tilt up and down (the only exceptions would be docking lights that are built into the hull near the bow or on the transom). Some searchlights are manually turned or tilted by a crewman who stands next to the light, but on most cruising boats with permanently mounted searchlights, the light is aimed or turned by remote control from a lever or wheel at the helm. Some have mechanical linkage—rods, levers, and gears or wheels which you turn by hand—while others have electrically operated remote-control systems that include a built-in motor which turns or swivels the light when the control switch or dial is manipulated.

Most manually controlled systems have a vertical control rod that projects down through the cabin top, and a lever attached to the end of this rod enables the skipper easily to aim the light by tilting or turning it as required. Some models use a single lever to control both movements—swiveling the lever swivels the light left or right, while tilting the lever tilts the light up or down. Other models enable you to tilt the light by tilting the lever, but in order to turn or swivel the light you have to twist the control handle (like a turning the handle of an outboard motor to accelerate). Still other models use the lever only for tilting the light up and down; a separate handwheel or knob is used for swiveling or turning the light from side to side.

Because so many of today's boats have flying bridges and upper stations, electrically operated remote-control searchlights are much more popular than the manually controlled models. These remote-control systems allow you to mount the light almost anywhere—up on the bow, on the front of the flybridge, or on top of the cabin. Electric controls also make it easy to control the light from more than one location—for example, you may have one control on the flying bridge and another one down at the lower station. All you have to do is add a second control unit and then wire it up according to the directions supplied.

When deciding where to mount your searchlight or spotlight, try to choose a location near the bow that will allow the beam to be aimed in all directions, including as far aft as possible. Try the light in this location at night if possible, using a temporary power cable or a portable battery to supply the necessary power for the light. Then swing and tilt the light to see if the beam can be aimed in the various directions and at the various angles where it is most likely to be needed.

Electric power for one of these lights should be drawn from

a cable that runs either directly to the battery or to a heavy bus bar, which is connected to the battery with wire that is at least as heavy as the wire recommended for your particular light. Don't just tap into any nearby "hot" terminal because it is conveniently close to where the light is installed.

In addition to searchlights, many owners of cruising boats and sport fishermen find it useful to install compact overhead floodlights (called "spreader lights" on a sailboat) to illuminate the cockpit or deck of the boat at night. These come in three basic styles: round, sealed beam units (similar to the kind used for automobile headlights) that shine almost straight down; rectangular, sealed beam units that are either 3 by 5 inches or 4 by 6 inches in size; and rectangular, quartz-type floodlights that are much brighter than sealed beam units.

Round, sealed beam lamps, although still widely used on sailboats as "spreader lights," are not often used on powerboats because they have to shine almost straight down and do not throw as wide or as bright a beam as most of the rectangular units. In addition, the rectangular-shaped lights have mounting brackets that permit you to install them on either a horizontal or vertical surface, and they allow the boat owner to adjust the direction of the light after the unit is installed.

CHOOSING AND USING DINGHY DAVITS

Towing a dinghy is not only a nuisance, it can also be a hazard when running in rough seas or when approaching a dock. And leaving a dinghy in the water means that its bottom soon becomes fouled and extremely dirty. That's why many boat owners prefer to stow their dinghy onboard, using davits of some kind to haul it aboard or to launch it when desired.

On larger yachts (more than about forty feet in length) a single crane-type davit mounted on the hardtop or on the bow deck is the usual type installed. Such cranes are mounted on poles that go clear through the hardtop or cabin top to the deck below—or in some cases to the stringers or hull below the deck. The crane can be equipped with a manual or electric winch, and there must be some kind of bridle or "strongback"-type rig that will permit raising or lowering the dinghy from a central lifting ring without it tipping or swinging.

Cruising boats that do not have room for a single heavy-duty crane will generally install stern davits that are smaller and lighter than cranes. These can be installed easily on boats as small as thirty feet in length and are very popular for those who carry inflatable dinghies, as well as the traditional fiberglass models. Most davits fall into one of two categories: the pivoting or clamp-on–type that is usually installed on the swim platform, and the more traditional davit that is usually mounted on the transom or stern covering board so it overhangs and projects out past the stern of the boat to lift the dinghy straight up out of the water by means of a rope-and-tackle arrangement that hangs down from the outer end of each davit.

Davits designed for mounting on a swim platform (sometimes referred to as clamp-on davits) differ from traditional stern davits in that they consist of compact locking brackets that are bolted to the outer edge of the swim platform (Figure 4.17). When the dinghy is brought alongside and aligned with these davits, the spring-actuated jaws on each bracket are literally clamped onto, or snapped into, matching ring-type fittings that are fastened to the side of the dinghy. After the dinghy is secured, it is tipped sideways up onto the swim platform until it rests or leans against the transom. It is then secured by tying one or two lines around and under it.

These pivoting or clamp-type dinghy davits that mount on the swim platform cost much less than traditional stern davits, and they are much simpler to install. Most are widely sold for use with inflatables, and some can also be used with rigid fi-

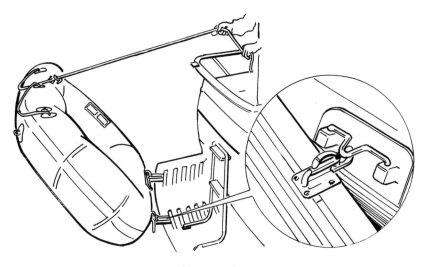

Figure 4.17

berglass dinghies. All work on basically the same idea—instead of hauling or lifting the dinghy straight up out of the water, these tilt the dinghy sideways up onto the swim platform so it leans against the big boat's transom and is secured there while under way. One drawback is that you must remove the dinghy's motor each time you bring the dinghy up onto the swim platform.

Traditional stern davits that lift the dinghy straight up out of the water are usually mounted in pairs on top of the transom or the covering board that goes across this. On boats that have an aft deck with no actual cockpit, they will be mounted right on the aft deck. Some models can also be attached directly to the outside of the transom with special mounting brackets that are made for this purpose.

Stern davits come in different sizes that vary in lifting power and height, as well as in how far they extend out past the stern of the boat (curved transoms will need davits with a longer reach than straight transoms will). There are also special removable transom davits available that are designed to be quickly removed when not needed—providing full access to the

Tips on Installing Transom Davits

⚓ When installing stern davits, the covering board or transom on which they will be mounted will need some type of heavy backing plate under the deck or covering board. This backing plate should be at least 10 inches wide by 20 inches long to spread the load properly, and for a transom installation it should consist of two layers of ⅝-inch plywood covered by a sheet of ¼-inch-thick aluminum (rather than using washers under the nuts).

When davits are mounted on the transom covering board, additional bracing usually will be required to prevent distortion of this covering board—although this will vary with individual boats. One excellent method for reinforcing this transom covering board is to install an inverted stainless steel tripod directly under this mounting surface as shown in Figure 4.18. Consisting

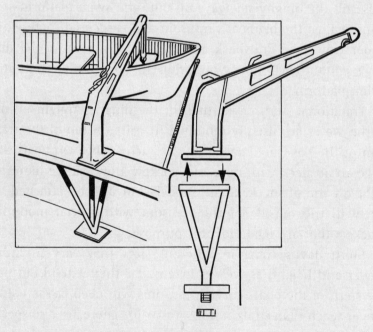

Figure 4.18

of a three-legged brace that fits under the covering board and rests on top of the deck below the board, this brace can be made up by any boatyard or welding shop that works with stainless steel. When installed as shown, it will help absorb both the crushing and tearing forces that are exerted on the covering board by transferring these forces to the deck below.

swim platform and getting them out of the way when fishing or swimming. These have a base that slides into a stainless steel "shoe" that is permanently bolted to the covering board or aft deck. A locking pin keeps the base of the davit from sliding out unexpectedly; yet when this pin is pulled out, the davit can be slid out easily without need for tools of any kind.

SIMPLE SALT-WATER WASH DOWN

An inexpensive way to add a salt-water wash down to the cockpit of a small open boat without drilling holes for a through-hull fitting is to use a bilge pump. Select one that that is rated at about 800 gph and comes with a mounting base that permits side mounting. This is installed on the outside of the stern as shown in Figure 4.19 so that it will be just below the waterline. A length of plastic tubing and a couple of elbow fittings are connected to the discharge port of this pump so that when the pump is running, water is carried over the top of the transom to the inside of the cockpit. A threaded plastic fitting is attached to the end of the plastic tubing so that a short length of garden hose can be attached to it when you want to use the wash down. The electric wire needed to supply power to the pump is brought out through a scupper in the transom, and both this wire and the plastic hose are secured to the transom with plastic wire clamps. A waterproof switch

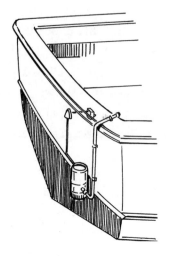

Figure 4.19

inside the cockpit controls the pump, and a red indicator light
is wired into the circuit to indicate when the switch is on.

NONSKID STEPS AND TREADS

An important safety precaution on any boat is to provide a
nonskid surface where people are most likely to slip, especially
in wet weather—for example, on smooth ladder steps where
people step when climbing on or off the boat, and on smooth,
polished deck areas where crew members need secure footing
while handling lines or attending to docking chores. There are
two simple ways you can accomplish this.

The quickest and easiest way is to apply self-adhesive plastic
strips that are sold for this purpose in all marine stores, as
well as in hardware stores and home centers. The other, more
permanent way to add a nonskid finish, especially on larger
areas, is to coat the surface with a nonskid paint—a paint to
which a nonskid, granular aggregate has been added.

The plastic, nonslip adhesive strips are usually sold by the
foot off large rolls, but they are also available in precut strips,

sheets, and oval-shaped treads of various sizes. Some companies make them in colors, as well as in the more common beige or off white. Applying them is simply a matter of peeling off the backing, then pressing them down where needed. However, in order for them to adhere properly, it is important that the surface to which they will be applied be absolutely dry and thoroughly cleaned beforehand by wiping down with a solvent such as alcohol or paint thinner.

To paint on a nonskid finish, you can use any good-grade deck enamel to which you have added a nonskid granular additive (sold in most marine supply outlets). This is not sand—which would not last very long—it is a special aggregate that is marketed by marine paint manufacturers for just this purpose. The additive must be thoroughly mixed in with the paint to ensure a uniform blend, adding no more thinners than absolutely necessary to permit even application. It can be applied with a brush or a long-nap roller.

Neater Rolled Curtains

Rolled-up canvas or plastic curtains on the flying bridge or aft deck of a cabin cruiser often look unsightly because it is almost impossible to roll them evenly and smoothly without their taking on a wavy, sagging look after they have been tied up. Here is a simple and inexpensive method to prevent such sagging and uneven rolling.

Cut a length of 1- or 1½-inch diameter white PVC (polyvinyl chloride) plastic pipe long enough to match the width of the curtain. Hold this along the bottom edge of the curtain and mark the pipe to indicate the location of each snap along the bottom edge of the curtain (the snaps that hold the curtain in place when it is rolled down). At each of these marks drill a hole of the right size to permit installing the base half of a screw snap—the half that will mate with the snap on the curtain.

Now all you have to do after you unsnap the curtain and

are ready to roll it up is to snap the length of PVC pipe onto the bottom edge of the curtain. Then you can roll the curtain up with the pipe on the inside. This will form a much neater roll that will not sag, even on hot days.

HOSE HOLDER

When washing your boat with a hose that is connected to the water supply on the dock, often when you lay the hose down for a moment, it slips overboard—especially if the pressure is still on. The nozzle then falls into the muddy bottom (if the

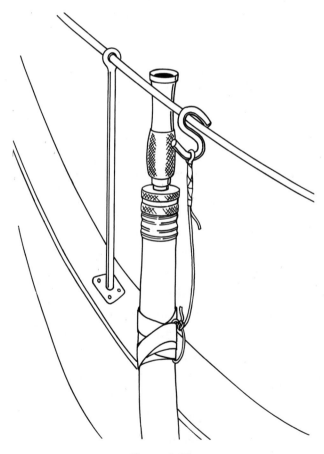

Figure 4.20

water is shallow), which creates a mess that takes time to clean up and is a nuisance to pull up each time. To keep this from happening each time you lay the hose aside, tie a small metal S-hook to the end of the hose as shown in Figure 4.20, using a short length of cord lashed to the hose just below its nozzle. To prevent the lashed cord from sliding farther down the hose, wrap it with a few turns of plastic tape. Now, each time you want to put the hose aside for a minute, simply hook this over a lifeline to hold the hose within easy reach until you are ready to use it again.

SECTION 5
CRUISING POINTERS

ONBOARD SAFETY

Every sensible skipper makes safety a top priority and tries to make his boat as accident-proof as possible.

For example: Because boats are always subject to some rolling or rocking motion, every boat should be equipped with plenty of strategically located handholds that people easily can reach when climbing aboard or moving about the inside or outside of the boat. This should include a sturdy railing around the bow deck to provide something to hang on to when anchoring or securing dock lines, as well as lifelines or railings around the side decks. If the side decks are not wide enough to allow for stanchions or a railing, there should be grab rails mounted against the outside of the cabin or on the cabin top so that there will be something to hold on to when going forward.

Inside the boat, there should be a long handrail running fore and aft the length of the cabin that is fastened securely to the overhead so that anyone walking through the cabin while under way will be able to steady himself while in rough

Safety When Cruising

⚓ • Make up a checklist of chores that must be taken care of each time you cast off for a cruise—and check off all items on this list before you start untying dock lines. Include such items as checking fuel and water levels, disconnecting and stowing shore cords, testing all electronic and navigation gear (don't wait until you need help to see if the radio works!), closing ports or hatches that could take on water, securing the dinghy, etc.

• When under way, never allow anyone to sit on the bow or deck with their feet hanging over the side (besides being unsafe, this is also against the law in many communities). Warn passengers and crew never to use arms or legs to fend off pilings or piers when maneuvering away from or into a dock, and don't allow crew members to go barefoot while running around on deck to tend lines—it's too easy to stub a bare toe or accidentally step on a piece of deck hardware with sharp edges.

• Someone should be on visual lookout at all times when under way, even if you are running under radar or if there seems to be no other boat in sight for miles. Never leave the helm unattended, even when on autopilot.

• In rough seas, make certain you know where everyone is at all times, especially if there are children onboard. If it is necessary for someone to go forward in a choppy sea, make sure that person is wearing a life jacket.

• If passengers go swimming while at anchor, insist on the "buddy system"—one person onboard must keep an eye on their "buddy" while he or she is in the water.

• Be constantly on the alert while fueling up, and never leave this chore for anyone else, unless it is a mature, experienced member of your own crew. Before starting to pump fuel, close all hatches, ports, and windows, and make sure all flames are extinguished inside the boat as well as outside. Shut off engines and electric motors, and make sure the fuel nozzle is firmly grounded to the fill pipe at all times. Don't allow fuel to overflow; but if it does, wash off spills immediately. After fueling, open all ports, hatches, and windows, and run the blowers for at least five minutes before turning on the ignition key. As a final check, sniff around down below to make certain there is no gasoline odor present before you start the engine.

seas. There should also be extra hand grips inside the head and galley areas, as well as alongside the boarding ladder and wherever one has to climb up or down a set of steps.

Ladders should have nonskid treads. If made of wood, they should be unpainted or covered with self-adhesive nonskid strips. If wood steps must be painted or varnished, then the coating should have an antislip additive mixed in with the paint or varnish. Ladders that have rungs made simply of round metal tubing (without wooden or plastic treads on each rung) should be replaced—these are an accident waiting to happen.

Coast Guard regulations spell out the number of Personal Flotation Devices (PFDs) required on each boat, as well as requirements for other safety gear such as navigation lights, fire extinguishers, flares, and a horn, whistle, or bell. However, it is still your responsibility to make certain that all this equipment is in good working order and ready for use. In addition, the items should be located where they are accessible for instant use when needed, and all adults onboard should know where safety equipment is stowed. Children as well as adults should be taught how to put life preservers on quickly in an emergency—and where they are stowed.

Remember that Coast Guard regulations spell out only the *minimum* requirements for your boat—it is often a good idea

Tips on Electrical Safety

⚓ • When plugging your shore cord into a dockside 120-volt AC receptacle, it is important that you maintain correct polarity. All 120-volt circuits consist of a white or "common" wire, a black (or red) "hot" wire, and a ground wire (usually green). The black or red wire and the white wire both carry the same current, but the green wire is never supposed to carry any current. Accidentally reversing polarity by connecting the "hot" wire in one circuit to the white or common wire of another circuit can be hazardous. It could cause electrical appliances or fixtures onboard to become "hot" so that a person touching it will get a lethal shock. In addition, reversed polarity can also cause serious electrolysis problems on your boat. This can happen when you plug into a dock receptacle that is not correctly wired and has the white and black wires reversed.

• To prevent plugging into such a defectively wired dock receptacle, it is a good idea to check it first with an outlet circuit tester (sold in most electrical supply houses, as well as in many marine supply stores). Neon lights on the top will tell you if there is reversed polarity, or if there are other potentially dangerous conditions in the dock wiring.

• The boat's storage batteries should be protected with a ventilated cover that will prevent anyone from accidentally coming in contact with the terminals, as well as protecting against sparks or shorts if a tool should accidentally drop on the terminals.

• Electric distribution panels for the boat's internal wiring should be covered or enclosed in a suitable cabinet to prevent accidental contact with exposed terminals.

• Switches, fuses, and circuit breakers should be clearly labeled so that you can find the right one in a hurry when there is an emergency.

> • When adding circuits or equipment, be careful to maintain polarity at all times—"hot" or positive wires should never be connected to the negative or grounded side of any circuit.

to have more than the Coast Guard regulations require. For example, the Coast Guard doesn't require your boat to carry an anchor, but you certainly wouldn't think of leaving the dock without one. The same holds true for an Emergency Position Indicating Radio Beacon (EPIRB). It's not required, but carrying one of these automatic emergency beacons certainly makes sense for any boat that does a lot of offshore cruising or fishing.

Fire extinguishers should be inspected twice a year to make sure they are still fully charged, and the skipper should make certain everyone knows where they are located and how to use them if fire does break out.

Most boat fires start in or near the engine room, so installing an automatic fire-extinguishing system that floods the compartment with Halon or CO_2 as soon as a fire starts is a very worthwhile investment for boats that have inboard engines. In addition, it is a good idea to install some type of gas detector that will give a visual or audible warning of the accumulation of dangerous fumes.

Spilled fuel or oil should always be carefully mopped up as soon as possible. Before the beginning of each cruise, check for fuel leaks by shining a bright light all around the engine room and along each fuel line and its connections. Don't start the engine(s) until all fuel or oil leaks are repaired and the spills or drips cleaned up. A clean engine room and bilge is not only neater, it also makes spotting future leaks a lot easier and it is a lot safer to work in—lessening the chance of fire and accidents caused by oily surfaces. That is why periodically inspecting and cleaning the bilges is important.

While doing this, you should also check all seacocks to make certain they can be closed quickly in an emergency. Inspect the hose clamps on each through-hull fitting to be sure they are still tight, then inspect the hoses connected to these fittings. Replace any that feel soft or look swollen.

PREVENTING AND FIGHTING FIRES ONBOARD

A small fire is a lot easier to put out than a large one; since most fires start out small, it is essential to take prompt action as soon as a fire is discovered—which means there should be plenty of good-quality portable fire extinguishers around (preferably more than just the minimum required by the Coast Guard).

For example: On a fifty-foot motor yacht, regulations call for only four extinguishers, but no sensible owner of a yacht of this size should settle for only four. Most experts recommend that there be one extinguisher near the entrance to each stateroom, including the salon; one near the galley; one near each helm station (including up on the flying bridge); one near each set of steps connecting lower levels with the aft deck; one on the aft deck; and one outside *each* means of entry to the engine compartment.

In a yacht this size, the wise skipper also installs an automatic extinguishing system in the engine compartment, even though there are no regulations requiring such systems. These are self-contained units that have heat sensors that will automatically discharge the contents of a large cylinder full of fire-extinguishing gas when fire breaks out in the engine compartment. The extinguishing gas will quickly flood the compartment and smother the fire before it can spread to other parts of the boat—in many cases before it can even do much damage to the engine.

To ensure fast action when fire is discovered, all portable

fire extinguishers should be located where they are easy to see and can be quickly reached. Every member of the family or crew should be familiar with where these extinguishers are located; in fact, it is a good idea to periodically have a practice drill to see how quickly an extinguisher can be located near a potential source of fire in various parts of the boat. It's also important that everyone (including youngsters) know how to use these extinguishers without having to read the directions first.

In addition to having an adequate number of extinguishers onboard, all should be inspected at least twice a year to see if they need recharging (dry-chemical units usually have a gauge that will indicate this). If any units do need recharging, have the work done by a competent professional—this is not a do-it-yourself job. With dry-chemical extinguishers, it is a good idea to also take them out of their bracket each time you inspect them and shake them vigorously because the powder tends to cake up on the inside if left undisturbed for many months.

Since the vast majority of boat owners never actually get to discharge a fire extinguisher, it is a good idea to set up a schedule where one extinguisher (the one that has the oldest inspection label on it) is discharged each year, then promptly brought in for recharging. Start a fire—on shore, *not* on the boat—using oily rags or a similar flammable material. Then demonstrate the proper way to use and handle an extinguisher for putting out this fire while the rest of the family and crew watches. Just remember that a typical 2½-pound portable extinguisher (which is all that is required on most pleasure boats) will discharge its entire load in less than ten seconds, so you can't waste much time after activating the discharge.

The stream should always be directed at the base of the flames or directly onto the burning material fueling the fire, not at the flames themselves. Try to get close—most portable units are effective only at distances up to about ten or fifteen feet—but never close enough to actually endanger yourself.

Fires are classified by three categories: A, B, or C. Class A fires are those involving common combustibles such as wood, paper, and fabric. Class B fires are those involving fuels such as gasoline or diesel, as well as oil, grease, paint, and flammable solvents. Class C fires are electrical fires that involve live wiring or electronic equipment that has current flowing through it.

The most effective extinguishing chemical you can use on a Class A fire is water—something that would seem to be readily available on boats. Realistically speaking, however, not many boats actually have fire hoses, or even large buckets that can be used to scoop water from over the side. That is why even though the Coast Guard only requires extinguishers that are rated for Class B and C fires (for pleasure craft up to sixty-five feet in length), it's still a good idea also to have at least one or two extinguishers onboard that are rated for all three types of fire—A, B, and C—especially in the salon and on the aft deck where paper or fabric fires are a distinct possibility.

If your galley is equipped with an alcohol or kerosene stove, make sure it is an approved marine model that is securely fastened down at all times. Ideally, it should also be gimballed so that it will stay level when the boat pitches or heels while the stove is in use. Never use camp-type outdoor stoves that have a built-in fuel tank or that have fuel tanks which are mounted next to the stove.

If your galley is equipped with a gas stove that uses propane or compressed natural gas, make sure there is an easily reached shut-off valve mounted at or near the tank. The tank should be mounted outside the cabin in a properly vented locker that will protect the tank from the elements, yet allow adequate circulation of air (in case a leak develops). The line connecting it to the stove must be an approved-type fuel line or gas line that is securely fastened in place.

Since propane is heavier than air, leaking gas will accumulate in the bilge if the gas finds its way belowdecks, producing a potentially explosive mixture. That's why these tanks should not be installed inside enclosed cockpits or enclosed aft decks unless they are properly vented directly to the outside (sizable openings at the bottom that will carry gas outside the hull and directly over the side).

Here are some other fire-prevention measures that all boat owners and crew members should know about:

• Never allow anyone to smoke in bunks or beds—an important fire-prevention measure that is all too often ignored, but is one of the most common causes of fires that start in sleeping quarters.

• If your boat has gasoline engines that are enclosed or belowdecks, make sure you run the engine compartment blower(s) for at least five minutes before you start those engines. Even then, play it safe and open the engine compartment and sniff for fumes before you turn the ignition key on for the first time.

• The engine compartment blower should be mounted high enough to protect against splashing of bilgewater, but ducts connected to the intake should draw air from the lower one-third of that compartment (Figure 5.1). Ideally, the intake should be below the engine if possible, but high enough to keep it out of the bilgewater at all times.

• Dispose of greasy or oily rags, paper towels, and similar flammable waste materials on shore as soon as possible. If you must carry these materials onboard (for example, while you are away from a dock), store them in a closed metal container out on deck.

Figure 5.1

• Get in the habit of inspecting all high-voltage and high-amperage electrical connections and terminals at least once a month. This would include battery cable connections, starter cables, alternator connections, 120-volt terminals, plugs and outlets, and anywhere else where there is a possibility of a spark or "short" occurring. If the dockside shore plug or connector seems to be a loose fit, or if it starts to corrode, the connection can overheat and start a fire.

• Your monthly inspection should also include a close examination of all fuel lines in the engine compartment, since even the slightest leak can be the cause of fire or explosion. If repairs or replacements are required, make sure you use only approved-type fuel lines. Also, make sure there is an easily reached shut-off valve at the tank that can shut off the flow of fuel in an emergency.

CRUISING EMERGENCIES

Although it may be impossible to prepare for every emergency while cruising, the most important step is to do everything possible to *prevent* emergencies from happening. A precruise inspection of gear and equipment is probably the most important step the boat owner can take in this respect, so here is a simple checklist that all boat owners can use as a guide before leaving the dock:

• Test the steering mechanism, the throttle controls, the gear shifts, and all radios, electrical, and electronic equipment to make sure everything is working smoothly.

• If you have an inflatable life raft, make certain it has been serviced and tested by an authorized technician or the manufacturer within the past year.

• If you will be cruising beyond reliable VHF radio range, you should carry an Emergency Position Indicating Radio Beacon (EPIRB); before the start of each cruise make sure its battery is still good and has at least 50 percent useful life remaining.

• Be sure that at least one other person onboard knows how to run the boat well enough to bring it back to shore or within hailing distance of help if the skipper is incapacitated (especially when cruising with family or friends). Someone onboard also should know how to use the radio to call for help and how to use flares or other signaling devices in case of an emergency.

• The boat should carry enough CG-approved fire extinguishers for a boat its size, and these should be located where they can be quickly reached when needed. Make sure everyone knows where they are all located.

• All loose gear should be secured inside the boat, as well as on deck. This includes dock lines, fenders, boat hooks, fishing gear, and sports equipment, as well as lamps, galley utensils, tools, and even clothing and boots.

• Inspect all life jackets, flotation cushions and other PFDs to be certain none are mildewed or torn. Make sure young children wear their life jackets at all times while they are on deck.

Unfortunately, no matter how careful and thorough the skipper is, there inevitably will be times when he will be faced with an unexpected emergency. Being prepared can make the difference between saving or losing his boat—or even saving the lives of those onboard. Here are a number of frequently encountered emergencies, along with suggestions as to how you can prepare for and cope with them:

Problem: A hose in the bilge, connected to an underwater through-hull fitting, breaks or splits, allowing water to rush in. You try to close that seacock, but it cannot be shut off because the handle is frozen in the open position.

Solution: Make up a tapered soft wood plug of the right diameter and shape to fit snugly inside each seacock. Tie one to the handle of each through-hull fitting and seacock so that in an emergency all you have to do is loosen the hose clamps and pull the hose off (cut it off if you have to), then hammer the wood plug into the opening to stop incoming water. (You can buy ready-made wood plugs from some marine stores).

Problem: You have struck a sunken log or run hard aground, and the boat is taking on water too fast for the bilge pumps to handle.

Solution: You can use the boat's main engine—or the engine that powers your auxiliary generator—as a large-volume emergency bilge pump. Here's how: Shut off that engine and disconnect the intake water hose that comes from its through-hull fitting to the engine (if it won't pull off easily, you may have to cut it; have a sharp knife and a pair of heavy-duty wire cutting pliers handy). After the hose is free, cover its end with a piece of screen mesh to keep out debris (tear the screen out of a hatch or porthole if necessary), then shove this end of the hose into the bilgewater and start the engine again (Figure 5.2). It will then draw its cooling water out of the bilge— it is hoped fast enough to keep you afloat. But make sure someone keeps an eye on the end of the hose to make sure it stays below water and does not get clogged.

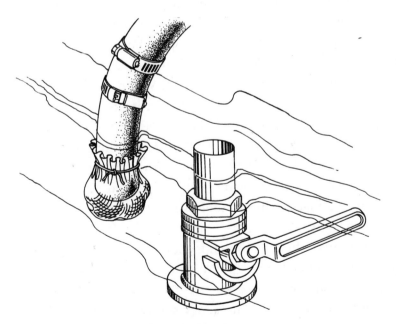

Figure 5.2

Problem: Your boat is involved in a collision that has punched a small hole through your hull at or below the waterline.

Solution: Carry some quick-setting epoxy putty onboard—the type that will set under water. Jam a wad of this into the hole, then force a cushion, a sizable piece of bunched-up canvas, or something else on top of the epoxy to hold it in place until it sets. Even better, keep a package of some water-activated fiberglass cloth onboard (Syntho Glass, available at marine stores and plumbing supply outlets, is one brand). The cloth can be wadded up and forced into the hole to close it. The resin is activated by salt water or fresh water and should be held in place for about ten minutes until it starts to set up.

Problem: An accident or collision has punched a sizable hole in the hull—too big a hole to fill or block up with epoxy while working from the inside.

Solution: Carry a small tarp or piece of heavy canvas onboard with grommets in each corner and ropes tied to each of these grommets. Two of the ropes should be long enough to go completely under and around the boat so they can be tied to something on the other side. When the boat is holed, tie the two short lines to some deck hardware on the damaged side of the boat, then pass the two longer lines under the boat and tie them to the other side. Move the canvas around until it is directly over the hole, then tie it securely in place. The pressure of the water will help hold this temporary "patch" in place while under way until you reach port—if you go slowly.

Problem: The boat is taking on water and the batteries have been flooded. Your radio is now useless and you cannot call for assistance.

Solution: Keep an emergency source of battery power onboard. It can be a few dry cells wired together in a suitable

Emergency Supplies

⚓ In addition to the usual complement of spare engine parts, oil filters, and extra lubricating oil, your onboard stock of emergency supplies should contain such items as:

• A set of basic tools, including several pairs of different size and style pliers, an assortment of flat-blade and Phillips-type screwdrivers, a set of open-end wrenches and one or two adjustable wrenches, a hammer, a sharp rust-resistant knife, a pair of Vise Grips or similar locking pliers, wire cutters, a hand drill, a hammer, a file, a putty knife/scraper, an all-purpose saw that will cut metal or fiberglass as well as wood, and an assortment of screws, bolts, nuts, and other fasteners.

• Several epoxy patching materials, at least one all-purpose adhesive, duct tape, and sail-mending tape.

• A moisture-displacing lubricating spray and a penetrating-type anticorrosion spray.

• Spare propellers and cotter pins, plus the tools needed to install them.

• A fully stocked first aid kit that includes sunscreen, prescription medicines needed by crew members or guests, and a good first aid manual.

• Spare drive belts for every V-belt in the engine room, including those on water pumps, bilge pumps, etc. Also, spare impellers for all these pumps.

• Spare hoses in all the lengths and diameters needed to replace any water hose or fuel hose inside the boat, plus an assortment of extra hose clamps in all the sizes needed.

• Spare bulbs and fuses for all navigation lights and for each piece of electronic equipment.

• An extra anchor rode and a second anchor heavy enough to hold in a blow, to be used for kedging off in an emergency when you go aground. Also, extra fenders and lines—in case you have to be towed (there should enough line to rig a towing bridle amidships).

• An aerosol-type air horn, or a manually operated horn that can be used in case your electric horn fails, or in case you want to take it with you when necessary to signal from a dinghy or life raft.

• Bottled drinking water and emergency food supplies that need no refrigeration or cooking—crackers, candy bars, canned meats, etc. (These should be packaged in waterproof plastic bags so you can throw them into a dinghy or life raft when in a real hurry). Don't forget a can opener.

• In cold weather, carry thermal blankets that fold into a compact package and store them with the first aid kit.

• A couple of powerful, waterproof flashlights, with plenty of extra batteries and spare bulbs.

• A compact emergency antenna for your VHF that can be hooked up quickly in an emergency if the boat's antenna gets damaged.

• A portable handheld VHF, in case the ship's radio breaks down or you lose power. This is also useful because you can take it with you if you have to leave the boat and get into a dinghy or life raft.

• Wide strips of reflective tape that can be affixed to the cabin top or to the sides of the boat to make it easier for rescuers to spot your boat, especially at night. Tape can also be used on life jackets and throwable rings or buoys.

holder, or you can buy one of those compact storage batteries that are sold for use in motorcycles, lawn mowers, and similar equipment. Be sure you store this battery at a high point in the boat where water can't get at it, and make sure such rechargeable batteries are fully charged before leaving the dock.

MAINTENANCE WHILE CRUISING

Being properly provisioned before leaving on a cruise is important to the safety and comfort of all onboard, but it is equally important to follow a preventive maintenance routine every day—including days when you are tied to a dock—either because of bad weather or because of an actual "break" in the cruise.

While under way, you should go below and inspect the engine compartment at least two or three times a day. Shine a light around to examine the fuel lines and fittings so you can check for fuel leaks. Also, do the same with all water hoses and lines.

Anchoring out, whether for an afternoon swim or for the night, is one of the most popular cruising pleasures, but it can turn into a nightmare if your ground tackle is not secure. So pay extra attention to the condition of your ground tackle during every cruise. Inspect the anchor rode and its chain, as well as all swivels, shackles, and other hardware each time you use the anchor. If the line shows signs of chafing, replace it as soon as possible; if the hardware is starting to corrode, spray with a moisture-resistant coating or lubricant. Have a second anchor rigged and ready for use at all times, in case you get caught in a blow or are forced to cut the original line.

When swimming around the boat while at anchor, take time to don a face mask and snorkel and take a quick look at the propellers and rudders to see if there is extensive fouling and to see if all the protective zinc anodes are still in place. Another chore that can be taken care of while spending an afternoon at anchor is to scrub off the slime and "grass" that inevitably accumulates along the waterline.

The same holds true for exhaust stains on the transom—cleaning these off periodically during the cruise will be a lot easier than cleaning them off later on. You can do these jobs while treading water near the boat if you attach one of those suction-type hand holds to the hull to give you something to hang on to while scrubbing with the other hand; or you can work from your dinghy if you have one.

During a cruise, powerboats will be fueling up much more often—sometimes at an exposed dock where the boat will be subject to rocking or pitching from the wakes of passing boats. This makes fuel spills and accidental chipping of the gel coat more likely (if the metal nozzle gets dropped on deck). Prevent this by putting down a canvas fueling "apron" to protect the fiberglass. This can consist of a piece of heavy canvas or carpet several feet square with a hole cut in the center to expose the fuel-fill opening. Lay this over the deck or gunwale with the hole over the fuel fill when you take on fuel so that spills will be caught by the "apron" and the gel coat will be protected against chipping if you should accidentally drop the nozzle.

Paint and varnish also takes more of a beating while on an extended cruise, so don't ignore minor scratches, scrapes, and gouges—especially on varnished brightwork. Small breaks in the film will allow water to seep into the wood, creating dark stains that will be much harder to remove later on. Moisture that penetrates will also hasten the day when the rest of the varnish will start letting go. To prevent this, always travel with a small can of matching paint and some varnish onboard, as well as a few small touch-up brushes.

Cleaning off dirt and stains that develop around the outside is equally important. Removing stains as they occur will not only make things easier for you at the end of the cruise, it will also keep such stains from becoming so deeply embedded that they will be very difficult—or even impossible—to remove later on.

Daily Cruising Checks

⚓ • Check fuel and lubricating oil levels before casting off each day.

• Before you take off, make certain the dinghy (if you have one) is secure, and make sure the crew understands how to launch it in a hurry if needed.

• Inspect each dock line as you coil it to see if there are any signs of chafing, particularly on permanent eye splices.

• Turn on all navigation and running lights, including anchor lights, to make certain all work properly.

• If you have a holding tank, check to see how full it is and plan your itinerary so you will be near a pump-out station when you think you will need one.

• Examine your shore cord as you unplug it from the dock. If the three-pronged male plug on the end looks scorched or corroded, take time to clean it off with steel wool or fine sandpaper before plugging the cord in again. If the prongs are loose, wobbly, bent, or badly burned, the plug should be replaced as soon as possible.

• Open the hatches and inspect the water level in the bilge. If there is more water than usual, the bilge pump's float switch may be stuck. Also check for signs of oil or fuel leakage, and at least once a week check for stuffing box leaks (don't forget the rudder stuffing box).

• Before plugging your shore cord into a strange dock, test the receptacle with a portable polarity tester. Reversed polarity could create serious electrolysis problems for your boat, as well as a potential shock hazard.

• Go through the inside as well as the outside of your boat to make certain all loose gear is properly stowed before you cast off. Lamps, TV sets, and other small appliances should be thoroughly secured or carefully stowed before you take off. All doors and cabinets should be closed and secured.

Warmer Steering Wheel

Many boats have a modern, stainless steel "destroyer"-type steering wheel. These are attractive looking and easy to handle, but on cold mornings, the bare metal can feel cold and uncomfortable to the touch, unless you wear gloves. A solution to this problem is to slip a length of inexpensive foam-type pipe insulation over the rim of the wheel. It is sold in plumbing supply outlets, as well as in hardware stores and home centers, and comes in tubular form and in various diameters to fit different size pipes. Buy the size that best fits the rim of your wheel (usually ¾ inch) and slide this over the wheel rim on cold mornings. It is not only warm to the touch, it is also more comfortable to hold on to when running for long hours. It will usually stay in place by itself, but if necessary you can wrap each end with masking tape to keep it from slipping.

FOR TROUBLE-FREE CHARTERING

Most well-established charter companies will show their customers through the ship to familiarize them with all operating systems and equipment. However, if you are dealing with a private owner, or with a yacht broker who does not charter on a regular basis, then you may have to insist on such a tour. Ask to be shown where all the water valves and pumps are located, where the fuel shut-off valves are located, where the fuses and circuit breakers are mounted, and what circuit each of these control (if this is not marked on the panel).

Ask the agent to start up the generator (if there is one) and to show you how the anchor windlass works. Note where boat hooks, docking lines, and fenders are stowed, as well as where anchors and anchor lines are stored, and inspect the lines and hardware used on each anchor. Also, locate all fire extinguishers and make certain they have been inspected during the past year. If you are chartering in the United States, make sure the yacht has been Coast Guard inspected during the year, and ask where the life preservers, flare guns, and other items of safety equipment are stored.

While checking all this, insist that each piece of electronic gear—loran and radar units, radios, depth finders, etc.—be turned on and activated, not only to familiarize yourself with how these pieces of equipment work, but also to make sure that they *do* work. If the boat has a dinghy, make sure you know how to launch it. Check its condition and start its motor if it has one to make sure it is in good condition.

Check the compass to see if it has been compensated and reads accurately. If there is more than one compass on board, they should read alike (if not, find out why). One good way to check a compass you are unsure of is to use a hand-bearing compass on the dock (away from all magnetic influences) to take a bearing on something prominent. Then see if the ship's compass matches this when you use it to take the same bearing.

It's important to check all operating gear and equipment to see if it works before you leave the dock—not only for your own comfort and safety, but because otherwise you may get charged for repairing these items after the boat is returned. To avoid such misunderstandings, make note of all defects in writing, including damages to fiberglass or paint and varnish, and have the agent sign this before you leave.

All reliable yacht charter services will insist that the boats on their list are properly maintained and are equipped with essential items, but remember, not everyone agrees on what is "essential." That's why you shouldn't depend entirely on the charter agent to make sure the boat is properly equipped for *your* comfort. For example, no one will argue with the fact that a first aid kit is essential, but not everyone will agree on what that first aid kit should include. Ask about this beforehand so that if there are other items you feel are needed these can be added before you take off.

One item every charter boat should have onboard is a basic kit of tools, but again, what does this include? Many find it worthwhile to carry along a few extra tools that may not be found in the onboard tool kit supplied by the owner, preferably stored in a compact roll-up canvas holder. Included should be an extra flashlight, plus extra batteries for that light. Also advisable would be a couple of tubes of all-purpose adhesive, plus a tube of "instant" glue and a small package of quick-setting, two-part epoxy adhesive.

In addition to tools and some essential spare parts (filters, hoses, lubricants, etc.) you should also have all the operating manuals on hand for the various appliances and other equipment on board. Remember that the charter agent is usually responsible for the cost of repairs due to a mechanical breakdown after you take off, but they are not always willing to pay for repairs to a clogged head, stalled dinghy motor, or other minor breakdowns unless this work is done at their own dock. To avoid arguments, ask how such problems will be handled after you are on your way. Before you sign your charter contract read it carefully.

Many of the better chartering outfits supply all the charts and cruising guides you will need as part of their service, but if they don't, make sure you pick these items up before you leave the dock—you may not be able to locate them later on. Ask the charter agent to give you a list of local distress and calling frequencies for your radio, and ask about arrangements for contacting the home office (especially in off hours) if you need help.

All cruising boats have only a limited amount of storage space, so be choosy about the amount of clothes you bring along. Select all-purpose wash-and-wear shorts, slacks, shirts, etc., that won't wrinkle easily—and that can be stuffed into small cabinets. Luggage should be duffel bags or other soft, collapsible pieces that can be rolled up and jammed into corners, and for footwear stick to sneakers or soft-soled boat shoes rather than open sandals.

GUIDE TO DINGHIES

Dinghies come in a very wide range of sizes and styles, but most fall into one of two broad categories: inflatables and rigid models. The amount of maintenance required varies, but all need some regular care to keep them serviceable and presentable in appearance.

Inflatable Dinghies: Most often made of some type of vinyl, neoprene, or similar rubberlike synthetic material, inflatables are often touted as being maintenance-free, but this is not entirely true. Even the best-quality models get grungy-looking if not regularly cleaned and if not protected from the sun when not in use for days at a time. However, there are simple precautions one can take to preserve and protect the appearance of all inflatables.

One mistake often made is to overinflate them in an effort to make them "stiffer." This places severe stress on the seams, and after the dinghy has been out in the hot sun for a while, pressure can build up enough to cause excessive fatigue to the fabric itself, thus shortening its life considerably. Careless beaching of the dinghy or dragging it up onto a rough shoreline where there are sharp rocks can also cause damage to, and shorten the life of, any inflatable. Even very coarse sand can abrade or tear the fabric. Sand that accumulates on the inside can also be a serious threat, regardless of how durable or strong that material is, because sand is an abrasive that will damage any inflatable material when it gets rubbed around on the inside. Avoid such damage by hosing out the dinghy after each use, or at the end of each day's cruising. Also wash the outside to get rid of salt and oil or fuel stains.

Long exposure to sunlight causes fading, oxidation, and discoloration, so at least once a year it is a good idea to apply a protective coating that is sold for this purpose. First wash the material with a mild detergent and allow the fabric to dry thoroughly, then apply the coating according to directions on the package. Another good way to protect your inflatable against fading and the deterioration caused by the sun is to cover it with a lightweight plastic or fabric cover when it is not in use (available from most canvas shops).

If the inflatable is left in the water constantly, it should be hauled out regularly and the bottom scrubbed to get rid of marine growth and slime—not only to make towing easier, but also to minimize possible damage to the fabric when the dinghy is dragged up out of the water. The best protection is to paint the bottom of your inflatable with an antifouling paint that is suitable for use on this material.

Every inflatable comes with a repair kit that includes an assortment of patches, plus a special adhesive for making permanent repairs. This kit, packed in a waterproof container, should be with the dinghy at all times so you can make quick repairs in an emergency. But remember, most of these glues or adhesives have a limited shelf life, so don't forget to replace them before the expiration date.

Rigid Dinghies: The vast majority of rigid dinghies are made of molded fiberglass and are most often finished with gel coat on the outside. Like any other fiberglass vessel, these should be frequently washed and given a coat of wax or polish about twice a year to maintain the gloss and to help resist fading, dulling, and oxidation of the finish.

Although some fiberglass dinghies have no wood trim, many have at least some varnished wood trim to dress them up—for example, along the gunwales and the seats. Some models also have varnished wood deck boards on the bottom to add to the appearance, and to help keep your feet dry.

Since poorly maintained brightwork will make any boat (including a dinghy) look drab and forsaken, it's worth the effort required to maintain this small amount of varnished trim. Hose off the brightwork and wipe it down with a chamois or towel at the end of each day. Maintain the finish by applying a fresh coat of varnish at least twice during the season, sanding lightly before each coat. Be careful to avoid dripping varnish onto the fiberglass since this will leave ugly stains that are hard to remove.

Fiberglass dinghies that spend most of their time in the water should have the bottom painted with an antifouling paint, but this is not necessary (or even advisable) if the dinghy is stored out of the water on deck or in davits. If the dinghy is normally hauled out and carried onboard in davits, make sure there is a drain in the bottom that is left open to keep the dinghy from filling with water when it rains or when under way in heavy seas. If the dinghy is stored on deck, either keep it covered or store it upside down—again to keep it from filling with water.

Towing Your Dinghy: When under way, the skipper must never forget that he is towing a small boat behind him, so it's essential that he keep looking behind at frequent intervals—or arrange for someone onboard to take this responsibility. Otherwise there is the possibility that the dinghy will suddenly "disappear" over the horizon without anyone remembering when and where it was last seen, especially when running in rough weather.

For towing, the dinghy should have an eyebolt securely mounted low in its bow. The towing line is most often attached to the big boat by fastening to one of the stern cleats, but a much better arrangement—especially in rough weather—is to rig a bridle across the stern so the tow line will be centered

Inflatable vs. Rigid Dinghies

⚓ Although it cannot be said that one type of dinghy is "better" than the other, there are differences. Understanding these differences may help you decide which type to buy.

• If you intend to carry the dinghy suspended over the stern of your cruising boat—on davits or mounted on a swim platform—an inflatable is usually much lighter in weight and thus much easier to haul onboard. It will also have less effect on the trim of your boat, especially when running in rough seas.

• Inflatables are generally more stable and less likely to tip or swamp, even when you step on one side. However, without rigid floorboards on the inside, inflatables are not as steady or as stable to move around in. Also, they are often harder to keep dry on the inside because puddles are harder to mop up.

• Most inflatables have lower freeboard than comparable-size rigid dinghies, so in choppy waters they tend to take on more spray, especially on a windy day.

• If you want a dinghy for rowing, then a rigid dinghy will be easier to handle—especially when you have to fight wind or current. With a rigid dinghy you build up momentum as you row so that it keeps gliding forward between strokes; an inflatable tends to lose way and stop as soon as the oars come out of the water.

• If the dinghy is to be powered by a small outboard, then either type will perform satisfactorily, but in choppy waters more power is required to get the same speed out of an inflatable. However, the performance under power will be much better if the inflatable is equipped with floorboards. A special motor bracket, which often must be purchased separately, will also be needed.

- If you want a sailing dinghy, forget about an inflatable. Although a few manufacturers of inflatables have come out with kits that include sails, none have proven very satisfactory. An inflatable cannot heel properly, and it must use leeboards instead of a center board. Also, they have difficulty tacking and coming about because they lose way so quickly.

when under way. The length of the towline should be adjusted when you are at cruising speed so that both boats are on or near the crest of a trough (on the upward slope of the wave) at the same time. This will ensure that the towline remains under relatively constant tension at all times—it should not snap back and forth from very slack to very taut. You certainly don't want the dinghy to come running up against the stern of the parent boat as it races down a large wave.

Braided nylon line is probably the strongest and safest towline, but many prefer polypropylene because it floats. It is usually strong enough for most dinghies, but remember that this type of rope does deteriorate with constant exposure to sunlight, so keep it under cover when not in use. The towline cannot be ignored when coming into a dock or approaching a mooring—even if it does float. Someone should be delegated to haul in excess line and keep an eye on the dinghy while docking because the line can get sucked down and into the propeller when backing down or when maneuvering around a dock. If there is no one available to keep a watch, then the dinghy should be pulled close and tied alongside the stern quarter (on the side away from the dock).

DOCKING AIDS

Although good boat fenders can protect your boat against most accidents when docking at a marina, even the most experienced boat owner will appreciate some of the aids and accessories that are available to make docking or undocking easier and to help to protect the boat while it is tied up at the dock:

Mooring Whips: Resembling oversize fishing rods or outriggers, mooring whips are widely used to keep boats from banging into or rubbing against docks and pilings, especially on docks or piers that are located along canals and bays where there is a lot of marine traffic. Properly installed, a set of mooring whips eliminates the need for fenders between the boat and its dock because they hold the boat away from the dock by several feet, even when the boat is subject to strong surge action or "wash" from passing boats, or under strong current and wind conditions.

Mooring whips consist of two solid fiberglass rods that fit into special sockets which are bolted to the dock (Figure 5.3). The rods or whips are flexible and tapered at the top so that when bent under tension, the upper part bends much more than the bottom. A line secured to the top is tied to cleats on the boat—one at the bow and one at the stern—after pulling the line tight enough to bend the whip and apply the required tension.

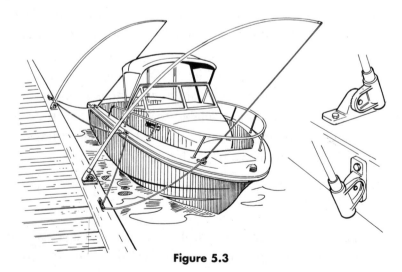

Figure 5.3

This tension is enough to hold the boat away from the dock, but the usual fore and aft dock lines are still required (but not fenders). Although the boat is held off the dock by these whips you can still pull the boat in quite easily for boarding—or you can simply release the tension on the mooring whips and allow the boat to drift in close to the dock when desired. When the whip lines are untied, the flexible poles spring upright, leaving the lines dangling where they can be easily picked up by someone onboard when the boat returns to the dock.

Mooring Arms: Although similar to mooring whips in function, mooring arms are not flexible, so they do not bend. Instead, the spring-mounted, stainless steel, telescoping-type arms are bolted to the dock or bulkhead so they project out horizontally above the boat's cleats as shown in Figure 5.4. When the short lines attached to the end of each arm are tied to the cleats on the boat, they serve to hold the boat away from the dock, while eliminating the need for separate bowlines and

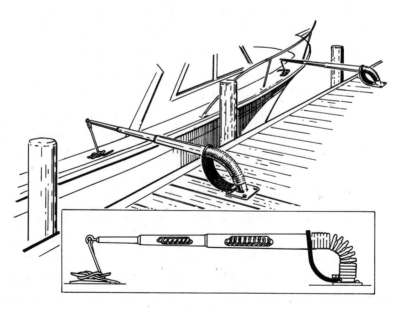

Figure 5.4

stern lines. However, spring lines are still required to prevent back-and-forth movement in most installations.

The spring-loaded mounting base for each arm swings it up to a vertical position when the lines are untied, thus keeping the arms out of the way when the boat leaves its slip. The telescoping sections of these tubular arms are also spring loaded, so that even though they are strong enough to hold the boat away from the dock in a severe wind, they still allow for a reasonable amount of sideways boat movement without placing undue stress on cleats or chocks.

Homemade Docking Aid: The only way to get a dock line ashore when there is no one on the dock to take a line is for someone to jump from the boat to the dock—assuming, of course, that the skipper can maneuver the boat in close enough to accomplish this safely.

To overcome this difficulty, especially when docking alone or when a crew member is reluctant to jump from boat to dock, boat owners can make up a special mooring line about seven to eight feet in length with a big open loop at the end, similar to one shown in Figure 5.5. This has a regular eye splice at one end with a much larger, permanently open loop at the other end. As the boat approaches its dock, the eye splice is dropped over the bow cleat on the boat. The other end (with the larger eye splice that is big enough to fit easily over a dock cleat or piling) can then be easily dropped over a dock cleat or piling by any crew member still standing in the boat. The size of the loop can vary, but it should be at least 18 inches in diameter to fit over most pilings.

Before making the large eye splice loop, feed that end of the line through a piece of rubber hose or tubing slightly larger than the diameter of the rope. The length of this hose should equal what is required to go around the circumference of the finished loop, but with enough extra length of rope sticking out of the hose to permit splicing the eye. Before splicing, fold

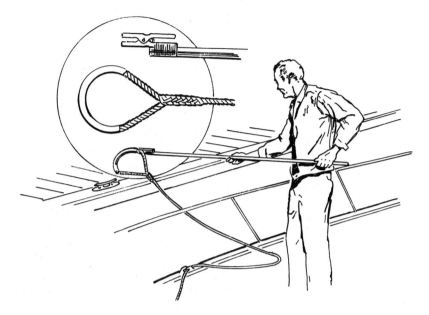

Figure 5.5

the hose in half and tape the ends of the hose together to keep the line and hose folded, then complete the splice as usual.

To simplify extending the finished line to the dock and placing it over the cleat or piling, use a long boat hook with a large spring clip or clothespin attached to the end. When the dock is in reach, the boat hook is used to drop the eye over the dock cleat (or piling), then pulled back sharply to release the line. The line can then be used to take up the slack and haul the boat more tightly into the dock.

Color-Coded Docking Lines

Most boat owners make up a permanent set of docking lines for use at their own marina dock. Usually these lines vary in length, according to which dock cleat they will be secured to. The skipper then must tell the dock boy—or whoever is helping from the dock—which line is intended to be dropped over which cleat on the dock.

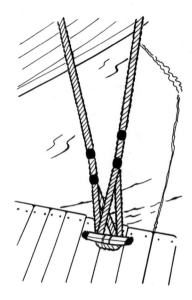

Figure 5.6

To avoid the confusion this often creates—with helpers on the dock as well as with your own crew—stick a colored strip of plastic tape to each dock cleat, using different colors for each cleat. Then add a strip of matching colored tape to the eye of the particular line that is supposed to go on to that cleat. This makes it easy to pick out the right line each time—all you have to do is say to anyone helping you, "put the line with the red tape on the red cleat, and the line with the blue tape on the blue cleat."

SECTION 6

SPRING COMMISSIONING AND FALL LAYUP

ORGANIZING YOUR SPRING COMMISSIONING

Spring commissioning is a hectic period when most boat owners are constantly pressed for time—especially those who don't organize and plan their commissioning tasks before getting started, or those who don't make certain they have everything needed to complete each job when they climb onboard. To avoid wasting time and effort during this crucial period, here is a common-sense plan that every boat owner can follow:

Belowdecks

Tools and Materials Needed: Scrub brush, rags and paper towels, bilge cleaner, large pails, small pump, oil or grease for seacocks and water pumps, assorted wrenches, several screwdrivers, extra hose clamps, flashlight, wire brush, waterproof grease, tape measure (for measuring hose if replacement is needed).

• Scrub the bilge thoroughly with bilge cleaner used at four times its normal strength. Flush out with fresh water, but do *not* pump the oily water overboard. Instead, pump it into pails or drums, then get rid of the contents at a safe disposal site onshore.

• Test each seacock to make certain it opens and closes smoothly (Figure 6.1). Clean and lubricate as necessary, and repair or replace those that do not work properly.

• If you disconnected your freshwater system to drain it before the winter, reconnect the hoses and tighten all hose clamps securely. Replace any clamps that are corroded. Connect up the freshwater pump, fill the water tank, and test the entire system, using a flashlight to see if there are any leaks while the pump is turned on and all faucets throughout the boat are shut off (if the pump cycles on and off even when

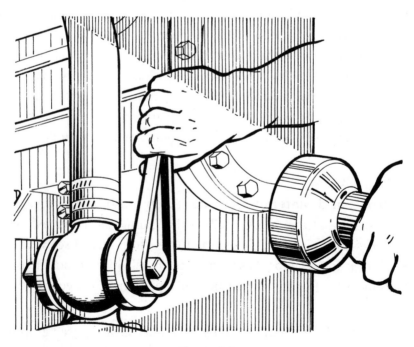

Figure 6.1

there is no faucet or appliance calling for water, this indicates there is a leak somewhere).

• Test the bilge pump(s) by turning on the manual switch. Test the float switch by pouring enough water into the bilge to activate the switch, or by taking the switch off and lowering it into a bucket of water.

• Clean the posts on each storage battery with a wire brush, then connect the cables and coat both the cable ends and posts with petroleum jelly or waterproof grease.

• Inspect engine hoses by squeezing each one. If a hose feels soft, replace it. Make sure all hose clamps are tight with double clamps on all through-hull fittings that are below the waterline (Figure 6.2).

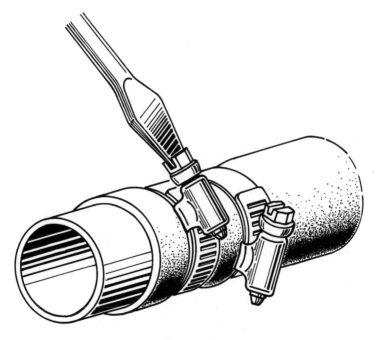

Figure 6.2

• After the boat is in the water, check the stuffing boxes to see if they are leaking (don't forget the rudder stuffing boxes). A slow drip is tolerable and often expected, but faster drips while at rest or while under way may indicate a need for tightening. For this you will need a wrench and large pair of slip-joint pliers (or two wrenches). If tightening does not stop the leak, then new packing may be required.

Electrical and Electronic Gear

Tools and Materials Needed: All electronic equipment that was taken off in the fall, weighted length of light line (for testing depth sounder), spare bulbs for each navigation light, moisture-displacing spray, electrical continuity tester, electrical crimp fittings and crimping tool, screwdrivers, wrenches and pliers, electric tie wraps, electrical tape, extra plug for AC shore cord.

• Hook up your radio and all other electronic gear, then turn each piece on and let it run for a couple of hours to make certain it is working properly. If it isn't, now is the time to send the equipment out for service—before the season begins.

• Calibrate your depth sounder to make certain it takes into account the difference between the lowest part of the keel and where the transducer is actually mounted. Use a weighted line to check the depth of the water while the boat is at rest, then check this against the reading on the sounder. Recalibrate if necessary, following the directions in your manual.

• Turn on all navigation lights to see whether any bulbs need replacing. Spray a little moisture-displacing, nonconducting lubricant into each light socket before installing a new bulb.

• Test all switches and circuit breakers by turning them on and off several times to make certain they are working properly. Replace those that stick or show signs of sparking.

• Examine all electric terminal blocks, junctions, and electrical connections. Look for signs of corrosion and clean these off with an abrasive pad. Test each terminal screw to make certain it is tight, and pull lightly on each wire to make certain the crimp fittings are not working loose. Then spray all connections with a moisture-displacing protective coating.

• Electric cables and wires should be secured at 18- to 24-inch intervals so that they cannot move or swing around and chafe when under way. Exposed wiring should always be covered with a protective conduit or molding of some kind.

• Inspect the full length of your electric AC shore cord to see if there are cuts or damaged spots on the insulation. If so, wrap with waterproof plastic tape or patch with silicone adhesive compound. Inspect the electric plugs at each end to see if prongs are bent, corroded, or discolored due to overheating. If you see evidence of this, replace the plug. Don't forget to inspect also the various cord adapters or Y-type connectors that you normally carry aboard for use at other docks.

Head and Galley Areas

Tools and Materials Needed: Rags and paper towels, marine wax, plastic polish (for countertops and cabinets), liquid detergent plus an all-purpose spray cleaner, a mildew-removing spray, baking soda, carpet cleaner, silicone lubricant, vacuum cleaner with attachments, old toothbrush or nail brush, toilet bowl cleaner, and toilet repair kit.

• If the galley sink is made of stainless steel, scrub thoroughly then give the inside of the sink a light coat of marine wax. This will make it less susceptible to water spotting and easier to clean in the future. Coat all plastic laminate countertops and cabinets with one of the polishes sold for this purpose.

• Clean the inside of all cabinets and drawers in both the head and the galley. If there are signs of mildew, wash with a solution of one part liquid laundry bleach and four parts water, or spray with a mildew-removing spray. To get rid of odors inside cabinets where food has been stored, place an open container of baking soda on the inside and leave it there.

• Scrub the inside of the icebox or refrigerator, then place an open container of baking soda on the inside.

• If the cabin has a vinyl-covered floor, wash thoroughly to clean it, but don't apply wax (too slippery). If the floor is covered with carpet, shampoo with a suitable cleaner. Better yet, if the carpet can be removed, take it off the boat for cleaning.

• Use silicone spray to lubricate all drawers and sliding cabinet doors. Clean out the tracks on which sliding doors ride by using a vacuum equipped with a narrow nozzle.

• Scrub the head and shower with a detergent and wipe down with a solution of liquid laundry bleach and water (see above) if there are signs of mildew. Be especially careful to clean all corners and crevices, using a toothbrush or fingernail brush in tight places.

• Give your marine toilet a spring "tune-up" by cleaning and lubricating moving parts as recommended in the owner's manual. Buy an overhaul kit for your toilet and replace the gaskets, seals, impellers, and other expendable parts included.

Clean and deodorize the toilet bowl, then disconnect the discharge hose and shine a bright light into the hose to see if it is partially blocked with a chemical buildup. If it is, replace the hose with a new one of comparable size.

Staterooms

Tools and Materials Needed: Mildew spray, vacuum cleaner, rags, sponge, lemon oil or cream-type polish, carpet stain remover.

• On a sunny, dry day, remove all mattresses and bunk cushions and lay them outside to air in the sun for several hours. Examine each piece for signs of mildew. Vinyl-covered cushions can be treated with a mildew spray, but cloth-covered cushions should be professionally cleaned if mildew is found.

• Use a vacuum cleaner to remove dust from vinyl headliners and interior bulkhead linings, as well as interior carpet or other upholstered surfaces that are not removable. If there are stains in the carpet that won't come out easily, rent a carpet cleaning machine from a local dealer.

• Interior wood that is varnished or finished with a clear sealer should be wiped down with a mild household cleaner to remove dust, oily grime, and soil. Then apply a light coat of lemon oil or a cream-type furniture polish. If the finish is really dull, apply one or two coats of a hard-drying penetrating sealer like Minwax Antique Oil Finish. Wipe on with a rag, then wipe excess off after about five minutes and buff vigorously.

• Open all hanging lockers, drawers, and other storage areas and clean out the insides with a vacuum. Use a damp cloth to remove caked-on dust or dirt and leave all doors and drawers open for a day or two to allow air to circulate.

• Inspect life jackets and other Personal Flotation Devices (PFDs) to look for rips, tears, or signs of mildew. Also, check all the fire extinguishers to see if any of them need to be recharged or replaced. Make sure flares are not outdated.

Around the Outside

Tools and Materials Needed: Marine-grade caulking, putty knife, scraper, grease or oil for windlass, sandpaper, paint thinner, rags, sponge, silicone lubricant spray, plastic polish for windshields and vinyl curtains, windshield wiper blades, assorted screwdrivers and wrenches, silicone rubber bedding compound, metal polish, boat cleaner, marine wax.

• Examine caulking around windows, hatches, port lights, and doors; inspect all joints where caulking is required. Scrape out any sealant that looks dried out or cracked, then replace with fresh material.

• If you have been troubled by leaks around window frames, don't depend on a fresh bead of caulking around the outside to stop the leak. You will have to completely remove that window or porthole frame on the outside. Scrape away all of the old compound, then spread on a liberal layer of fresh silicone rubber sealant or similar marine-grade caulking before replacing the frame. Make certain that before inserting the screws or bolts, you squirt some of the sealant into each of the holes also.

• If your boat has an anchor windlass or winch, lubricate as recommended in the owner's manual. Some windlasses have a regular grease fitting, while others have an oil sump that must be filled regularly.

• If there is any varnishing to be done around the outside, wait until the weather is dry and reasonably mild (above 55 degrees), but you don't have to wait until then to do your sanding—you can do this at any time. When you are ready to apply the varnish, wipe down the sanded surfaces with a rag wet with paint thinners just before applying your first coat.

• Inspect canvas curtains, bridge enclosures, and cockpit covers to see if there are any broken zippers or other fasteners that need to be replaced. If any repairs are needed, send this work out now so that the canvas will be ready before the season gets under way. Spray zippers, snaps, and other fasteners with a silicone lubricant to keep them from corroding and sticking.

• Use a wet cloth or sponge to wash the clear vinyl "windows" in each curtain. Do the same for all plastic windshields, port lights, and doors. Apply a polish or wax-type protective coating that is sold for use on such plastics (available in marine stores).

• If, like most boat owners, you haven't replaced the windshield wiper blades during the past year, then it's a good idea to do this now—sun and salt causes the rubber and metal on these blades to deteriorate rapidly, even if they have not been used.

• Use a screwdriver and wrench to make certain all screws and bolts that hold deck hardware in place are tight. If any of these fasteners are badly corroded, replace them. If a chock, cleat, stanchion, or other piece of deck hardware seems loose or wobbly, it may be advisable to take it off completely so that you can replace the bedding compound underneath before tightening the fasteners.

• As you inspect each piece of deck hardware, clean it with a metal polish, then give it a protective coat of wax or one of the clear coatings sold for use on chrome and stainless. This is especially important for aluminum hardware because even anodized aluminum will tend to oxidize in salt water.

• The last spring maintenance job is to give the whole outside of the boat a good scrubbing down, then wax all fiberglass and gel coat with a good-grade marine wax. Touch up the painted boot stripe if necessary.

SPRING COMMISSIONING A TO Z

No matter how well organized the boat owner is when planning his spring commissioning, there is always the possibility that something will be forgotten. To help prevent such omissions, here is a complete alphabetical list of commissioning chores that anyone can use to make sure that *nothing* is omitted accidentally:

A

AIR CONDITIONER: Connect the compressor's cooling water hoses to their through-hull fittings, making certain that all are double clamped with stainless marine-grade clamps. Open seacocks and run the unit to make sure there are no air locks in the hoses, and make sure strainers are clean.

ALARMS: After engines have been commissioned, turn on the ignition and see if the engine temperature and oil pressure alarms sound. If the boat is equipped with a security system (burglar, fire, and/or smoke alarm), test each as directed in the owner's manual.

ALTERNATOR: Readjust V-belts that were loosened in the fall and tension each to manufacturer's specifications (typically, a deflection of about ½ to 1 inch when 25 pounds pressure is applied between two pulleys).

ALUMINUM TRIM: Wash with freshwater and mild boat soap. Polish to remove oxidation or pitting, then apply a boat wax or clear protective coating that is sold in marine stores for use on aluminum.

ANCHOR LINES: If the line was not washed in the fall, do so now. Take it out on the dock and soak in a large bucket of mild detergent solution, then rinse with plain water and spread out to dry. Replace anchor line if there are signs of chafing.

ANCHORS: Examine shackles, swivels, and other hardware, and inspect chain carefully for signs of corrosion. Replace if it looks bad. Check mounting brackets that hold anchor on deck to make sure they are secure.

ANTENNAS: Replace those that were removed for the winter. Inspect connections and cables to see if any need to be replaced or repaired.

B

BATTERIES: Replace batteries that were removed in the fall and reconnect cables after cleaning posts and cable ends. Coat posts and terminals with anticorrosion grease, then top off cells with distilled water. Test with hygrometer for specific gravity of 1.275 inches.

BELTS: Check drive belts on pumps, engines, and generators for signs of cracking and fraying. Replace those that look doubtful. Test tension on each to see if adjustments are needed.

BILGE BLOWER: Turn on each blower to make sure it works properly. Make sure intake opening at end of hose is at lowest point in bilge. Spray electrical connections with a moisture-displacing lubricant.

BILGE PUMPS: Reconnect hoses that were disconnected in the fall and make certain each has a double clamp at each end. Replace clamps that are corroded and test each pump and its float switch.

BILGE: If it was not cleaned out in the fall, do so now. Use a bilge cleaner at double the normal strength and let soak overnight before pumping it out. Make certain limber holes are clear and remove all debris. After scrubbing, leave hatches open for a day to air out the bilge area.

BOOT STRIPE: If the boat has a painted boot stripe or waterline that has not been repainted in the past two or three years, chances are it needs a touch-up or a fresh coat of paint now. If tape was used to create the boot stripe, then cleaning may be all that is needed. However, if the tape is scratched or torn in places, peel it off and replace with new tape.

C

CABINETS: Use a vacuum and a damp cloth to clean inside cabinets and drawers. If there is a musty smell, spray with a mildew remover and leave the door or drawer open for a couple of days.

CANVAS: Unroll curtains, cockpit covers, etc., and spread them out on deck. Wash each piece, then examine for signs of wear to see if repairs are needed. Lubricate zippers and snap fasteners with silicone lubricant.

CARPET: Vacuum and clean as necessary. If the carpet was rolled up and taken off the boat, unroll it onshore and examine for signs of mildew or insect infestation before replacing it.

CAULKING: Inspect caulking around window frames, portholes, hatches, doors, etc. Dig out compound that is cracked or coming loose and replace with fresh material.

CHAFING GEAR: Replace any that looks worn or cracked, using factory-made units that can be purchased at marine supply outlets, or using short lengths of garden hose.

CHARTS: Bring back all charts, tide tables, cruising guides, etc., that were stored at home over the winter. Replace those that are outdated and see if any additional ones are needed.

CIRCUIT BREAKERS: Be sure each one is labeled to indicate the circuit it controls, and examine the terminals in back to make sure they are tight. Spray with a moisture-displacing lubricant.

CLEATS AND CHOCKS: Test bolts and screws to be sure they are tight. If one is loose, remove it and squirt some silicone caulking into the hole before replacing and tightening that fastener. Spray each piece of hardware with a clear metal protective coating or good boat wax.

COCKPIT: Scrub clean, then examine drains and scuppers to make sure they are clear and not clogged with debris.

COMPASS: If the compass was taken off and stored at home, replace it now. Check for deviation after all equipment is onboard by taking some known bearings to make sure it does not need to be compensated.

CONTROLS: Run each control lever back and forth through its full range. There should be no binding or sticky points in its travel. Lubricate cables, linkage, and other moving parts with light oil. Check for wear or kinks in any of the cables.

COUNTERTOPS: Wash with detergent, then wipe dry. Polish plastic laminates with one of the products sold for this purpose.

CURTAINS: Wash with mild boat soap and water, and lubricate zippers and snap fasteners with silicone spray. Send out for repairs if needed.

D

DECKS: Fiberglass decks will need a good scrubbing after all mechanical work on the boat is done. Teak decks should be thoroughly wet down, then scrubbed with a mild, one-part teak cleaner (use two-part cleaners that contain acids or caustics only if necessary—they tend to raise the grain).

DEPTH FINDER: Reinstall on the boat and turn it on for at least an hour. Recalibrate if necessary by checking actual depth in shallow water with a weighted line.

DINGHIES: Inflatables should be pumped up and tested for air leaks. Patch where needed, then give dinghy a good washing, inside and out. When dry, apply one of the preservatives that are sold for this purpose. Rigid dinghies should be scrubbed clean, then painted and varnished where necessary.

DOCK LINES: Examine the full length of each line for signs of chafing or wear—especially the loop at the end. If not done previously, mark lines to indicate length and/or use (bowline, stern line, etc.).

DOORS: Lubricate hinges, locks, and latches. Varnished doors should get a fresh coat of varnish before the season begins, painted doors a fresh coat of paint. Doors made of clear plastic should be washed with boat soap, then dried with paper towels and protected with a coat of marine wax.

DRAWERS: Open and close each one to make certain it slides freely. Remove drawers and vacuum dust out of slides, as well as the inside of the drawer. Wood drawers should be coated with shellac to prevent swelling.

E

ELECTRICAL WIRING: Make sure all boat wiring is properly secured with clamps spaced no more than 18 inches apart. There should be grommets, sleeves, or protective collars where wires pass through metal or fiberglass. Test terminal screws and mounting lugs of bus bars and junction boxes to make certain they are tight. Clean off all connections and spray with a moisture-displacing protective coating.

ELECTRONIC GEAR: Test each item by letting the equipment run for several hours before you leave the dock for the first time.

ENGINE ROOM VENTS: If these were sealed off or covered during fall layup, uncover them now. Replace Dorade-type vents that have been removed from the deck and make sure that at least one of them faces toward the prevailing wind.

EXHAUSTS: Remove plastic and tape that was used to cover the exhaust openings. Use mineral spirits (being careful to vent fumes sufficiently to avoid a fire hazard) to remove glue deposits left by tape before reassembling exhaust components.

F

FASTENERS: Test each nut, bolt, and screw to make sure it is tight. Look for signs of severe corrosion and replace those that look doubtful, but make sure you use only marine-grade bronze or stainless steel fasteners.

FENDERS: Scrub each with a fender cleaner, then apply a protective coating that will help shed dirt (the same coatings sold for use on inflatables and shore cords). Check the lines tied to each fender and replace those that are frayed.

FIBERGLASS: Scrub entire hull and cabin sides with a good boat soap, then apply one or two coats of a marine-grade wax or clear polymer coating.

FIRE EXTINGUISHERS: Check date of the last inspection on larger models and if more than a year has passed, have extinguishers reinspected by a professional service. Smaller units have an indicator to show condition of charge, or they can be weighed.

FLARES: Check the expiration date on each one and replace those that have expired. If you have a flare gun, clean and lubricate it to make sure it will work smoothly if needed.

FREEZER: Wash out inside and check carefully for signs of mildew. If present, wash with mild solution of laundry bleach and water (one part bleach to five parts water).

FRESHWATER SYSTEM: Reconnect all hoses and reinstall water pump if it was removed in the fall. Fill water tank and turn on all faucets to expel air from the system. Examine all water lines and connections for leaks (if pump keeps running with all faucets off, there is a leak somewhere). If system had been filled with a nontoxic antifreeze (instead of draining), run water until all color is gone and refill tanks—or run dockside water through all lines till taste and color are gone.

FRESHWATER TANK: Reconnect water line if it was disconnected in the fall. Flush tank several times if it was filled with nontoxic antifreeze.

FUEL TANKS: Inspect portable outboard motor tanks to see if there is any rusting or leaking. If replacing, buy plastic fuel tanks to avoid corrosion and to prevent metal flakes from migrating through the fuel system. Treat gasoline left in the tank with a fuel stabilizer.

FUSES: Fuse panels should be labeled to indicate what each fuse controls. In-line fuses (not on the panel) should also be labeled. Make a list of where each in-line fuse is located so you will know where to find each one in a hurry (put a label on the outside of the cabinet where the fuse is located, or put a sticker on the piece of electronic equipment to tell you where its fuse is). It's a good idea to tape a spare fuse alongside the one in use.

G

GALLEY: Clean thoroughly, washing all counters and cleaning out the inside of all cabinets and drawers. Also scrub out the inside of the refrigerator or ice box, and reconnect water lines to each appliance.

GEL COAT: After washing, inspect all gel coat surfaces for signs of chipping, nicking, and/or scratching. Repair all defects before waxing the boat. After patching, allow repair to cure, then apply a coat of marine polish or wax.

GENERATOR: Reconnect seawater cooling lines to their through-hull fittings, making certain each end of the hose is double-clamped. Inspect hose to see if there is any sponginess, and if so replace it. Replace and readjust V-belts that were loosened in the fall and follow all steps described in owner's manual for commissioning of engine.

H

HALYARDS: Inspect wire halyards for signs of corrosion or broken strands that stick out. Wipe down with oily rag, paying particular attention to the condition of the splice where the wire is joined to the length of rope at its end. Examine rope halyards for signs of chafing or fraying and replace those that look doubtful. Use color-coded lines to simplify identifying the right one in a hurry.

HATCHES: Lubricate hinges and locks on hatches and inspect gasket or weather stripping around each rim. Replace stripping that is dried out or cracked. Plastic hatches should be coated with wax and buffed to protect against scratching and to help shed dirt.

HEAD: Scrub walls and shower stall, as well as sink and counters. Wash inside of medicine cabinet and check inside other cabinets and lockers for signs of mildew. Replace first aid supplies that were taken home over the winter.

HOLDING TANK: Flush out tank and inspect discharge for signs of calcification. Reconnect all hoses and inspect each for signs of cracking or sponginess.

HOSE CLAMPS: Test each with a screwdriver or wrench to make sure it is tight, and make certain there are two clamps on each through-hull fitting (at both ends of the hose). Only marine-grade stainless steel clamps should be used, especially on through-hulls that are below the waterline.

HULL: Wash with boat soap and soft brush. Use a stronger hull cleaner if there are stubborn stains that won't come off, or if there are oil or exhaust stains along the waterline. Wax fiberglass and gel-coated surfaces. If the boat was stored in the water over the winter, it should be hauled so the bottom can be cleaned before the season gets under way.

HYDRAULIC SYSTEMS: Fluid levels should have been checked and topped off in the spring, but if it was not done then, do it now. Also check all lines for signs of leakage, especially at fittings.

I

ICE BOXES: Wash out the inside and rinse thoroughly with fresh water. Leave door open (or cover off) for a day or so to make sure interior dries thoroughly. Wash with dilute solution of laundry bleach and water (one part bleach to five parts water) if there is a musty odor on the inside.

ICE MAKER: Reconnect water lines and clean out the inside.

INSULATION: If your boat is very noisy when under way, this is a good time to add more insulation. Nonflammable marine insulation can be ordered from boat yards and marine outlets, or direct from companies that specialize in these products. This insulation will be especially helpful under engine hatches in the cockpit, or under the salon hatches.

L

LADDERS: Inspect ladders leading to the bridge to see if any treads or steps are loose or cracked. Repair or replace as necessary. Also examine boarding ladders and swim ladders to make sure they are sound. Don't forget to check the condition of the mounting brackets that hold them in place when in use.

LAUNCHING: If possible, arrange to be present when your boat is launched. That way you can make certain slings are properly positioned in the travel lift to avoid marring or damage to underwater parts. (Workmen also tend to be more careful if they know you are watching.)

LIFELINES: Wash with a mild detergent and check tension to make certain there is a slight amount of slack in each lifeline. They should not be pulled tight, or left so loose that they drape noticeably. It is a good idea to also apply a light coat of wax or polish to each lifeline as this will help them shed dirt better. Inspect all turnbuckles and other hardware for signs of corrosion or possible metal fatigue.

LIFE PRESERVERS: Spread flotation devices out in the sun for several hours. Replace those that are mildewed, torn, or otherwise defective.

LIGHTS: Test all navigation lights to see if bulbs need to be replaced or if there are problems with the switches or the wiring. Before installing a new bulb, spray the base of the lamp and the inside of the socket with a moisture-displacing spray. Make sure your spare parts inventory includes spare bulbs for all these lights, as well as for all interior lighting fixtures.

LINES: Lay out dock lines and mooring lines to check for signs of chafing or severe wear. If chafe is evident only near one end, you may be able to cut that end off and still use it as a shorter line.

LOCKERS: Use a vacuum and damp cloth to clean out the inside of each. Leave doors open for a day or so, then hang a bag of dehumidifier inside each locker.

LOCKS: Test each door lock, padlock and combination lock to make sure it works easily. Spray with graphite, or with graphite-containing lock lubricant.

M

MAST: If the mast was taken down in the fall, examine its full length before the yard replaces it. Pay particular attention to masthead fittings and spreaders, tightening all fasteners that are loose and replacing any that show signs of corrosion of bad oxidation. Wash the mast and coat with a clear protective coating made for use on aluminum. If the mast is wood, give it a fresh coat of varnish or paint after sanding the old finish.

MASTER BONDING SYSTEM: Inspect all connecting wires and cables to see if any are broken, and check all connections to make sure they are secure and still making good electrical contact. Inspect master zinc on the outside of the hull and replace if needed.

MATTRESSES: If they were left on the boat, turn them over and inspect underside for signs of mildew. If mildew is evident, spray with mildewcide or have them cleaned.

MOORINGS: Before the mooring is put back in the water, make certain all hardware, chain, and rope are still in good condition. Replace chain or hardware that looks badly corroded, and replace line that looks chafed or partially rotted. Pay particular attention to swivels and shackles since they are easy to replace and are often the weak link in the system.

N

NAVIGATION EQUIPMENT: Make sure your charts and other publications used for navigation and cruising are current. Also check your navigation instruments—including dividers, mileage scales, pelorus, and binoculars. Replace items that are not in good condition. Don't forget pencils and marking pens needed for plotting courses, making notes, etc., and a reliable watch or clock.

NUTS AND BOLTS: Lay a wrench on every one of the engine's nuts and bolts to make sure vibration hasn't loosened any. Tighten as necessary.

O

OIL: Change crankcase oil now if it wasn't done during fall layup. Don't forget to run the engine for ten to fifteen minutes before draining or pumping the oil out. Install a new oil filter at the same time.

P

PAINT: Wash down painted surfaces, then look for places where the paint is cracked, peeling, or flaking off. Scrape off loosened paint, then sand smooth and dust thoroughly. Touch up with two or three coats of paint—enough to build up to the original film thickness.

PANELING: Vacuum with a soft brush on the nozzle, then wipe down with cloth. If finish is dull, wipe on a wood polish or liquid wax. Touch up scratches with one of the colored touch-up pencils sold in most paint stores.

PLUMBING: If your boat has a pressurized freshwater system, hook up the water pump after all hoses and water lines have been reconnected, then allow water to run from each faucet until all air is expelled from lines. Let pump run for another ten or fifteen minutes with no faucets open to see if pump comes on. If it does, there is a leak in one of the lines or fittings.

PROPELLERS: Inspect each blade for nicks and gouges. Minor imperfections can be smoothed up with a file, but more serious nicks and deep scratches require the services of a professional propeller shop that will also rebalance the propeller.

PUMPS: Make sure there is a spare impeller on board for every pump, including freshwater pumps and toilet or macerator pumps. For engine raw water pumps, it's best to replace the old impellers if they are more than two or three years old.

R

RADAR: Turn it on and let it run for three or four hours to make sure it is working properly and will keep on working. Look at the scope every thirty or forty minutes to be certain you are getting a clear image, and try the unit at various range settings.

RADIOS: Reinstall those that were removed in the fall, then turn each one on and let it run for at least an hour. Try transmitting and receiving, and spray all cable connections and terminals with a moisture-displacing penetrating lubricant.

RAILINGS: Metal railings should be washed, then wiped down with a liquid metal polish. Buff to remove excess so the railing will not be slippery. Make sure all fasteners and attached fittings are tight. Wood railings are usually varnished, so early in the spring they will need a light sanding and at least one or two coats of fresh varnish.

RAW-WATER COOLING SYSTEM: Reconnect all hoses that were disconnected from seacocks and engines when the boat was hauled and make sure each has double stainless steel clamps at each end.

RIGGING: Inspect stays, shrouds, and all other rigging to look for signs of chafing or wear. Replace hardware that looks doubtful and adjust tension on all lines and cables. Spray turnbuckles with rust-preventive coating and grease or oil winches according to manufacturer's specifications. Don't forget also to inspect and lubricate running blocks, turning blocks, and snatch blocks.

RUDDERS: Turn the wheel hard over from left to right to make sure it works freely with full movement. Check stuffing boxes to see if they are leaking excessively. A slight drip is acceptable in most cases, but not really necessary. If leaking is slight, a simple tightening of the packing nut is all that may be required, but if this doesn't stop the leak, repacking may be required.

S

SAIL TRACKS: Clean and lubricate all tracks and travelers, and test bolts and screws to make sure they are tight. Move hardware back and forth along each track to make sure there are no rough spots or worn areas that might snag.

SEACOCKS: If these were not tested and lubricated in the fall, do it now. Move the handle back and forth on each to make sure the valve can be opened and closed easily. Tie a tapered wood plug that is a snug fit for the through-hole opening next to each seacock. That way if the seacock fails or gets damaged, you can plug the hole in an emergency.

Searchlights: Test to make sure bulbs and switches are operating. Spray swiveling and tilting mounts with penetrating lubricant, and if the unit is remotely controlled from helm, make sure all controls are still working properly.

Shore-Power Cords: Spray plugs at each end with moisture-displacing lubricant. Inspect prongs on plug to see if they are burned or badly corroded; if so, replace the plug. Clean cord with a fender cleaner or special cleaner sold for this purpose—do not use acetone or lacquer thinner on the outside of the cord because these solvents will attack the insulation.

Shower: Wash down walls and floor and use a mildew-removing spray to get rid of any signs of mold or mildew. Wash shower curtain and replace if it is mildewed. Run water through shower to see if drain and sump pump are working properly.

Shower Sumps: Clean out debris. Pour water into sump to test float switch action and operation of pump. Check strainer in line coming from shower drain.

Snaps: Lubricate each with a silicone spray or wipe on a small amount of clear petroleum jelly. Replace snaps that are badly rusted.

Spars: Paint or varnish wood spars as needed, and apply clear metal coating to aluminum spars. Make sure all hardware attached to spars is still securely fastened in place and there are no loose screws, bolts, or rivets.

Stanchions: Test fasteners to make certain the mounting is tight, then wash each stanchion and base and apply a coat of boat wax. Replace those that are bent or are damaged in any way.

STEERING SYSTEM: Lubricate all cables, chains, and other moving parts. Don't forget sheaves and pulleys through which the cables run, as well as gears and rotating shafts. Turn wheel at helm all the way over from one side to the other several times to make sure it works freely and does not bind at any point.

STOVES: Before reconnecting propane stoves and ovens, carefully inspect all lines and hoses, as well as all fittings that connect them. Test for suspected leaks by brushing soapy water over the suspicious area.

STRAINERS: Engine strainers should have been cleaned out in the fall, but if they weren't, check them now. Clear plastic strainers can be inspected visually to make sure they are clean; others will have to be opened to check the inside. Don't forget strainers on other water lines, such as toilet inlet water lines, shower sumps, etc.

STUFFING BOX: Wait till the boat is in the water, then start the engine and watch the stuffing box to see if it leaks—and how much. Slight dripping is acceptable while the shaft is turning (put the engine in gear to check this), but if water is being sprayed around in the engine room, or if there is a fast drip, then the packing nut will have to be tightened. If tightening doesn't slow the leak, then new packing is required. If there is no drip at all, touch the outside carefully after the boat has been underway for several minutes. If the metal is too hot to touch, then the packing nut is too tight and should be loosened (or new packing might be needed).

Switches: Flick each one on and off several times to make sure the power comes on and goes off each time, without sparking. Make sure terminal connections are tight and spray all with a moisture-displacing, corrosion-resistant spray.

T

Teak: Scrub teak decks and trim with a mild solution of ammonia and water, scrubbing across the grain to avoid rubbing out the soft wood in the grain. Check condition of sealer in joints and recaulk where necessary. Coat teak trim with teak oil or sealer. If teak trim is varnished, apply a touch-up coat to all bare spots and then a new coat of varnish as soon as possible.

Through-Hull Fittings: Inspect connections where bonding wires are attached, and check bolts or screws that hold fitting in place to make certain fasteners are tight. Make sure attached hoses have double clamps on the end.

Toilets: Reconnect hoses that were disconnected for the winter, and replace those that feel spongy or are partially blocked by chemical buildup or hardened sediment. Flush toilet several times to make sure it works properly. Test operation of Y-valve, if installed, and run treatment device, if installed. Flush out holding tank and add deodorizer.

Tools: Go through your tool box and inspect all items to make sure all are still in working condition. Replace any that look doubtful, and add those that have been lost, or that you think may be needed next season. Spray a light coat of protective lubricant over tools that are likely to rust—or wrap them in oily rags.

TRAILERS: Make sure tires are properly inflated, and inspect each tire for signs of wear or cracks in the sidewall. Paint exposed metal frame of trailer, including tongue, and grease hitch assembly. Test braking system and stoplights before loading up for the first time. Also check air pressure in each tire, including spare.

TRIM TABS: If you didn't do it in the fall, scrape off all marine growth now. Sand lightly and coat with antifouling paint after applying a suitable metal primer. Make sure zinc anodes are in place and not worn more than one-third down.

TRIM/TILT: Run stern drive and outboard motor drive legs up and down two or three times. Then check the lift pump fluid level, topping off as necessary. Visually inspect the lift ram hydraulic lines to make certain the connections are snugged down tight and not leaking. Also inspect the full length of each line to make sure it is free of cracks or breaks.

U

UPHOLSTERY: Vacuum all upholstered furniture on the inside, and wash all vinyl cushions or upholstery in the cockpit or on the bridge deck. One of the special vinyl cleaners sold in marine supply stores works best for this. After washing, allow cushions to dry in the sun if possible. Have repairs made where tears or open seams are visible.

V

VARNISH: Wash varnished trim with boat soap and look for areas that are worn or need to be touched up. Sand these areas and touch up with at least two coats of varnish, sanding lightly between coats. Plan to revarnish all these surfaces with a full two coats as soon as time and weather permits.

VENTILATION: If boat does not have vents that will allow air to flow through the interior when the boat is closed, plan to install hatches or mushroom-type vents that will allow air to circulate through boat at all times.

W

WASHING MACHINE: Reconnect hoses that were disconnected in the fall. Turn on machine and watch for leaks while testing operation of all cycles.

WATER FILTER: Change cartridge in freshwater-system filter (if you have one) and make sure you have at least one spare cartridge on hand at all times.

WATER HEATER: Reconnect water lines that were disconnected in the fall and turn on the circuit breaker that controls power to the heater. After water pressure has been turned on, check tank and all connections for water leaks.

WATER PUMP (FOR FRESHWATER SYSTEM): Hook up water hoses that were disconnected in the fall, then test for leaks after pump is running again. Replace impeller (or diaphragm) if it is more than two years old. Make sure there is a spare-parts kit for this water pump onboard.

WATER TANK: After connecting water lines, flush out thoroughly. If nontoxic antifreeze was used for the winter, several flushings may be required.

WINCHES: Grease or lubricate as recommended by manufacturer. Apply metal polish to protect finish and to prevent corrosion.

WINDLASS: Follow directions as to lubrication required, if any, then run it a few times to make sure it is turning freely and the switching mechanism is operating properly.

WINDOWS: Replace caulking or sealant around frame where necessary, and clean out tracks of sliding windows. Make sure drainage holes and vent holes in window track are not clogged. Wash plastic windows with mild detergent, then coat with a wax or polish made for this purpose.

WINTER COVER: After removing the cover, spread it out on the dock or on a paved surface to dry. Inspect to see if repairs are needed and, if so, take the cover in to a canvas shop now. If not, fold neatly and store in dry location out of the weather.

Y

Y-VALVES: Often installed in toilet discharge line to direct waste overboard when out at sea, these can stick or jam if neglected. Work handle several times to make sure it moves freely, and inspect the inside with a bright light to make sure there is not a heavy buildup of accumulated sediment. If so, clean it out before reassembling.

Z

ZINC ANODES: Inspect the sacrificial zincs mounted on inboard powered hulls, propeller shafts, and rudders. After removing what is left of the old zinc, scrape the surface clean and sand down to the bare metal before bolting on the new zinc. Don't forget also to inspect cooling system zincs. If there is less than 50 percent of the zinc remaining, replace it.

ZIPPERS: Lubricate each with a silicone spray or with a stick-type lubricant sold in hardware stores. Test each one to make sure it works easily, and replace those that are difficult to open or close.

....
SPRUCING UP DURING SPRING COMMISSIONING

In addition to doing the many chores that must be completed to commission the boat each spring, you might also expend a little extra effort on sprucing up the boat.

For example:

• Before waxing the fiberglass, look it over carefully to see if there are any nicks, scratches or other repairs that are needed. Use a gel-coat repair kit to fill in scratches and nicks; use an epoxy patching compound for larger damages. Allow these repairs to cure completely before waxing.

• Painted names on a fiberglass transom need recoating after two or three years in most cases, especially if they have not been protected with wax. If the letters are of the stick-on vinyl kind, replace old ones that are scratched or have pieces missing.

• Paint and/or varnish the dinghy if you have one, since its condition contributes to the overall appearance of your boat.

• If your boat has a mast or boom, or if it has a painted davit or crane for hoisting the dinghy aboard, paint these before the boat is launched.

• When polishing railings and deck hardware, don't forget also to polish the narrow metal bands and metal strips found on fiberglass antennas, as well as chrome or stainless steel hardware and fittings on compasses, radar units, boat hooks, ladders, rod holders, and similar items. This not only protects against and removes corrosion, it also helps spruce up the boat's appearance.

• Chrome-plated deck hardware that is pitted, worn-looking, and starting to lose its plating should be taken off and replaced or replated. Before deciding to have fittings plated, however, check the price—it may be cheaper to buy new hardware (especially if you have only a few pieces to be plated).

• Use a vinyl shampoo to clean and restore cockpit cushions, padded dashboards, and coamings around the cockpit. If the vinyl is so far gone that cleaning no longer brightens it, then you actually can paint the vinyl with one of the special paints sold for this purpose.

• Teak decks and teak trim should be cleaned and coated with a sealer (or varnished) as soon as the finish starts to dull. Don't wait until the old coating has become completely dull, or until the bare wood is exposed in places.

• If the clear plastic curtains that enclose your cockpit or flying bridge plastic are so badly scratched, dull-looking, or cloudy that they cannot be restored with polish, have the clear plastic "windows" replaced—not only to improve visibility, but also because this always spruces up the appearance of your entire boat.

• Wash the bright yellow shore power cord and the fenders with a good fender cleaner—again because this always makes a boat look better. Use a mild kitchen abrasive pad to get all the dirt off, but do not use acetone or other strong solvent. These solvents will attack and soften the plastic, leaving it sticky to the touch.

TEN FREQUENTLY FORGOTTEN COMMISSIONING CHORES

1. **Toilet's Vented Loop:** Toilets located below the water-line have a vented loop in the discharge line, similar to the one shown in Figure 6.3. It has a small one-way,

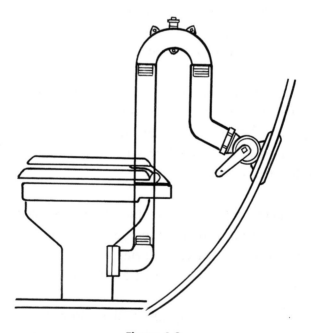

Figure 6.3

flapper-type valve at the top that allows air to enter (to prevent back-siphoning of seawater), but prevents waste-water from escaping when the toilet is flushed. Sometimes this air vent becomes clogged, or the rubber or leather flapper on the inside gets stuck. To prevent this, clean out the vent opening by pushing a pointed wooden toothpick down through the little hole in the top, then flush the toilet and see if water spurts out through the vent opening. If it does, take the vent fitting off and wash out the inside, including the internal flapper. If it still doesn't work properly, replace the vent valve.

2. **Shower Sump:** Boats that have a shower usually have a sump with a pump in it to get rid of water that drains out. These sump-and-pump combinations have to be cleaned out in the spring, and periodically throughout the summer, to get rid of hair, soap curds, and a buildup of sediment.

3. **Fuel Filters:** When changing the engine's fuel filters at the beginning of each season, many boat owners forget about the secondary fuel filters that are installed in many boats, especially those with diesel engines. These prefilter the fuel before it gets to the engine filters, and they are usually mounted on a nearby bulkhead, not on the engine itself.

4. **Anchor Winches:** These often require periodic lubrication, but many owners forget this in the spring. Some have oil reservoirs while others have grease fittings. Check your owner's manual if you are in doubt. Stainless winch cables should be wiped down with an oil-soaked rag or sprayed with a moisture-displacing lubricant at the beginning of the season.

5. **Bonding System:** In a master bonding system all metal seacocks, through-hull fittings, rudders, propeller shafts, and other underwater components are electrically con-

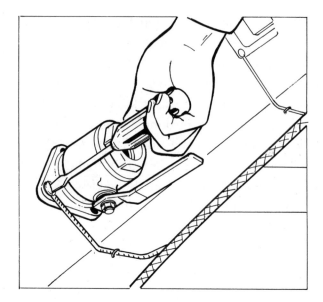

Figure 6.4

nected to a large zinc anode mounted below the waterline on the outside of the hull. If these electrical connections are not complete, protection is lost, so test all terminal screws where bonding wires are connected to make sure connections are tight (Figure 6.4). The master bonding cable—a heavy bare copper wire or a braided metal cable—should also be checked to make sure that it is unbroken and solidly connected to the through-bolt that connects it to the master zinc on the outside of the hull.

6. **Engine Zincs:** In addition to checking the sacrificial zincs on the outside of the boat, don't forget the engine zincs. Usually located in or near the heat exchanger or the raw-water pump, these consist of a threaded brass plug with a zinc "pencil" threaded into the inside so that it projects down into the engine's cooling water. To inspect this zinc, unscrew the brass plug to which it is attached and pull it out (Figure 6.5). If the zinc looks worn, or if it crumbles when tapped, replace it.

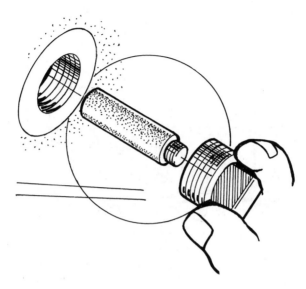

Figure 6.5

7. **Stuffing Box:** A slight drip in a stuffing box is permissible, and even preferred by some to ensure against overheating, but it should never leak so much that it sprays water out while running. Spraying water usually means that it needs to be tightened. You can use one wrench and a large pair of channel-lock pliers or two wrenches to accomplish this, one to hold the packing nut in place and one to loosen (and then tighten) the locknut (Figure 6.6). Tighten the packing nut just enough to stop the dripping, then wait until you take the boat out and feel the outside of the stuffing box after you have been under way for about fifteen minutes. If it gets too hot to place your hand on it, you have overtightened it. Loosen it just enough to permit a very slow drip, then test again. If tightening won't stop the leak, then repacking is required.

8. **Propeller Shaft Alignment:** If the engine shaft and propeller shaft are not properly aligned when the boat is commissioned, considerable vibration—and even dam-

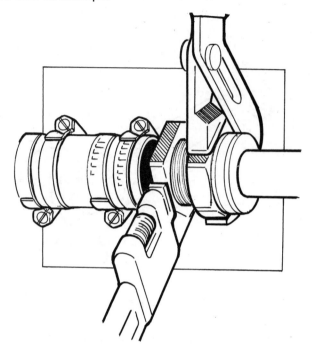

Figure 6.6

age to engine and transmission bearings—can result
when the boat is running. The face plates on each half
of the coupling must be flush up against each other
where the two couplings are bolted together. This is
checked by using metal feeler gauges between the couplings, or by using a special rotary alignment gauge that
some pros prefer. Adjustments are made by raising or
lowering the engine mounts, but this is a fairly tricky
job best done by a professional marine mechanic.

9. **Propeller Blades:** Before the boat is launched, you
   should personally inspect the propeller(s) to see if there
   are nicks, bends, or deep scratches in any of the blades.
   If so, the propeller needs to be serviced—preferably before the boat is launched.

10. **Toilet Discharge Hose:** Disconnect the waste line
    coming from your toilet and shine a light into it to

examine the inside. If the hose is coated with a thick lining of sediment, it will seriously interfere with its flow and could affect flushing efficiency, so replace the hose before the season starts.

FALL LAYUP CHECKLIST

Those who live where winter normally brings below-freezing temperatures normally "decommission" their boats for the winter months. Since this layup routine involves many chores, it is wise to think about and organize your work before the first cold weather arrives. To make sure nothing will be forgotten, here is a comprehensive list that will serve as an easy-to-follow decommissioning checklist for boats that are to be hauled out and stored on land for the winter.

• Clean off the bottom as soon as the boat is hauled by using a pressure washer to remove barnacles, grass, and slime while the bottom is still wet. This growth will be a lot harder to wash off after it dries. Use a scrub brush along the waterline, and in stubborn places where washing is not enough. Pay particular attention to cleaning off the waterline and the transom and don't forget to clean off the propellers, shafts, struts, rudders, and trim tabs.

• After washing, clean out through-hull openings by using a large screwdriver or similar tool to poke up inside each opening. Make sure there is no marine growth left on the inside.

• Take the storage batteries off the boat and store them in a dry, heated location onshore where they can checked regularly and charged with a trickle charger as necessary. Water levels in each cell should be replenished at the same time.

• Spray electric circuit breakers, junction boxes, and terminal boards with a moisture-displacing lubricant, then test each connection to make certain it is tight.

• Remove roll-up curtains, canvas cockpit covers, and bridge enclosures before putting on the winter cover. Make sure these curtains and covers are clean and dry before storing them, and do not fold or crease clear plastic curtains. Have weak seams and tears repaired as soon as possible, and make sure all zippers, snaps, and other fasteners are in good condition.

• Winterize seacocks by disconnecting the hose connected to each one. Open and close the handle a few times to make sure it works easily, and lubricate as recommended by the manufacturer. Leave all seacocks open so trapped water can escape harmlessly.

• Protect deck hardware against pitting and corroding by applying a moisture-displacing spray or clear metal protective coating to all chocks, cleats, stanchions, winches, anchor windlasses, and similar hardware—or coat each item with marine wax and do not buff the wax until next spring.

• Fill the fuel tanks. Leaving tanks partly full is hazardous because of explosive vapors, and can cause condensation problems during the winter. Completely draining them is impractical, so keep fuel tanks full during the layup period and add fuel stabilizer to minimize the possibility of algae growth.

• Clean the cockpit and empty the lockers and lazarettes around the outside of the boat. Also, make sure cockpit scuppers are clear so that rain and melted snow can run out. Remove and store boat hooks, boarding ladders, rope, and other loose gear.

• Use heavy line to tie down the winter cover securely and make sure each line is protected against chafing where it goes under the keel or around sharp corners. Use pieces of old carpet or foam padding to protect the lines from chafing when whipped around by the wind (Figure 6.7).

• Provide vents or openings near the top at each end of the cover (use flaps or stove pipe elbows to keep rain and snow from entering). Hang small fenders along the bottom edge of the cover as shown in Figure 6.8 to keep the canvas from lying tight against the hull. If there are zippered "doors"

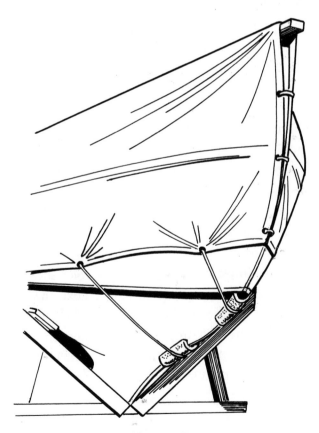

Figure 6.7

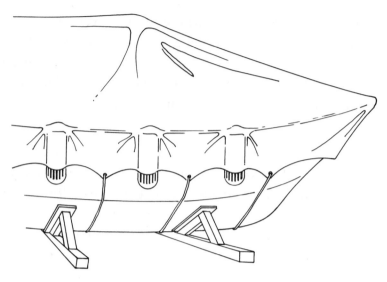

Figure 6.8

or entrance flaps to provide access to the inside, lubricate these zippers and snaps liberally to keep them from freezing up.

• Winterize the freshwater system inside the boat by either draining all lines or filling the system with a nontoxic antifreeze that is sold for this purpose. To drain the system, you will have to disconnect each water line at its lowest point and also disconnect the hoses going to and from the pump and the tank. Then open all faucets and leave them open. If you winterize the system by using a nontoxic antifreeze, make certain you let the water flow out of each faucet until the antifreeze color shows up. Then shut that faucet off before going on to the next one.

• Remove the rubber impeller from each water pump so that it won't take a "set" or trap water inside the pump's housing. Leave the impellers out until spring commissioning.

• Drain the hot-water heater and leave the hoses disconnected. Turn off the heater's circuit breaker and put a tag on it to remind you to refill the tank before turning the hot-water heater back on in the spring.

• Remove electronic equipment and other portable items of value that are likely to attract thieves, including radios, TV sets, VCRs, stereo equipment, binoculars, cameras, flare guns, foul weather boots, and even dinghy oars or motors.

• Clean the galley and head and take off all canned and bottled items that can freeze. Also take home foodstuffs that will attract insects or rodents.

• Take home first aid kits and medical supplies so that each item can be inspected and replenished if necessary before next spring. Discard outdated medicines. After emptying cabinets, lockers, and drawers, wash out the inside and spray with a mildewcide to discourage mold.

• Scrub galley counters and sinks to eliminate food stains on which mildew can thrive. Coat Formica countertops with a light coat of wax to help repel dirt.

• Drain and winterize toilets as recommended in the owner's manual, and do the same for waste-treatment devices (if any). Don't forget also to drain and flush out the holding tank, then add antifreeze to the tank, the pump, and the Y-valve (if there is one installed).

• Clean carpets, curtains, and upholstered furniture to remove dust and stains and vacuum carpeting that must be left onboard—mildew thrives on dirty materials. If there are stains left by spilled food or beverages, use an upholstery-cleaning foam or rug-cleaning solution to get them out after vacuuming.

• Remove linens, blankets, towels, and clothing to minimize chances of mold and mildew. This includes bathing suits and swim wear, as well as snorkeling equipment, scuba gear, shoes, luggage, and foul-weather gear.

• Bunk mattresses and cushions should be vacuumed and then propped up to allow air to circulate around and under them. Don't cover mattresses or furniture with bedspreads or sheets, and hang bags of a dehumidifying chemical inside cabins and large lockers.

• Wash out bilge with a heavy concentration of bilge cleaner, then pump the dirty water out into large containers and dispose of this in an approved manner onshore. If there are fuel or oil odors in the bilge, spread liberal quantities of baking soda around.

Spring Clamps Hold Tarp in Place

When trying to cover a boat with a large plastic tarp during fall layup, most people have trouble getting the tarp in place when working alone because the wind often blows the lightweight plastic off on one side while you are trying to tie down the other side. A simple solution to this problem is to use a few spring-type workshop clamps to hold one side down while the other side is being secured. A piece of light line about six feet long is tied to the center of each clamp, then the other end of the line is run through the handle of a plastic milk bottle that is filled with water. As soon as the tarp is roughly in position, snap the clamp to that side of the fabric. This will serve to hold it down while you finish tying or securing the tarp on the other side of the boat. You can adjust the weight of the filled bottle so it doesn't pull the clamp off the fabric by simply pouring some of the water out of the bottle.

STORING YOUR BOAT IN THE WATER

Wet storage—storing your boat in the water over the winter—often costs less than having it hauled and stored on land, as it can eliminate the cost of hauling and launching during peak seasons. But for many, the most appealing attraction is the weeks it adds to their boating season by allowing them to continue using their boat later into the fall. Another benefit is that when spring rolls around they can get their boat back into commission earlier—no waiting until the boats in front are launched. Also, while workers are waiting for other boats to be launched, they will often start working on boats that are already in the water.

Storing a boat in the water is also better for the hull. A boat floating in water is in its natural habitat and is not under any kind of unnatural stress or strain because it is being supported more effectively than even the best of custom-made cradles.

Of course, not everyone should choose wet storage. Storing a boat in the water is only for those who live reasonably close to where the boat is stored, and those who are willing and able to visit and inspect that boat regularly during the winter. The boat should be boarded at least twice a month to check the docking lines, the overall condition of the boat and its winter cover—including the tie lines that hold the cover in place—and to make sure all fenders are in place. This is especially true after a heavy snowstorm or ice storm.

When deciding on wet storage, shop around carefully for a yard that is equipped for this. It's always safer to store your boat where there are other boats in wet storage, and where there they have adequate deicing equipment for below-freezing temperatures. Make sure the yard has adequate maintenance personnel to check on this equipment regularly—especially in the event of a power failure. Find out if the yard also shovels the docks and parking lot after a snowstorm so you can get to your boat to check it.

Bear in mind that many yards only install enough de-icing equipment to protect their pilings and docks—they may not really make a serious effort to also keep ice away from all the boats that are in the water. Also, try to select a marina that is not located on open water where boats are likely to be exposed to moving ice (due to commercial traffic during the winter, or due to strong currents).

Boats stored in the water tend to stay cleaner than those stored on land, but problems with corrosion and mildew will still be a problem, so it's especially important to make certain the winter cover is well ventilated with vents at each end, and that there are panels that can be opened to permit you to climb onboard easily when you visit the boat.

Most of the routines followed when laying up a boat on land also apply to those laid up in the water, but there are a few items that should get special attention:

• Check with your insurance broker to make certain you are covered for wet storage. In some cases, a special rider may have to be added to your policy.

• Lines that hold the winter cover in place should go completely under the keel from one side of the boat to the other. Use nylon or polypropylene lines, and make certain chafing gear is used where the lines rub against the hull.

• Hang twice the number of fenders normally used when docking in the summer, and allow the winter cover to overlap these fenders so that air can circulate under the cover. Double up on each fender line.

• Dock lines should also be doubled, and extra lines should be run from the far side of the boat to docks or pilings on the far side of the slip in order to help hold the boat away from the dock in a strong wind. Since winter storms can subject lines to a great deal of stress and chafe, don't use old lines that have started to wear. Also, use heavier lines than you would in the summer and make sure each is protected by adequate chafe guards.

• Don't allow dock lines and electric shore cords to sag or hang into the water. Heavy accumulations of ice can start forming on them, much in the way that ice forms on overhead power lines—and this could cause them to break.

• Pay extra attention to batteries and bilge pumps because these will be called into action if a leak develops. Batteries should be kept fully charged (charged batteries won't freeze), and the bilge should be cleaned of debris that could clog the pumps.

• Make sure all seacocks are closed and all cockpit drains are open.

• Remove as much electronic gear as you can, and remove binoculars, navigation instruments, TV sets, and other portable valuables that might be a temptation to thieves (boats stored at a dock are easier to board than those up on cradles on land).

GETTING A FALL START ON SPRING COMMISSIONING

Fall is actually a good time to get started on some spring commissioning chores. For example, although every boat owner does his varnishing in the spring, during fall layup he could get some of the preliminary sanding out of the way. This will enable him to get his boat back into commission that much quicker next season; with the sanding done in the fall, all he will have to do in the spring is wipe the sanded wood down with a rag dipped into paint thinner, then start applying his first coat of varnish.

Another important way to minimize spring commissioning chores is to diligently follow manufacturer's recommendations for winterizing the engines and the auxiliary generator (if you have one) so that there will be less work to do in the spring.

• Drain all gasoline out of the carburetor and fuel lines.

• Drain the salt-water side of the engine's cooling system, including the heat exchanger, the engine block, and the water jackets around the exhaust system.

• Replace the antifreeze in the freshwater side of the engine's cooling system now—to avoid having to do this in the spring.

• Change the oil in the crankcase and replace the oil filters and the fuel filters.

• Flush out and drain the engine water pumps and remove the rubber impellers from water pumps that have them (so they won't take a "set" over the winter).

• Spray a rust-preventive lubricant into each cylinder on gasoline engines, and clean out and lubricate the carburetor.

• Take apart and clean out all intake water strainers in the engine's cooling system.

Here are some other chores you can complete in the fall when decommissioning the boat that will help give you a head start in the spring:

• When cleaning engine water strainers, do the same for those installed in air-conditioner inlet lines and toilet intake lines.

• Clean the bilges thoroughly by pouring in a good bilge cleaner and adding water as necessary. Slosh this around vigorously by agitating with a long-handled brush, scrubbing where necessary to free up grease and dirt. Then drain all the water out by pulling the bilge's drain plug (if the boat is out of the water) or pump the water out.

• While winterizing the toilet, overhaul it by replacing the gaskets, impellers, and other components that need annual servicing.

• To prevent corrosion of exposed electrical connections, plugs, terminal posts, and other components of the boat's wiring systems, spray all fittings with a light film of a penetrating, rust-preventive lubricant such as WD-40 or Boeshield T-9.

• Wood ladders, hatch covers, and other removable wood items that will need refinishing should be taken off and taken home during layup so that you can sand and refinish them over the winter.

• Inspect underwater running gear after the boat has been hauled and the bottom cleaned to see if there has been any damage done to propellers, rudders, shafts, or trim tabs. If needed, make arrangements to have the necessary repairs or replacements made over the winter—don't wait for spring when yards and shops are jammed with rush orders.

• While checking underwater metal parts, also inspect all the zinc anodes that were installed to prevent electrolytic damage. This is the best time to replace any that are more than one-third eaten away, or any that seem spongy and crumbly. Don't forget zinc buttons on trim tabs and rudders, and zinc collars on shafts. When you remove the old zinc, be sure to clean the metal underneath until it is shiny before installing the new zinc.

• If your boat has a master bonding system with a big underwater zinc, make sure the bolts that form the electric connection between the zinc and the bonding cable on the inside are still in good condition. It's also a good idea to go inside the boat and check the bonding cables at the same time—to make sure all connections are still solid.

• Washing the boat before covering it for the winter will make the job of cleaning the boat in the spring a lot easier. Caked-on dirt, muddy footprints, and oily stains will be a lot harder to clean later on.

• Polish chrome and stainless deck hardware, including stanchions, winches, railings, cleats, chocks, etc. After the metal is clean, wet a rag with a rust-preventive lubricant, then wipe on a light film of this oil and leave it there over the winter. Or, wipe on a light coat of boat wax, but don't polish or buff it—leave the buffing for next spring.

• If your boat has ports, hatches, or windshields made of Plexiglas, Lexan or similar plastic, wipe on a light film of white paste wax, then leave this on—without buffing—until spring.

The wax will help minimize scratching that often occurs when these surfaces get coated with dust and dirt, or when canvas is dragged over them.

• Remove all canvas and vinyl curtains, as well as folding tops and cockpit or flying bridge covers before covering the boat for the winter. Clean or wash these over the winter and store them in a dry place without folding. Do *not* leave navy tops or bimini tops up and then lay winter covers directly on top of these when storing the boat.

• Take home dock lines, shore cords, fenders, and other gear that normally needs a good scrubbing in the spring. Clean them at home during the winter so you won't have to waste time next spring. At the same time you will also be able to make needed repairs or replacements over the winter so they will be ready to go when spring arrives.

• Your dinghy (if you have one) will also need cleaning or waxing, and possibly some painting or varnishing, next spring—so you can save time by doing as much of this work as possible in the fall.

INDEX

Pages containing figures and illustrations are in italics